Women Creating Women

Richard Fallis
Series Editor

Women Creating Women

Contemporary Irish Women Poets

Patricia Boyle Haberstroh

Syracuse University Press

Library of Congress Cataloging-in-Publication Data

Haberstroh, Patricia Boyle.
    Women creating women : contemporary Irish women poets / Patricia
Boyle Haberstroh. — 1st ed.
        p.   cm. — (Irish studies (Syracuse, N.Y.))
    Includes bibliographical references (p.) and index.
    ISBN 0-8156-2671-1 (cl : alk. paper). — ISBN 0-8156-0357-6 (p :
alk. paper)
        1. English poetry—Irish authors—History and criticism.   2. Women
and literature—Ireland—History—20th century.   3. English poetry—
Women authors—History and criticism.   4. English poetry—20th
century—History and criticism.   5. Strong, Eithne—Criticism and
interpretation.   6. Boland, Eavan—Criticism and interpretation.
7. Ní Chuilleanáin, Eiléan, 1942–   —Criticism and interpretation.
8. McGuckian, Medbh, 1950–   —Criticism and interpretation.   9. Ní
Dhomhnaill, Nuala, 1952–   —Criticism and interpretation.
10. Irish poetry—Women authors—History and criticism.
11. Ireland—In literature.   I. Title.   II. Series.
PR8733.H33   1995
821'.914099287'0899162—dc20   95-33075

In Memoriam
Ethan Charles Haberstroh
1966–1993

Patricia Boyle Haberstroh is an associate professor of English at La Salle University in Philadelphia, where she teaches courses in Irish Studies and Women's Studies. She has served as Women's Studies Advisory Editor for *Éire-Ireland* and has published many articles on contemporary literature.

Contents

Illustrations

Preface

As an American who has not lived for any length of time in Ireland, I began this study with some limitations; not having been raised in the culture, I was an outsider looking across the Atlantic to a country my parents had left many years ago. As I began to read Irish women poets, however, I noticed how much they had in common with other women poets I had read, and this observation gave me the foundation on which my book rests. Therefore, while I touch upon the "Irishness" of these poets, that is not my central concern.

This study is finished at what I believe is the early stage of work on a subject to be carried on by many scholars, in Ireland and elsewhere, in the years to come. There is much more to be said about the women I cover in this study, many different approaches to women poets writing in Ireland that others can take, and poets coming into print who deserve recognition. As anyone who writes on contemporary literature knows, a study like this is already almost out of date as it goes to press, and I kept wanting to cover more poets and more topics, but I knew I could go on for a very long time. Nevertheless, I hope that my outsider's view offers some insight into an area where not enough has been published and that it complements some very good work on this subject now being done in Ireland and beyond.

Many people have been generous with their time and help, especially some of the poets I discuss in this book. Eavan Boland encouraged me many years ago to undertake this study; Eiléan Ní Chuilleanáin has been especially helpful in discussing her own poetry and directing me to the work of women poets I had not read. Eithne Strong, Medbh McGuckian and Nuala Ní Dhomhnaill also talked to me about their poems. My decision to include Ní Dhomhnaill, who writes in Irish, was influenced by the availability of translations and by the sense that she is an important poet in redefining an image of Irish womanhood. In most quotations I have included the Irish, not only because this is Ní Dhomhnaill's chosen language but also because some who will read my book already read, or may wish to learn to read, her poetry in the original.

My colleagues in the American Conference for Irish Studies, who heard some of this material in papers, and my friends who are specialists in women's writing at La Salle University and elsewhere gave me valuable feedback as I worked on this book, for which I am very grateful. Small parts of chapters one, three, and four have appeared in the *Canadian Journal of Irish Studies* and the *Irish University Review*. Research grants from La Salle, as well as from the British Council, allowed me to travel to the Republic and to Northern Ireland for research and interviews.

Acknowledgment is made to the following for permission to reprint poetry or photographs in this book: Leland Bardwell, Eavan Boland, Anne Le Marquand Hartigan, Ruth Hooley, Jessie Lendennie, Maeve Kelly, Lynda Moran, Medbh McGuckian, Paula Meehan, Janet Shepperson, Eithne Strong, Carcanet Press, Dedalus Press, Gallery Press, W. W. Norton and Company, Poolbeg Enterprises, Raven Arts Press, Salmon Publishing, Wake Forest University Press, Oklahoma State University English Department, and *Irish Times*.

My most heartfelt thanks go to my husband, Charles, who served as first-draft editor, and also read the poetry, and to my daughter, Karintha, who grew into young adulthood hearing more than any teenager wants to know about women poets. This book is dedicated by all three of us to our son and brother, Ethan, who died just before it was completed.

Melrose Park, Pennsylvania   Patricia Boyle Haberstroh
February 1995

Women Creating Women

1

Introduction

Not so many years ago, reading Seamus Heaney's *Field Work*, I stopped to consider the vision of Ireland and of the speaker in the poems. Born in Northern Ireland, living in the Republic, Heaney appeared to embody a broad image of the Irish; he is also a very good poet. The central symbol of the book spotlights the relationship between individual and land that informs much of Irish contemporary poetry. When I finished the book, I asked myself whether a woman would or could write these poems. My immediate response was no: this was a man's vision of Ireland, for field work, even with all the racial, familial, social, and aesthetic connotations Heaney draws from the image, seemed essentially man's work.

More importantly, I realized how little I knew about contemporary Irish women poets—how hard it would be to envision their image of Ireland. And what would they write about? I ignored the voice that whispered "house work," and set out on a journey that became as interesting as the potential answer to my question. Down on my knees to reach books buried on the lowest shelves in bookstores, through the tunnels to the dust-covered Early Printed Books at Trinity College, on to the National Library and to University College at Belfield, all over Dublin, and then beyond, I went hunting for books by women poets. It was not easy. Quickly I dismissed the major presses; women poets had not made too many of their lists. Searching for out-of-print volumes and out-of-the-way presses, I began to get some sense of what any person who wants to read Irish women poets, even contemporary ones, was in for. I would ask women poets for names of others to read; some passed on volumes to me, but too often I was told, "This is out of print," or "A collection of hers hasn't been published yet."

Gradually a picture of women poets in contemporary Ireland emerged: publishing slowly but steadily in poetry periodicals, gathering in workshops all over Ireland to read and listen to one another, seeking out presses like Attic, Arlen House, Beaver Row, or Salmon that were willing to publish and publicize their poems,[1] but unknown to the mainstream reading public. In recent years, Gallery Press in Ireland and Wake Forest University Press in the United States, both small presses who often bring out different editions of the same work, have published individual volumes by Eiléan Ní Chuilleanáin, Medbh McGuckian, and Nuala Ní Dhomhnaill, but in general women poets were almost invisible.

As I read the poems I collected, searching for a volume like *Field Work*, I found poems by and about women: daughters, mothers, grandmothers, children—often about what goes on inside the home—that created a vision of the world of Irish women with broad connotations. I began to see another kind of "field work," and, more importantly, to recognize the aesthetic implications of such a world. I also saw that this was a vision available to few readers.

While I would like to report that the situation for women poets has changed drastically since I first began this work, the news is not that good. More opportunities have opened up, but the voice of women is still underrepresented inside and outside of established Irish poetry circles; this fact is even more significant given the recent visibility of Irish poets in the European and North American literary communities. Some of the women I cover in the following chapters have achieved a degree of prominence, but they are generally not as well known as their male colleagues. More importantly, there are many good Irish women poets who remain unread.

Recently I asked several people who read Irish poetry in English what women poets they had read; most had not read any. I also asked who they thought had been the most influential poets in modern Irish poetry, suggesting some correlation between my two questions. The common choices were ones I expected: William Butler Yeats and Patrick Kavanagh. Thinking about the impact of these poets on the course of twentieth-century Irish poetry in English, I considered what effect this might have had on women poets. Although studies have been devoted to ways in which Yeats and Kavanagh may have influenced the major male writers, almost nothing has been devoted to the impact of these poets on women writers.

The attitudes of Yeats and Kavanagh themselves towards women writers is an interesting area for study. Isolated examples can be found to

---

1. Catherine Rose was a guiding force as publisher at Arlen House (which, like Beaver Row, has folded). Attic is still the most productive publisher of women's writing in Ireland. Salmon, established in Galway, concentrates on poetry and is now being published under Poolbeg.

illustrate Yeats's support for writers like Kathleen Tynan and Dorothy Wellesley, but that support is sometimes patronizing. At the end of the year in which she first met Yeats, Dorothy Wellesley reports: "W. B. Y. is for ever trying to revise my poems. We have quarrelled about this. I say to him: 'I prefer bad poems written by myself to good poems written by you under my name'" (Yeats 1964, 46).[2] Likewise, the role that George, Yeats's wife, played in the creation of his work is still nebulous; her automatic writing involved a complex collaboration in which George may have contributed more than Yeats gave her credit for. As Margaret Mills Harper says, "although her husband directed the Script by his questions, it has not been known until recently that many—perhaps most— seminal ideas of *A Vision* originated in the mind of George Yeats" (Harper 1988, 49).

Yeats's poetry also indicates his attitudes towards women. In a poem like "Friends" (Yeats 1990, 119), praising Lady Gregory, the novelist Olivia Shakespear, and Maud Gonne, Yeats is primarily concerned with their relationship to him. Olivia Shakespear, with whom Yeats had a love affair in the 1890s,[3] receives praise as a writer, yet the focus is on her lifting his "dreamy load," so that he is "changed," and "labouring in ecstasy." And in "In Memory of Eva Gore-Booth and Con Markiewicz" (Yeats 1990, 241–42), though Gore-Booth was both poet and dramatist, Yeats immortalizes these sisters as he wants to remember them, as "innocent" and "beautiful," as "Two girls in silk kimonos, both / Beautiful, one a gazelle."

Even more instructive is any attempt to define Yeats's attitudes towards the roles women should play. The Maud Gonne who appears in his poems needs to be seen as Yeats's invention, someone he loved and lost; the real Maud, as some recent studies have shown, was someone else altogether.[4] When we turn to poems like "A Prayer for My Daughter" (Yeats 1990, 185–86), we find a conventional view of the ideal Irish woman: "rooted" in her husband's home, she should be beautiful, courteous, innocent, "a flourishing hidden tree." While this poem suggests that silence is a good trait in women, "A Prayer for My Son" (Yeats

---

2. Wellesley continues: "When he has made a suggestion for altering a certain line in my verses and I demur saying: 'I shall make a note saying this line was altered by W. B. Y. otherwise I am cheating,' he says, 'No! it has always been done in a company of poets,' which is true. He adds: 'Lady Gregory wrote the end of my 'Deirdre' on my fundamental mass.'

However I shall do as I intend" (Yeats 1964, 46).

3. For details, see Kline 1983.

4. See, for example, Ward 1990.

1990, 218–19) insists that the boy's destiny depends on his breaking out of silence, and away from his mother, to deal with the world:

> Though You can fashion everything
> From nothing every day, and teach
> The morning stars to sing,
> You have lacked articulate speech
> To tell Your simplest want, and known,
> Wailing upon a woman's knee,
> All of that worst ignominy
> Of flesh and bone.

While drawing generalizations in a contrast of this type has drawbacks, the expectations for the male and female child in these two poems differ. Keeping this in mind, we begin to understand the problems a woman might have with a poet who wants her "hidden" in a world of "custom" and "ceremony." Though all contemporary Irish poets have to face the Yeatsian legacy, women must confront issues not only of aesthetics but also of gender.

Examining Yeats's early love poetry in her essay, "Yeats: The Anxiety of Masculinity" (1991), Elizabeth Butler Cullingford discusses some of these issues and concludes:

> The politics of Yeats' historical situation, his love for a "New Woman," the indeterminacy of his gender identity, and the obliquity of his relationship to the canonical tradition, make it impossible to categorize his love poetry in any simple way. In approaching his early work, therefore, I find myself compelled to alternate between a recuperative and a suspicious hermeneutic. (1991, 65)

My own sense is that as we begin to examine Yeats more fully in this light, his later poetry presents a similar problem. In defining his concept of Unity of Being, Yeats attempted to identify a masculine and a feminine side of himself,[5] but much of that defining involves stereotypical definitions of male and female, masculine and feminine. In *The Last Courtly Lover: Yeats and the Idea of Woman*, Gloria Kline examines Yeats's view that women are the center of order in the life of a man or a culture: "The problem with this symbolical function is that it does not assure the Unities of Being and Culture to the woman. If she is herself an artist or a scholar, she must be so in terms of the masculine definition because no other exists. If she finds her identity in serving as the fixed center of

5. Yeats's concept of Unity of Being is explained in *A Vision* (Yeats 1978).

things, then her intellectual activity, being 'masculine' in nature, is somehow exterior to herself" (1983, 3).

When we turn to Kavanagh, the problems are equally complex but even more relevant to the contemporary Irish literary scene. Kavanagh waged his own battle with Yeats and the heritage of the Literary Revival. He saw himself, and others saw him, as an outsider, a rebel against the literary establishment. His groundbreaking 1942 poem, *The Great Hunger,* attacks the idealistic world of Irish nationalism and Yeatsian romanticism. Robert Garratt, in *Modern Irish Poetry: Tradition and Continuity from Yeats to Heaney,* defines Kavanagh's conflict with Yeats:

> For Kavanagh the conflict was inescapable: Yeats was the rootless force creating its own base and context, conceiving a literary nationalism that sought its validation in a rural fiction, "from contact with the soil," while remaining essentially urban. Kavanagh, in contrast, represented rooted experience, which knew too well the realities of rural life. The fact that Yeats was the dominant presence in Irish poetry made Kavanagh's difficulty more pronounced. He had to walk the thin line between admiration and recognition of genius on the one side, and imitation and assimilation on the other. (1986, 165–66)

Ironically, it was not long before Kavanagh himself became the measure against which other poets might be judged. Garratt's study, among others, details the major influence Kavanagh had on the poets who followed him. But these studies are devoted to male poets, and if we were to consider the questions of admiration, recognition, imitation, and assimilation that Garratt brings up and apply them to the woman writer, Kavanagh can present the same problems for her that Yeats presented for him.

Undoubtedly, for Kavanagh, writing was a male prerogative. In an essay on "The Irish Tradition" in his *Collected Pruse* (1967), Kavanagh defines a poet, speaking in the cocky voice he became known for:

> If I happened to meet a poet—and I have met poets—I would expect him to reveal his powers of insight and imagination even if he talked of poultry farming, ground rents or any other commonplace subject. Above all, I would expect him to be excited and have my horizons of faith and hope widened by his ideas on the only subject that is of any real importance—Man-in-this-World-and-why. (233)

Reinforcing the vision of poet as male embodied in these words, Kavanagh shows elsewhere in *Collected Pruse* that for him women could not be writers, as he falls back on reductive, stereotypical images: "The body with its feelings, its instincts, provides women with a source of wisdom, but they lack the analytic detachment to exploit it in literature. The great writer is the man who has in him some of this feminine capacity for perceiving with the body" (1967, 27). Garratt shows that Kavanagh himself often lacked "analytic detachment," misreading Yeats when it suited his purpose and attacking the work of rival poets (1986, 138–46). Nevertheless, Kavanagh's reputation and influence grew dramatically. As Dennis O'Driscoll says, "It is mandatory in any discussion of Irish poetry to quote Patrick Kavanagh as frequently as possible. His is the commanding voice among modern Irish poets, wielding an authority much greater than that of Yeats" (1989, 38).

Acknowledging the difficulty of assessing how attitudes like Yeats's and Kavanagh's might contribute to the relative invisibility of the woman poet, we can also say that their ideas and judgments are not untypical, having been passed down within Irish poetry circles, which male poets and critics have dominated. In twentieth-century literature, no woman has received the recognition that the major male poets enjoy, and the depiction of women in this poetry has often been filtered through the imagination of many male poets who share Yeats's and Kavanagh's views about women.

Recently, however, attempts have surfaced to challenge the authority of males in the Irish poetry canon. Nuala Archer's collection of contemporary Irish women's writing, published in the Winter 1986 issue of *Midland Review;* Ruth Hooley's 1985 collection, *The Female Line: Northern Irish Women Writers;* and Ailbhe Smyth's *Wildish Things,* an anthology of new Irish women's writing published by Attic Press in 1989 all feature women poets and demonstrate that outside the mainstream literary tradition, Irish women have been writing for a long time, often without recognition. A. A. Kelly's *Pillars of the House,* the first anthology of verse by Irish women, published by Wolfhound in 1987, also brought before the reading public the work of women poets.

The publication of these anthologies has not, however, been without problems. The issue of mainstream versus margin soon surfaced, with some critics maintaining that anthologies devoted exclusively to women further marginalized them, condemning them to a ghetto on the fringe of established literary territory.

Responding to such arguments, Ailbhe Smyth, the editor of *Wildish Things,* in the introduction to the volume, argued vigorously for publishing women writers together:

This anthology virtually imposed itself, as a necessary statement of the fact of Irish women's writing now. A statement of its breadth and depth, its power and variety, in Irish and in English, in poetry and fiction. It is important for us to make that statement, because if we do not, our work will continue to be altogether denied, ignored or only grudgingly admitted to the jealously male-guarded territory of "Irish literature." (1989b, 15)

Another point of view, published in 1988 in the *Letters from the New Island* series from Raven Arts Press, appears in Katie Donovan's provocative essay, *Irish Women Writers, Marginalised by Whom?* Because Donovan argues against using the category "Irish Woman Writer," any discussion of contemporary women poets will eventually come round to some of the issues Smyth and Donovan raise.[6] The question "Marginalised by Whom?" in the pamphlet's title brings up a host of questions feminist literary critics have been discussing for some time. Although Donovan does not address some of these questions, they influence the answers one might give to the major question she raises.

According to Donovan, resorting to the category "Irish Woman Writer" exacerbates the problem of marginalization by focusing an "isolating spotlight":

> isolating women writers into a single category has the self-defeating effect of further marginalising them from the literary mainstream. If their claims to be given an equal place alongside their male peers are to be taken seriously, women writers must be pushed into the flood, there to sink or swim on their own merits. Self-proclaimed feminist publishing houses place their protegees in a custom-made pool where they hover, maternal life-guards, ready to buoy up their charges. Such books will be bought by other feminists—a converted audience—and will not reach the audience amongst whom they might effect some of the attitude-changes they desire. (1988, 5)

Responding to Donovan, however, we might raise some additional questions that she does not consider but that are at the heart of arguments like Ailbhe Smyth's. How exactly does a writer get into the mainstream, and who does the "pushing"? If we admit, as Donovan does, that

6. In Donovan's analysis, her comparison of several women novelists with male counterparts leads to some valuable insights based on gender. But Donovan also makes connections between women writers, suggesting, for example, that their narrators emphasize personal biography more than public history.

women have been marginalized by male critics, they may not get a push and the very important opportunity to sink or swim on their own merits. When we examine the mainstream of Irish literature in English, or consider the question of the influence of poets like Yeats and Kavanagh, the issues get even more complicated. One can just as well imagine this "flood" as a larger, custom-made pool with a school of male swimmers, watched over by hovering, paternal lifeguards. Jumping into this water (or being pushed in) certainly is not as easy as Donovan makes it seem. Many factors—social, political, and literary—and many forces—including writers, critics, publishers, even academics—come into play here.[7]

Donovan's warnings against the classification "Woman Writer" presupposes that a poet who finds herself in this category will never make it into a mainstream. But one can also argue that an isolating spotlight gets women into print, where they eventually have the chance to sink or swim on their own merits. Eavan Boland, whose early work was brought out by Arlen House, which set out specifically to publish women writers, is a good illustration of this point. Likewise, Attic Press's growing list of books and pamphlets has become an invaluable resource in publicizing the achievement of women writers and the significance of women's issues.[8] And the Salmon Press, which is not exclusively a women's publisher but has published more poetry by women than any other press in Ireland, has highlighted the work of many women writers ignored by larger publishing houses.[9]

Most publishing houses have isolating spotlights, whether acknowledged or not, and writers who make it into the mainstream often do so as protegees. Publishers have traditionally promoted a particular category of writing or writer they think needs to be heard. The Dolmen Press, for example, was, according to Sebastian Barry in his introduction to *Inherited Boundaries: Younger Poets of the Republic,* responsible for "single-mindedly and single-handedly creating the means to the literature of the Republic, at least in poetry" (1986, 13). Many of the major Irish poets writing in English today, including Thomas Kinsella, John Montague, and Richard Murphy, benefited from their association with Dolmen.

7. Increasingly, poetry taught in university courses has an impact on a poet's reputation. There is little evidence that, until recently, courses in Anglo-Irish poetry included women poets. I discuss some of these ideas in more detail in "Literary Politics: Mainstream and Margin" (1992). On the related issue of book reviewing, see Sherry 1991.

8. Ailbhe Smyth's editorship was a major force in the success of Attic Press.

9. A cofounder of Salmon Publishing, Jessie Lendennie, has almost single-handedly overseen its growth. Salmon has also been responsible for more interest in writers not based in Dublin.

However, Dolmen, because it published so few women, was in part responsible for the domination of male poets in contemporary Ireland. Barry's anthology, published by Dolmen, illustrates the problem: his younger poets of the Republic are all male. Ironically, in his introduction Barry complains about the spotlight focused on the poets of the North, and suggests that the English publishers Faber and Faber have been partly responsible for this. One could just as easily accuse Barry and Dolmen of failing to notice the many women poets writing in the Republic.

In "Irish Women Poets: Breaking the Silence" (1990), Dennis J. Hannon and Nancy Means Wright reveal the results of a 1983 survey which showed that 89 percent of Irish poetry published was by men, and that of the other 11 percent, 9 percent was brought out by Attic Press. They also point out that women are severely underrepresented in contemporary anthologies, like *The New Oxford Book of Irish Verse* (1986) where there are no women, and *The New Penguin Book of Irish Poetry* (1990), where the ratio is thirty-five men to four women. Because such anthologies are popular sources for Irish writing, the failure to include a substantial representation of women's writing will affect the perception readers have of Irish literature for years to come.

The recent publication of *The Field Day Anthology of Irish Writing* (1991), a three-volume, four-thousand–page collection of writing in Irish and English from the sixth to the twentieth century, has been criticized for sparse representation of writing by women. With no women editors and little space devoted to women writers, this anthology calls attention to the continuing problems women have in getting their works published and recognized. Because such anthologies in effect create a canon, they will continue to perpetrate a vision of Irish writing dominated by male writers. Responding to criticism, Field Day plans a fourth volume devoted to women, a venture that created its own controversy. The fact that the contributions of women to Irish literature are far from getting the recognition they deserve may be the strongest rationale for the value of presses committed to publishing work by women.

Donovan's implication that women writers are often protected by other women, or by feminist critics, needs to be examined. Response to A. A. Kelly's *Pillars of the House* is a case in point. While acknowledging the groundbreaking significance of Kelly's work, Patricia Craig in the *Times Literary Supplement* certainly points out what she thinks are the weaknesses in Kelly's selections (1988, 957). Likewise, Maureen T. Reddy, discussing Ruth Hooley's collection, *The Female Line: Northern Irish Women Writers,* in the *Women's Review of Books,* acknowledges the strengths of some of the selections but also complains that the characters in one piece "carry such a burden of feminist messages that they seem more like speaking position papers than dramatic personae" (1988, 9). Reddy, noting that many of the contributors to this anthology have turned to writing later in life or have written for a long time without an audience, says, "I am glad, despite my complaints, that *The Female Line* gives these women a forum" (10). As Dale Spender documents so well in *The Writing or the Sex? or why you don't have to read women's writing to know it's no good,* the overwhelming number of reviews have been, and still continue to be, written by men (1989, 60–92). In an ideal world, perhaps the reviewer's gender should not be so important an issue; in the real world of literary publishing and reviewing, it has been and continues to be.

More importantly, anthologies of literature by women, studies of women writers, or reviews of women writers by women critics, often call into question some mainstream critical standards developed primarily to judge literature by men. Research in language and linguistics has recently focused on gender differences and on the ways in which bias has trivialized the concerns and expression of women. When we begin to apply this research to the imaginative use of language, we must ask whether the critical standards used to evaluate literature suffer from the same bias. Once we do this, we identify potential prejudices inherent in the literary establishment's criteria, and arguments like Donovan's, which ignore all of these issues to support some absolute and unchanging mainstream critical judgments, need to be challenged.

An even more basic consideration may be whether fitting oneself into a tradition, a mainstream, is always the best way to find a voice. Ailbhe Smyth's essay in the *Irish Review* on the response to the monument to Joyce's Anna Livia Plurabelle (which Dubliners have "renamed" "The Floozie in the Jacuzzi") suggests that women must begin anew, not try to insert themselves into a literary tradition that posits them as Other:

> The problem is *not* how to negotiate entry *inside,* into a tradition, culture, discourse which designates the Other as necessary alien, necessarily *outside.* . . .
>   Nor even how the discourse can be so altered as to accommodate alien expression. Both strategies of assimilation, recuperation. Insertion. . . .
> *Tabula Rasa. Free Space*
> Uninscribed place of the future. This is what we must remember. (1989a, 21–22)

While Smyth's ideas reflect an ongoing debate within feminist criticism, Donovan's view typifies a great deal of Irish thinking on this issue.

The Irish woman writer's response to the issues of feminism, women's rights, and the situation of the woman writer are not easy to categorize. Hesitation about identifying themselves as women poets appears among some women, though they offer several different reasons for their reluctance. At base, the issue again seems to be a concern that mixing literature with a narrow view of feminism will limit the way people look at their work, or whether they are read at all. And there is good reason to believe that in Ireland this will happen. Some of the poets I have talked to indicated their ambivalence about what the term "feminist" connotes in Ireland; others, while identifying themselves as feminists, reject a separatist stance. Still other Irish women writers feel that to mix politics with art inevitably leads to trouble, an opinion they share with some contemporary male writers.

Even Eavan Boland, most outspoken on discrimination against Irish women writers, voices concern about what she calls "The Woman Poet: Her Dilemma":

> The dilemma I speak of is inherent in a shadowy but real convergence between new experience and an established aesthetic. What this means in practical terms is that the woman poet today is caught in a field of force. Powerful, persuasive voices are in her ear as she writes. Distorting and simplifying ideas of womanhood and poetry fall as shadows between her and the courage of her own experience. If she listens to these voices, yields to these ideas, her work will be obstructed. If, however, she evades the issue, runs for cover and pretends there is no pressure then she is likely to lose the resolution she needs to encompass the critical distance between writing poems and being a poet. (1986, 40)

Boland claims to be neither a "post-feminist" nor a "separatist," though she has often documented in her essays why women have cause to be either or both and defines herself as a feminist. For the dilemma that she describes, Boland believes that adopting a separatist stance may involve substituting one oversimplification for another. Her position may be most clearly stated in an article in the *Irish Times:* "You couldn't have a feminist poet anymore than you could have a Marxist poet. Poetry begins where those *isms* stop. It begins in all those ambiguities and powers of human feeling and the *isms* don't go that far" (1992b, 12).

The writer Evelyn Conlon, on the other hand, in describing the position of women within Irish literary culture, celebrates feminist writers and places Irish women writers in an international context of women who share the same experiences and problems. In the Autumn 1988 issue of the literary review *Graph,* Conlon documents the continuation of male domination in Irish literature, citing a number of examples to prove her point: a new literary award sponsored by Overseas Publications with four male judges; the reestablishment of *New Irish Writing,* where three men decide what gets published; a 1987 newspaper Arts Award for the year with seven male judges; a collection called *The Irish Mind* with thirteen essays on men by men and one by a women on Yeats; the all-male board of Field Day and the numerous pamphlets by males published by Field Day and Raven Arts.

Responding to the charge that a writer is a writer first, not a man or a woman, Conlon argues that women writers still confront a hostile environment that works against them. Defending the value of feminism for the woman writer, Conlon suggests its broader effects:

> Feminism is many things: one part of it is the emotional/political/philosophical movement which gives us a life-long licence to believe that our thoughts, words, and solutions matter in the overall picture. For many of us this is a new feeling. The good, the excitement, the truth that can come from it could easily be lost in a still hostile and again newly hostile anti-feminist world (I think this is our world in Ireland). A canon that doesn't include the books which have found life due to this worldwide movement, is not truly concerned with the dissemination of knowledge or ideas. (1988, 5)

Challenging the argument that "excellence is excellence," Conlon asks: "who decides?" She also mentions the often unchallenged assumption that writing by men is inherently more universal and important. Recalling Tillie Olsen's study of women writers in *Silences,* Conlon points out that the "lack of mothers writing has surely been one of the most dangerous silences in our world" (1988, 6).

The Northern poet Ruth Hooley maintains, on the other hand, that it is important for women to identify themselves as writers, not women writers, which she sees as a "dangerous" but "transitional" category. Hooley distinguishes between being a feminist and being a feminist poet, like Boland identifying herself as the former but not the latter. However, the fact that she is a woman informs her poetry, Hooley believes, and she suggests why this is significant: "I'm writing primarily from a woman's perspective. With a lot of my poems the gender of the poet wouldn't matter, but knowing the gender of the poet does make it different. It comes across in the imagery. A lot of the poems in *The Female Line* couldn't have been written by men. They couldn't have said the same things."[10]

If we read between the lines of this debate, and look at much of what is said and written on the subject of Irish women writers, a much deeper issue emerges. The traditional image of woman in Irish culture lies at the heart of this problem, and the expressions and ramifications of that image, so deeply embedded in the Irish psyche, are just beginning to be explored. If we are to understand the marginalized woman poet, we must first study the marginalized woman in Ireland. We might then answer Eavan Boland's question of why, in Ireland, people have had such trouble putting the words "woman" and "poet" together (Boland 1990a, 32).

The poet and critic Mary O'Donnell describes one aspect of this problem as it relates to contemporary women poets:

> The majority of male poets can probably spend more time in the actual process of writing insofar as they are ably supported by prevailing social structures and attitudes—whatever their endeavour—whereas many people have difficulty in responding to a woman who is a poet. A woman writer may find that her work is regarded as a "hobby"—a time-filler when she is unemployed or before she has children. One wonders how many men, upon the birth of their child, have been asked, "Well, I suppose you've given up writing now?", or on the resumption of employment are greeted with the following delirious comment: "It must be marvellous to have a proper job—you can forget about the writing!"
>
> Women writers regularly deal with this attitude, which clearly signals that a woman is expected to function within certain clearly-defined and rather narrow parameters. (1986, 16)

What, we might ask, are the "narrow parameters" O'Donnell mentions? While contemporary women's movements challenge most cultural mores, the threat they present to a communal and personal image of Irish womanhood cannot be overestimated. In *Women in Ireland: Voices of Change,* Jenny Beale claims that women in the Republic have traditionally had fewer rights than those in other European countries and fewer than women in Northern Ireland. Beale elaborates:

---

10. Hooley is quoted in an interview with Rebecca E. Wilson in Somerville-Arjat and Wilson 1990, 169–70.

Contraception was illegal, divorce was banned in the Constitution and abortion was a criminal act. Single mothers and separated women were ineligible for welfare payments, and women were openly discriminated against in education, employment and the tax and welfare systems. A marriage bar was in operation in the Civil Service and other occupations, forcing women to give up their jobs on marriage. Women had few rights under family law, and were in a highly vulnerable position if their marriages broke down. (1987, 3–4)

The 1937 Constitution of the Republic, a document that reflects the image of women as defined by political and church leaders, identifies the family as the "natural primary and fundamental unit group of Society" and "the necessary basis of social order . . . indispensable to the welfare of the Nation and the State." It also describes the role of women: "In particular, the State recognizes that by her life within the home, woman gives to the State a support without which the common good cannot be achieved. . . . The State shall, therefore, endeavour to ensure that mothers shall not be obliged by economic necessity to engage in labour to the neglect of their duties in the home."

As Beale points out, the terms *woman* and *mother* are used interchangeably in the Constitution. While claiming to protect women who wanted to carry out their domestic duties, the Irish government ultimately discriminated. The historian Margaret Mac Curtain, in an essay on "The Historical Image" in *Irish Women: Image and Achievement* (1985, 37–50), maintains that attempts to explain the status of women in Ireland center on the traditional value system of a rural society, but ignore other causes: "Rarely, if at all, is allusion made to the total exclusion of women from public life, and from responsibility for public morality. Woman's place was in the home" (1985, 49).[11]

At another level, the identity of many Irish women is strongly influenced by their experiences in the Catholic Church, which offers the image of Mary, virgin and mother, as the archetypal perfect woman. Asexual, comforting, and protective, Mary embodies concepts of domesticity and submissiveness, with motherhood her primary trait. Pope John Paul II evoked this image when he spoke in Ireland in 1979: "May Irish mothers, young women and girls not listen to those who tell them that working at a secular job, succeeding in a secular profession, is more im-

11. For more information on women in Irish history, see Mac Curtain and Ó Corráin 1979, Luddy and Murphy 1989, and "Women and Irish Politics" (1992), a special issue of the *Canadian Journal of Irish Studies*.

portant than the vocation of giving life and caring for this life as a mother" (quoted in Beale 1987, 50). The message here, that everything must be subordinated to a woman's primary vocation as mother, echoes through many of the pronouncements and laws of the Irish Republic and the Irish Catholic Church. The idea that a woman might choose neither to marry nor to have children is implicitly condemned.

Equally complicated is the issue of female sexuality. With virgin and mother as model, and a male, celibate hierarchy promoting unrealistic images of female sexuality, Catholic women in Ireland often had more to come to terms with than their counterparts in other countries. Control over reproduction, often crucial in determining the direction a woman's life takes, has been a particular stumbling block because of the Catholic Church's opposition. Although selling contraceptives became legal in the Republic in 1979, limitations included a provision that they were to be sold only for "bona fide" family planning (that is, to married people) and under prescription. Ailbhe Smyth maintained in 1983 that this plan was "virtually unworkable" and "that it would appear that a blind eye is turned on the activities of family planning clinics" (48). In 1973 the Catholic bishops agreed that the state need not uphold the teachings of the church; however, church leaders have frequently defended their views on female sexuality and sexual sins, and bans on contraception and abortion continue in the Republic. At the same time, what Beale defines as "voices of change" have challenged these views, leading often to acrimonious debate.

The situation for women in Northern Ireland may differ in some respects from that in the Republic, but it certainly is not easier. Living for years within a war-torn landscape, the women of Ulster have had to watch as the political turmoil over which they have so little control continually disrupts their lives. In "Women in the Community in Northern Ireland: Struggling for Their Half of the Sky," Avila Kilmurray writes that despite organizations like the Northern Ireland Women's Rights Movement and women's growing self-confidence as they struggled amid the fighting, consciousness raising did not flourish in the North. Because of the church's resistance to any attempts to examine attitudes towards family or personal relationships, women's issues got little attention: "Thus, by the mid-seventies it was clear that if the silence of working-class grievance was shattered across Northern Ireland, the particular issues of specific concern to women tended to be lost in the babble of demands—either being dismissed by political parties as 'red herrings'; marginalized as irrelevant middle-class feminism; or denounced as unrepresentative left-wing agitation" (1987, 180). As Liam O'Dowd demonstrates in "Church, State and Women: The Aftermath of Partition" (1987), institutionalized religion and politics have been overwhelmingly dominated by males in both Northern Ireland and the Republic, in effect disenfranchising women, separating the public and private spheres, promoting ideological images of women, and obscuring the role women played in Irish life and Irish society.

Despite these obstacles, changes in Ireland for women since the beginning of the 1970s have sometimes been both dramatic and disturbing, and these have spilled over into literature as well. Contemporary poetry by women reflects them all. As more women begin to speak for themselves, they create alternatives to stereotypical and idealized images and write realistically and explicitly about female experience. Any reading of contemporary Irish women poets will reveal just how varied and complex the responses to the problems women face can be.

Identifying common characteristics in poetry by Irish women is not easy, though with more reading and study, and more women in print, some generalizations can be made. But doing so is not so simple as it may appear; in the context of international gender, language, and theory studies, there are many approaches we can take. As in the debates over mainstream and margin in publishing, certain basic issues permeate these discussions.

An intriguing area for exploration centers on the question of voice and the aesthetic challenge for contemporary women to create female speakers. Lyric poetry presents a unique problem for women in creating a poetic "I." Traditionally, the better known and acknowledged Irish women writers have been novelists, not poets. In fiction, plot and setting allow writers like Somerville and Ross, Mary Lavin, or Edna O'Brien to imagine a world that often does not demand the same kind of personal voice a lyric poem does. Even if we consider the modernist poet's suggestion that the writer adopt a mask through which to speak, we soon realize that those masks and speakers, whether Yeats's or Pound's or Eliot's, were almost always male. Any exception to this convention, like Yeats's Crazy Jane, usually remains a filter through which the male poet expresses his own attitudes and personality.

Many of the Irish women poets I talked to, who had been brought up, educated, and begun to write in a literary tradition dominated by male voices, still search for ways to deal with the challenge of the lyric "I" when they are creating women speakers. Monique Wittig identifies a source of this difficulty:

In principle, pronouns mark the opposition of gender only in the third person and are not gender bearers, per se, in the other persons. Thus, it is as though gender does not affect them, is not part of their structure, but only a detail in their associated form. But, in reality, as soon as there is a locutor in discourse, as soon as there is an "I," gender manifests itself. (1986, 65)

The problem, Wittig explains, is that the "abstract form, the general, the universal, this is what the so-called masculine gender means, for the class of men have appropriated the universal for themselves" (66).

Raising the issue of a female "I" in poetry today immediately presents problems. In a poststructuralist world, we have been warned that to speak of an "I" as a unifying voice or center ignores the multiple ambiguities, ironies, contradictions, and diverse meanings of the nonsubjective language systems that some critics claim a poem describes. The critical theory that maintains that the reader creates the text warns us to ignore anything so absolute as the intention of the author or the subjective meaning of the poem.

Dealing with the issue of a specifically female "I" in lyric poetry also brings up questions of defining gendered thinking and language. Feminist critics have illustrated the numerous potential meanings embedded in words like *woman, female,* and *feminine,* pointing out that gender is a construction, that we have to be very careful to differentiate between biology and psychology. The dangers of accepting binary opposites like male/female and subjective/objective, which can marginalize women in culture and language controlled by men, have led both to calls to get beyond gender categories and to attempts to identify a specifically female language, *écriture feminine* or *womanwriting,* which I shall discuss in more detail in chapter 5. The broad dimensions of this discussion include not only issues of language but also the relationship of language to sexuality and gender. In the field of literary criticism, philosophical, psychoanalytical, and linguistic theories have influenced the growth of a number of different approaches to analysis of writing by women.

One of these approaches, based on the humanistic concept of a unified self that reflects a truth and reality beyond itself, places women within a gendered history and culture and sees poetry as mimetic. The woman speaking becomes the foundation for analysis, and interpretation often seeks to look at a poem as a reflection of a woman's experience and to uncover how women writers are often subverting patriarchal assumptions and societal codes. Usually associated with American feminists like Ellen Moers, Susan Gubar, Sandra Gilbert, and Elaine Showalter, this approach posits a female tradition in literature and proposes what Showalter defines as "gynocritics," a woman-centered critical framework for the analysis of women's writing (Showalter 1985).

Challenging these critics are several theories aligned with contemporary movements in philosophy, psychoanalysis, and linguistics. Influenced by the work of Freud, Derrida, and Lacan, these approaches focus less on "women" than on "woman" (what deconstruction critics call a signifier), and the debate is centered on language. Isolating woman from culture, history, and politics, proponents see gender as a construction and language as patriarchal. Following Lacan's theory that language becomes the substitute for the pre-Oedipal union with the mother, French feminists like Hélène Cixous, Luce Irigaray, and Julia Kristeva define a female language, *écriture féminine,* which, deriving from the mother, is neither logocentric nor logically coherent.[12] Emanating from the repressed unconscious, this female writing disrupts what is termed "phallogocentric discourse." Julia Kristeva, challenging the idea of a subjective speaking voice and a historical or cultural positioning of any voice, emphasizes language as process and sees style as the expression of repressed femaleness.

In *Gynesis: Configurations of Woman and Modernity* (1985), Alice Jardine suggests that the lack of a "conscious, Cartesian subject" denies the possibility of literature as representation of "Man's truth" (27). In "The Laugh of the Medusa," Cixous connects language with anatomy, and posits a new language connected with female sexuality. Not a logocentric system, this female language is fluid, nondiscursive, irrational, reflecting a process rather than a fixed subject. Style, rather than theme or meaning, defines the feminine, which, argues Cixous, is not restricted to writing by women (Cixous 1976).

From a different direction comes another challenge to a monolithic concept of woman writer or female voice: here the issue is often how class, race, or ethnicity might interact with sexual and gender identity. Objecting to the psychoanalytic critic's separation of text from both history and culture, these critics point out the importance of identifying the ways in which ideology informs both a culture and a literature, often unconsciously. Speaking of a woman writer or a woman's voice immediately calls into question the numerous identities a woman has, and to privilege gender more than all or any of these is to oversimplify.[13]

12. For more on French feminist theory, see Marks and de Courtivron 1981.
13. Todd (1988) sees this approach as influenced by Marxism and more popular in Britain.

Other recent critical theories warn about an essentialist approach—that is, assuming that there is a set of fixed and essential characteristics that define the female—or a mimetic approach, which emphasizes the ways in which writing by women is taken as the "real" or "true" reflection of women's lives. Tied in to these critical theories are questions about the relationship between art and autobiography, between personal experience and artistic expression. Challenges to the concept that literature reflects "true" representations of female experience or that poems necessarily express or depict an external reality have been raised in recent years as literary theory has grown much more complex.

The question of voice in lyric poetry, then, is not easy to discuss. Complicating these theoretical analyses is the idea that not to look at the persona of a poem as a woman may be to miss much of what the poet wants to say (keeping in mind Ruth Hooley's point, mentioned above, that knowing the gender of a poet does make the poem different). We can argue that voice, subjectivity, and a female persona may be very important as women move out of silence and that gendering the lyric "I" validates the importance of a woman's voice and experience and empowers the female speaker, who for so long has been unheard and undervalued. Some feminist critics look suspiciously at theories influenced so heavily by male philosophers and psychoanalysts, maintaining that such theories are just new attempts to deny meaning and status to the female voice.

Solving this problem is difficult because we could argue that the voice we identify as female depends on a definition which grows from a social construct, and is, therefore, not natural or essential to females at all. But we can also argue, as Eavan Boland does, that women are constructed by the construct and therefore live and write within its parameters (1990a, 36). To identify the "I" or voice in a lyric poem as nonsubjective, as some contemporary critics do, may also be to work from a scientific, phallogocentric base that will continue to ignore the voices of women.

Because the issue of self-identity has been such an important theme in poetry by women, identifying the "I" as female and subjective seems important in understanding and appreciating what many women poets are writing about. My own reading, as well as interviews with the poets I cover, shows that many of them are aware of the need to speak as women while they simultaneously develop their own individual voice and style. Creating a new image of women in Irish literature is a goal many of them share. What writing as woman ultimately means, however, certainly changes as we move from poet to poet.

Janet Todd at the conclusion of *Feminist Literary History* notes that the "epistemological revolutions" we have undergone have made both the subject and the unified speaking voice problematic. Maintaining that the concept of a dispersed subject with "its jaded contempt for anything but internal states and their narratives" may be just as problematic, Todd tries to negotiate a path between the two approaches:

> There seems little use in questioning everything at every moment. Such questioning can only prevent activity and reduce the time for listening to answers, however partial and determined. It may be that for any activity a certain intellectual deceit is necessary, some pretence of an identity that is not entirely identical, an acceptance of some history even if its status as rhetorical story is suspected. As long as we know that we are ultimately not speaking for all and all time, that at every turn the various marks of race, age, class and so on should be noticed, and as long as we understand the ultimate impossibility of comprehending the past except through present structures, we may have to accept the useful fiction of "women"; though we speak out of a cluster of conventions that have no necessary individuality or unity, we may have to hear a woman speaking as well as listening to speech "in the feminine." (1988, 135–36)

I find Todd's a sensible approach because it acknowledges that a woman speaking in a poem is necessarily a construction, a fiction, a created voice. But it allows for relating this voice to women's experience and to making some kind of connection between the woman poet and a woman speaker. This does not mean that we necessarily see women's poetry as autobiographical or "personal," though some women poets can be read this way, or that the poet is speaking only as woman to women. I find in Irish women poets a vast range of speakers: some clearly identified as women, some more gender neutral, some working within patriarchal structures to challenge conventional views of women, some illustrating a type of *écriture féminine*. Whether identity is "pretence" or not, it "means" something; in fact, the meaning of identity appears to me to be the most prominent theme in the poetry I cover. While I would not argue against the idea that a woman has multiple identities, nor for the concept that there are essential characteristics in all women's poetry, I do believe that women share certain experiences and that these, reflected in their poetry, are worth examining. Placing women poets in relation to one another brings these to the surface and illustrates some differences between poetry written by women and that written by men. Because my study is devoted primarily to imagery, I hope to show how images connect these women poets to one another and differentiate them from male poets.

In an article discussing three contemporary women poets, James McElroy suggests that in Irish poetry males put place before person and put less emphasis on the value of self, which tends to be a central question for women poets (1985, 36).[14] While this is true in one sense, and much has been written about the sense of place in recent Irish poetry, such an evaluation often depends upon narrow definitions of *self* and upon *place* defined as geography and land. I think again of Heaney's "field work," but abundant allusions to geography and land can be found in the work of John Montague, Thomas Kinsella, Paul Muldoon, Richard Murphy, and others.[15] On the other hand, in volumes like Medbh McGuckian's *On Ballycastle Beach* or Moya Cannon's *Oar*, geography and land play an important part in our understanding of the poems. But whether males put less emphasis on "self" is certainly a debatable point; the relationship between self and place underpins many of the poems by male poets.

We can attribute the emphasis on place in some of the better-known Irish male poets to specific sociological factors, the territorial battles of one version of Irish history reflected in the continual use of land as symbol. Much of this "place" imagery involves the male poet's response to Irish political history and the individual's relationship to his place in a divided land: his poetic "self" is often integrally tied to that history. While especially evident in the Northern poets, images of farms, towns, counties, cities, streets, and museums figure prominently in the work of poets from both Northern Ireland and the Republic, illustrating the more "public" life that men in Ireland have known. Their "self" is often seen in terms of this history.

Women poets, on the other hand, frequently circumscribe another kind of place: the predominance of internal spaces in rooms and houses clearly links them to one another. On the most obvious level, this is the world many women in Ireland inhabit, and they often identify with it more than with the "public" world of their male colleagues. However, we might see this imagery not as a difference between public and personal, or between place and self, but as a difference in how men and women poets identify self in terms of different "places." As more women

14. Although I have some disagreement with McElroy on this point, he has some valuable insights on women poets (see also McElroy 1989).

15. Seamus Heaney has published a critical work, *The Place of Writing* (1989). A book of essays edited by Andrew Carpenter (1977), *Place, Personality and the Irish Writer*, addresses some of the same topics.

are published, another kind of history and geography surfaces, which validates their image of place as equally important as the more "public" landscape Irish male poets often write about.

Irish women poets share this different sense of place (or space) not only with one another but also with women writers in other cultures. In her book on American poets, *Stealing the Language,* Alicia Suskin Ostriker explains how such imagery expresses a quest for self-identity: "it is immediately apparent that women who seek themselves will include the material of their daily lives and feelings in their poems. . . . The legitimization as literary of what has been excluded from literature is one result of all literary movements" (1986, 89). As Ostriker says: "When the republic of letters annexes a new province, it is immediately revealed to be different, and more complex, than we thought while it was a blank spot, like Conrad's Congo, on the cultural map" (90).

The differences and complexities Ostriker describes represent a challenge to traditional thinking and established images, and ultimately to mainstream critical criteria that define the significance of a literary work. Many of the attitudes about women expressed by Yeats and Kavanagh influence not only the invisibility of women writers but also the sentimentalized, unrealistic, and often negative portrayals of woman in Irish literature: from the passive victim, Mother Ireland, to the idealistic Cathleen Ní Houlihan; from the devouring female to the all-suffering, accepting mother.

In recent years women have begun to challenge these images as the creation of male thinking and writing. In "The Floozie in the Jacuzzi" (1989a), Ailbhe Smyth surveys such images in Irish life and letters. Describing the impact of demeaning, male creative fantasies, Smyth juxtaposes these with excerpts from the work of women, in a strategy she labels "intersextextual." Smyth quotes from writers like Catherine Byron, Paula Meehan, Julia O'Faolain, and Clare Boylan to illustrate how their works "resonate with different realities" (17).

Those realities can be seen often in contemporary poetry, in which the images, themes, and feelings described by Irish women are different, often unexpected, as personae struggle with the multiple roles they are expected to play. As women writers began to challenge sexual taboos, for example, they expressed a new view of female anatomy, which figures prominently in their imagery. Female sexuality also became a focus of self-identity. In 1980, Eithne Strong published *FLESH . . . The Greatest Sin,* which might be read as a female version of Patrick Kavanagh's *The Great Hunger;* in the same year Eavan Boland's *In Her Own Image* explored the effects of conventional sexual images of women; and in 1982,

Mary Dorcey's *Kindling* ignored the homosexuality taboo to depict lesbian sexual experience. Each of these, published in the early 1980s, signaled a disregard for restrictions the Irish woman poet had been expected to respect.

As women became more assertive about their voice, less hesitant about a literary life, more confident about their talent, a body of poetry with different emphases began to emerge. Poems about orgasm and masturbation, poems about wombs, childbirth, mastectomies, hysterectomies, anorexia created images of women not embarrassed about their bodies. Ostriker, noting this body imagery in much of women's poetry, reads it as the "release of anatomy" and a sign of liberation for the female writer:

> One of the ways we recognize a poetess—which is to say a woman poet locked into sentimentality by her inhibitions—is that she steers clear of anatomical references. As womanly inhibition declines, we grow aware of its sources in dualistic ideology, gender polarization, and the dread of female sexuality. One of the ways we recognize that a woman writer has taken some kind of liberating jump is that her muted parts begin to explain themselves. (1986, 92)

Challenging the stereotypes of submissive lover and joyous mother, the voices of women poets also echo with confusion, anger, and ambivalence. A poem like Leland Bardwell's unconventional "Lullaby" from *The Fly and the Bedbug* (1984, 25), for example, is anything but soothing:

> Lullaby sing lullaby
> To my sweet baby in his cradle
> Your daddy's gone but what is worse
> I wish that I had left him first
> Oh lullaby sing lullaby.

The love between mother and child is also the subject of numerous poems by women. In the work of Eavan Boland, Medbh McGuckian, Nuala Ní Dhomhnaill, and Eithne Strong, there are numerous poems about the value of motherhood, but the difficulties of mothering recur often in these poems. The celebrated 1992 case of a young girl brought back from England, where she had sought to abort a fetus conceived through rape, is the subject of Paula Meehan's poem "The Wounded Child," in which Meehan shifts the focus away from the fetus and towards that part of the young girl aborted in the humiliating and highly publicized political process. No longer silent on issues that concern women, these poets speak about female experience, often revealing how women are unfairly perceived and treated in Ireland.

Like some of their male counterparts in contemporary Irish poetry, many of the women poets condemn the traditional glorification of Irish battles, even though women are rarely credited with making any kind of comment on Irish history and politics. Eiléan Ní Chuilleanáin's "Site of Ambush," Medbh McGuckian's *On Ballycastle Beach,* Linda Anderson's "Gang-Bang, Ulster Style" (Kelly 1988, 144–45), among others, respond to the long history of conflict in Ireland; many of these poems describe the plight of the woman bystander. Margaret Curran's speaker in "The Ulster Widow's Tale" (Archer 1986, 98) describes her loss in terms of a family, not a cause:

> Now he's a number on a noticeboard
> Not my husband; kind father;
> Just 3079.
>
> And I'm left with a bullethole
> In the mind
> Plugged with valium.

Many of these poems lament the impact of war on home and family life, the bonds of love destroyed by the hatred that fuels war. Women poets write about their fear: "It is a time of hate / And I am nowhere brave. / I dread to be / slashed apart," says Eithne Strong's speaker in "The North in Any Direction" (1974, 14). Catherine Byron, in "The Black and Tans Deliver a Son—Galway 1921" (Archer 1986, 15), describes how soldiers destroy what women nurture:

> Didn't she step out into the yard
> God love her
> and see her own son's brains
> scattered like mash about the flags?
> And didn't she then kneel down
> and gather the soggy shards
> of her womb's child into her apron
> carefully, as a girl gathers
> mushrooms in the September fields?
> And didn't she then stifle
> the outbreath of her grieving
> till only a whistle
> or whimper of her lamentation

was heard in that place
lest the soldiers note her the more?

While Byron's conversational tone echoes Irish colloquial speech patterns, the insistent repetition of "didn't she?" forces us to view this poem as a demand for recognition of the sacrifices and enforced silence ("whimper of her lamentation") women have endured in the Troubles. Poems like this challenge the sentimentalized mothers of Patrick Pearse's well-known poem, "The Mother," which celebrates the generosity of women as they send their sons off to the glory of bloody battle for the cause.

For Eavan Boland, this mythology of war is part of a larger problem Irish women have to deal with, an image of a nation the woman speaker in "Mise Éire" (1990c, 78–79) will no longer accept. Rewriting Patrick Pearse's "I am Ireland," Boland's persona states another point of view:

I won't go back to it—

my nation displaced
into old dactyls,

oaths made
by the animal tallows
of the candle,

land of the Gulf Stream,
the small farm,
the scalded memory,
the songs
that bandage up the history,
the words
that make a rhythm of the crime

where time is past.
A palsy of regrets.
No. I won't go back.

The poem continues with an image of an emigrant woman, homesick and numb, holding a half-dead baby to her breast. Boland's speaker's words "unbandage" history and present another view of the "crime," pointing out the ways in which Irish songs and poems have created an image of Ireland with women either excluded or sentimentalized. The assertive, "No. I won't go back," voices the commitment of a woman poet to challenging a romanticized image of Ireland, particularly as this applies to women.[16]

Such issues often find their way into poems in which Irish women revise myth and history, creating new stories with alternative images. Again links with women poets in other countries can be made, for mythic revision, a common theme in women's poetry, reflects another aspect of the search for self-identity. In Nuala Ní Dhomhnaill's poetry, the hag of Irish folklore, a powerful, overtly sexual female figure, displaces the passive woman we often see in Irish literature. Roz Cowman's poems "Medea Ireland" (1989, 35), "Dionysia" (Kelly 1988, 134), and "Jocasta" (Archer 1986, 60), and Medbh McGuckian's "Venus and the Rain" (1984, 31) all represent new visions of ancient heroines, seen now from a woman's point of view. Shifting the focus from the males these mythic figures have been identified with, and away from the fantasy females some male poets have imagined, such poems attempt to give the female mythic figure a mind and voice of her own. New images also challenge traditional religious figures as women poets explore the impact of these models on the lives of Irish women.

At the beginning of my study, I thought of the female voice as a problem for women poets; I see it now as a challenge that contemporary Irish women have responded to in different ways, and often as the impetus for the uniqueness of each woman's work. Although I was originally looking for how Irish women poets share certain characteristics, I have also discovered the different ways in which they have responded to the challenge of speaking through a female voice, creating some of their best and most original poetry. I have also understood the need to identify the female voice as a human voice coming to us through a female speaker. These poets are not speaking just as women, nor are they speaking just to women, although at times they are doing both. Their experience as women gives them a valuable perspective on human experience. Because for so long that perspective has been missing from Irish poetry, the growth of interest in their work will have a great impact on a changing definition of Irish literature, literary tradition, and culture. Women creat-

16. A debate on the potential conflicts between Irish nationalism and feminism suggests that the strong undertones of nationalism evident in both politics and literature need to be examined in light of their impact on women. Gerardine Meaney points out that women themselves have cooperated in becoming "the scapegoats of national identity" (1991, 7). Edna Longley (1990) argues that this debate, because it often ignores the women of Northern Ireland and the relationship between women and Unionist politics, is too narrowly defined.

ing women, as these poets illustrate, can help us collapse one barrier between margin and mainstream.

So, after my journey through the work of contemporary women poets, what have I found to place with Heaney's *Field Work* to express a more comprehensive vision of Ireland and the Irish? There are more than enough good choices in the following pages. Eithne Strong's *Sarah, in Passing,* Eiléan Ní Chuilleanáin's *The Magdalene Sermon,* Eavan Boland's *Outside History,* Medbh McGuckian's *On Ballycastle Beach* all qualify, as do several other volumes written over the last twenty years. In the next chapter I will look at Eithne Strong's *FLESH . . . the Greatest Sin* and discuss the ways it covers territory left out of Patrick Kavanagh's *The Great Hunger.* In another chapter I will discuss Eiléan Ní Chuilleanáin's poem "The Lady's Tower," which the poet herself describes as a "feminist riposte" to Yeats's tower. In the final chapter, where I briefly cover the work of several poets, I suggest that Paula Meehan's poem "The Pattern" might be set beside Seamus Heaney's "Digging" to enlarge our vision of Irish family and social life.

In her essay "What Foremothers?" Nuala Ní Dhomhnaill addresses Anne Stevenson's support of a John Montague statement that women poets have not been discriminated against in Ireland. Supporting Eavan Boland's arguments, and maintaining that poetry in Ireland has produced a "diagrammatic and dehumanized image of woman," Ní Dhomhnaill points to many images of women that are "fictions of the imaginations of men" (1992a, 21).

My study is an attempt to illustrate the fictions of the imaginations of women. From one point of view, I could argue that the poetry I discuss in the following chapters represents another literary tradition, a margin on the mainstream. But I am less concerned with margins and mainstreams, or indeed with comparing poetry by women with that by men, than I am with exploring the work of some very good poets. Because I am not a good swimmer, I would never qualify as a maternal lifeguard, but I do think as women poets become better known, they swim on their own, as long as they get into the stream.

Eithne Strong.
Courtesy of *Irish Times*.

2

Eithne Strong

Private?

They objected, "These things are private,
you must not write about them." But
privacies are the stuff, the sine qua non
of writers: subtly placed, distanced,
transmuted, tangential—merely being,
they will out whatever shape,
the academicians' boon, ground for beavering.

—Eithne Strong, *Let Live*

With one of the longest careers among contemporary women poets, Eithne Strong seems to defy much of the conventional thinking about what the woman writer is or could be. Studies of women writers often point to the conflict between a writing career and domestic and maternal duties, using examples like Emily Dickinson or great nineteenth-century novelists like Jane Austen and Charlotte and Emily Brontë, who may have become successful writers because they never married. Indeed many of the married poets covered in this study have smaller-than-average Irish families. But Eithne Strong, married to the writer and psychoanalyst Rupert Strong, somehow managed to write almost without interruption while she raised nine children.[1]

Having left school early, Strong returned to complete a degree at Trinity in her forties, spent twelve years teaching, and continues to write and publish. In an interview in 1989, she told me that she worries little about literary reputation; when she is gone, she says, a body of work will

---

1. For the first five years after the birth of her handicapped son, Strong has said that she found little time to write (Maher 1980, 10).

be there for people to judge.[2] By 1993, Strong had produced five volumes of poetry in English, three in Irish, a volume of selected poems, a novel, a collection of short stories, and numerous uncollected poems and stories, which provide ample evidence of her prolific and sustained literary career.[3] How, we surely ask, was Strong able to accomplish all this?

Hers is an interesting story. In 1942, at nineteen, Eithne O'Connell left Glensharrold, her rural West Limerick home, for Dublin. Her parents were teachers, funds were scarce at home, and university scholarships were generally unavailable in Limerick. Of the few careers open to women, nursing held little interest for her, and teaching was restricted because the training colleges were closed. Though she tried the Civil Service, she left because she "loathed figures." She soon met Rupert Strong, an English writer twelve years her senior. Despite family objections, including an attempt to force her return to the West,[4] Strong stayed in Dublin with her future husband.

In 1943, Strong married Rupert and at twenty became a founding member of the Runa Press, a small publishing venture begun primarily for poetry. Runa published a number of poets, including Roy McFadden and Valentin Iremonger, and brought out Strong's first work in English, *Poetry Quartos* (published between 1943 and 1945), as well as her first collection, *Songs of Living,* in 1961. Strong notes that there was no Arts Council help for such a venture as Runa, and that early sales and distribution of the poetry involved canvasing door to door, which she willingly joined.[5] Given the few chances that women poets had to publish in Ireland, her association with Runa at such an early age no doubt worked to her advantage.

Not until 1961, however, when Strong was thirty-eight, did *Songs of Living* appear, with a tribute by Padraic Colum, an older, established poet celebrating the work of his female colleague. Colum's preface makes much of the Spae-woman image he found in Strong's poems. This an-

2. This, and comments I quote later in this chapter, are from talks we had in June 1989, at Strong's home in Monkstown, and in the summer of 1991 and the spring of 1992 in Dublin.

3. Strong's poems in Irish, which I do not include in my bibliography, are collected in *Cirt Oibre* (1980), *Fuil agus Fallaí* (1983), and *An Sagart Pinc* (1990), all published by Coiscéim. She has also published a collection of stories, *Patterns* (1981), and a novel, *Degrees of Kindred* (1979).

4. Strong describes this incident as a "kidnapping," saying that she answered the door one night and soon was on the train back to the country. She "escaped" again and soon returned to Dublin.

5. Mark Hartman (1971) has written an informative essay on the Runa Press, covering its beginnings and its achievements.

cient figure appears, says Colum, in her three guises of Maiden, Wife, and Crone, bringing "her knowledgeableness out in measured sayings" (Strong 1961, 7). Trying to explain the effect of Strong's poems on him, Colum suggests that "this voice has the tone of one who lives outside companies," one "speaking from herself and for no other one" (8). Such an acknowledgment from a well-known poet, with its emphasis on the originality of a modern poet reaching back to an older tradition, might be seen to mark the arrival of the Irish woman to the community of contemporary Irish poets.

Colum's preface, however, is not without reservations. "I have been troubled by their monotony of form—there should be more formal excellence, more diversity," he says (Strong 1961, 7), indicating perhaps not only a weakness in Strong's poems but also his own preference for certain conventions of stanza, meter, and rhyme. Even more notable is that Colum separates Strong from other women poets:

> We read poetry made by women in the context of poetry made by men. Often we find a defect in women's poetry—it tends to be self-centred, self-regarding, self-pitying. Read Christina Rosetti [*sic*], Elizabeth Barrett Browning, Edna Millay to judge this. But by going back to something ancient Eithne Strong writes of a woman's way of life in a way that takes her outside the context that so much of women's poetry has to be read in. We read hers as the utterances of the priestess, the druidess, the sybil. (Strong 1961, 7–8)

In evaluating one of the earliest volumes of contemporary poetry by an Irish woman, Colum calls attention to the fact that this is the work of a woman writer. While praising her work, he separates Strong from other women poets, insisting that she succeeds because she does not write like a woman.

Looking back over Colum's criteria and assessment, we must raise a number of questions. Should we always read the poetry made by women in the context of poetry made by men? Is women's poetry necessarily "self-centred, self-regarding, self-pitying," whatever these terms meant for Colum? Could not these words, depending on how we define them, also be applied to male poets—Yeats, or even Colum, for example? Should we dismiss the poetry of Rossetti, Barrett Browning, and Millay so quickly, or do "we" do this because their poems will not fit into a "context" of poetry made by men?

Most importantly, while arguing that Strong "writes of a woman's way of life," Colum also maintains that she speaks "from herself and for no other one" (Strong 1961, 8), as if she writes in some kind of limbo.

Turning Strong into the ancient Spae-woman allowed Colum to avoid facing the contradiction inherent in suggesting that she writes about a woman's life but does not write like a woman poet. While eager to listen to the voice of the ancient "priestess, the druidess, the sybil," Colum also appears less than ready to consider that a woman writing of a woman's way of life might be not only "speaking from herself," but also writing of, for, and to other women. Though this was 1961, and the door opened a crack, the welcome mat was not yet out for the modern woman speaking as modern woman in Irish poetry. Nevertheless, contradicting Colum's judgment, in "Twenty-five," one of the poems in *Songs of Living*, Strong declares: "I write like a woman."

Admittedly, we can be too harsh here on Colum, who was trying to recognize the value of a fellow poet's work. We can also say that the voice of the Spae-woman gives us a very good way to approach this volume, one that Strong herself might have appreciated. On the other hand, this image does not appear in some of the best poems in *Songs of Living,* and Strong has told me that although she was grateful for Colum's praise, she thinks that he made too much of the Spae-woman image. To be fair to Colum, many other poets and readers shared his assumptions about women's poetry, and his communal "we" was the most accurate way to present the judgments they made. Only by moving beyond the restrictions and assumptions on which these judgments rest, however, only by broadening and redefining the contexts Colum describes, can readers judge the success of Strong's volume, and indeed all of her poetry. Spae-woman or not, the persona in these poems belongs in a contemporary Ireland, and the value of *Songs of Living* rests on the ways in which the Spae-woman makes her way around a modern Irish landscape.

In poems like "A Woman Unleashed" (1961, 10), the Irish Spae-woman most clearly appears. Strong's knowledge of Irish literature, and her poetry in Irish, certainly influenced the development of this image, for the multidimensional female figure makes numerous appearances in Irish literary tradition.[6] The crone Colum mentions roams the world, "a Queen of blood," with "gluttony and fire / titanic destruction / sweeping away the life." Unlike the Christian Virgin Mary, she is:

6. Nuala Ní Dhomhnaill, who is the subject of chapter 6, has also used an ancient female voice quite effectively in a modern context. The source for both poets is, no doubt, Irish poetry. In my discussion of Ní Dhomhnaill's work, I examine more closely both the source and the use of this image. For more information, see Condren 1989 and Caldecott 1988.

Swift breed of sin
all the lightning fire
hell in the breast
a witch's sabbath
all the cauldron of gluttony and lust.

In other poems in *Songs of Living,* we hear this woman, in graveyards echoing with the sounds of death ("Ballad"), a singer attuned to a primeval song ("Unapprehended").

But in Strong's poems the Spae-woman's attributes also appear in contemporary females, like the woman in "To Lillie" (1961, 26), who is "black / and like a snake; / black / and like a woman of the ancient druids; / black / and like a lover whom I took; / but withal / beautiful." Seductive, mysterious, holy, brooding, threatening, the women in *Songs of Living* are timeless, both "Spirit-Bound" (1961, 14) and "Joy-Reft" (1961, 15). Strong's Spae-woman is a representative female and, as such, shares some characteristics with other figures. Strong combines attributes of the pagan goddess and the Christian Mary in poems like "She" (1961, 13): a woman with "black brows" and a "stabbing laugh" possesses the qualities of "gentleness" and "sympathy"; and, at the end, a death's head displaces the beautiful face with which the poem opens. By continually fusing the characteristics of the pagan goddess and the Christian Virgin, Strong transcends time and culture to create an image of woman that expresses complex physical, emotional, psychological, and spiritual dimensions.

Colum's praise notwithstanding, the poems in which the Spae-woman appears most prominently are, in some cases, the least successful in the volume. As she takes the form of "The Wanton" (1961, 38), for example, she speaks with an artificial poetic voice: "'I shall pluck the fruits of the valleys / and drowse my voluptuousness / in the drunkenness of opiate mists." Searching for an image of woman liberated from "the call of the sacred" and "the drivelling of the preachers," Strong stresses her physical and sensuous nature here but misses the poetry in the search, creating an abstract seductress idealized, in another poem "Woman" (1961, 64), in her power:

And there is no ache like unto that final ecstasy
when the man yields in the soul-quest,
giving to her with his eyes and lips
before the body's long love.

Such language betrays itself: "ecstasy" and "soul-quest" create a clichéd, romantic tone rather than a dynamic and realistic speaking voice. In some of the love poems in *Songs of Living*, Strong's search for the "soul" and emotion of women lead her to abstraction and stilted poetic diction.

But *Songs of Living* also introduces us to a maternal world, and we get a more realistic image when the Spae-woman's prophetic vision metamorphoses into a contemporary "Nightmare" (1961, 19):

> I saw a ghastly ugliness
> hanging on a tree to-night:
> a putrid body
> grey
> its one eye
> above the jutting gaping of the nose
> leering hideousness of mouth;
> and it was my mother
> dying in the blight of a March east wind
> in the utter barrenness of her own despair.

Like T. S. Eliot's sybil in *The Waste Land*, this hanging victim symbolizes lack of hope. But here she is also an Irish mother, unable to muster the strength to overcome her despair. She appears again, in a less gloomy portrait, in the poem "To My Mother" (1961, 17–18), where an overworked, weary woman struggles (mending, helping children with schoolbooks, carefully budgeting wages), to be left finally with the pain of children passing from her "out into the void." The poem describes her as a willful but loving woman, whose daughter, the speaker, is saddened by her plight: "And before sleep / with knowledge near to tears / I knew again your fight." The despair of the speaker in "Nightmare" does not appear here, but the "pain" of mothers is a central concern in both poems.

Such poems give us another view of Irish women, undermining clichés about the unending joys of motherhood. Loving their children, mothers also feel anger, pain, sometimes give in to despair. We also see them jealous of their own children or apprehensive about the males approaching their offspring, as in "Mother and Daughter" (1961, 62–63):

> Suddenly
> I am the old witch.
> The old witch watches

the beautiful gazelle
with hideous eyes of hate.

Matriarch I
in my jealous jungle
stalk tigers
aprowl
for the shapely gazelle.

The bulls flourish their malenesss
in the morning air
and snuff for the young odour.
The witch and the tiger
crouch for the smell of blood.

Here the image of woman as witch suggests the all-too-human weaknesses of fear and envy and the mixed emotions of a woman trying to hold on to a daughter she knows she must let go. This witch, another version of the stalking Spae-woman, is both a mother trying to protect her young and an older woman envious of her daughter's youth.

Several poems in the volume focus on children, on the ordinary but significant details of maternal love and fear: "Brita—One-And-A—Half," "Rachel," "A Brood of Six," "To Jenny—Aged 14 (or Virgin Love)" are anchored in Strong's everyday life, expressing the often confusing and conflicting emotions a mother experiences. Such is "Rachel" (1961, 41):

She sits in bed
dark eyes round-deep in thoughts untold
and careful-slow the small words come:
Rachel is my five-year old.

Careful-slow the small hands move:
Deliberation is her other name,
precision-thoughts selectedly
small words unfold to ordered frame.

I sit and watch this gypsy child
heart-poignant at her special mould:
this beauty tightens round the heart
as saddest song when twilight's tolled.

These quatrains, with frequent iambs and repeated rhymes, are deceptively simple but quite appropriate for the subject. Like a nursery tale, the form becomes a good illustration of the line "small words unfold to ordered frame." Multiple emotions generated by a child turn "Rachel" into a sad "song" in which a mother's feelings echo her daughter's "thoughts untold" and "deliberation." The twilight setting, linking this poem with the hushed groves where the prophetess speaks, makes the child's "small words" as significant as those of an ancient sybil or Spae-woman, her "dark eyes" likewise connecting her to the beautiful woman described in the poem "She." The poet, the mother, and the young daughter come together here as "small words" reverberate in meaningful female songs.

A hint of what is to come in Strong's later poetry appears in *Songs of Living* when a dark tone permeates a voice angry about problems women have to deal with. We hear this in "When Men Don't Love" (1961, 30):

> All in a room about a table
> the women gossip.
> Idle gabble.
> There they sit.
> Shrill slitters of one another.
> Destroyers of the true.
> Mind-squander of words in values
> on man-catching, body-trappings, face dressing.
> Tight pain of unfulfillment about the table.
> Blades slashing the air:
> proprieties, the artificial, surface-levels.
> Dances, men,
> again again—
> in never-ending hen-cackle
> cat-spitting, snake-hissing—
> and the quiet pulse of life
> beneath
> but for the pausing
> the silent knowing.

This portrait of women whose lives revolve around men brings something new to contemporary Irish poetry, especially in shifting part of the blame from the women themselves to the men who ignore them. Animal impulses surface in these women (hens, cats, snakes, they gabble, spit, and hiss) as they try to trap the men who evade them. But the speaker asks that we look beyond the surface to the "pain of unfulfillment." Probing the causes of their behavior, Strong advises us and them to consider "the silent knowing." There is no doubt, in this portrayal of bickering women, that Strong understands the pain of the unloved who mask their lack of fulfillment with defensive chatter. In describing the "mind-squander" of those who may never discover the values of a life beyond "man-catching, body-trappings, face dressing," Strong has some sympathy for women who, at first glance, seem to deserve little.

In his preface to *Songs of Living,* Colum describes "When Men Don't Love" as a poem about "the woman who passes through maidenhood and refuses to enter the next phase," a type of woman for whom Strong, says Colum, "has no tenderness" (Strong 1961, 8). But Colum misses the point of the poem, primarily because he disregards the title, "When Men Don't Love." He also fails to notice Strong's understanding of women who squander their mind on futile and quarrelsome attempts to define themselves only in terms of men. Colum describes these women much like the "self-centred, self- regarding, self-pitying" women poets he mentions, ignoring Strong's attempt to probe beneath the stereotype of the jealous, bickering woman.

In evaluating *Songs of Living,* there is validity to Colum's judgment that some of the poems lack formal excellence and diversity. Intended, as the title suggests, as songs, they are generally loose and irregular, with an occasional stanzaic form. Some experiment with a shorter line, like "On Listening to Bach" and "A Brood of Six" (which imitates a nursery rhyme), and a few might best be described as prayers. Although there is nothing distinctive about the form of these poems, Strong's problem is more often with poetic diction, as when she settles for an abstraction rather than a concrete image or relies on the hyphenated "passion-flame," "love-ache," and "soul-quest" to carry the poem. A melodramatic voice echoes through a few poems.

Yet *Songs of Living* is an important volume. For all his attention to the Spae-woman, Colum seems to have missed the significance of her contemporary incarnation: to provide Strong with a model and a voice for expressing a modern woman's concerns. With the Spae-woman, Strong challenged the virginal model of the silent Blessed Mother, the ideal woman of Irish Catholicism, to express a more complex image— one not quite so pure, passive, and unearthly. The physical and sexual nature of women comes through in these poems, and Strong's continual use of animal imagery reinforces this emphasis. Sexuality was to become a much stronger focus in her later poems, one she talks about in an interview with Rebecca E. Wilson many years later: "You find all kinds of new things coming in what women are writing: the single mother is there, the homosexual, the plural arrangement. Women talk about sexual things much more. This is something very new in Irish poetry" (Somerville-Arjat and Wilson 1990, 114).

Judging these poems, however, as Colum does, as "remarkable" be-
cause Strong speaks "from herself and for no other one" is a mistake.
With *Songs of Living*, Strong made her entrance into the world of
women's poetry, and the personae in these poems explore a range of
human experiences and emotions from a specifically female perspective,
one that had not been heard enough in modern Irish poetry. Love, ha-
tred, jealousy, pain, loss, sexual pleasure, children, rejection involve dif-
ferent experiences and responses for women and men, and ideas and
feelings expressed by women often differ from those by men. In Strong's
poems, intended for both female and male readers, we can see those
differences.

Though some of the voices in these poems, particularly the love
poems, reveal no specific gender, others, like "Worship" (1961, 54–55),
declare the value of a woman's recognition of her own worth, in this case
as the bearer of a child:

> I
> white woman
> of the cold North,
> look upon this boy
> born out of the torrid earth
> and know swift ecstasy
> because of life.
>
> Shattering of joy:
>
> Now mute of heart
> in overflow
> as for the sudden sun
> the open sky
> the broken cloud.

This is one of the voices of the Spae-woman, but the white woman of the
cold North is also the Irish mother whose "I" we hear continually in
Strong's poems. Some of her themes and her subjects, her settings and
her images, rather than separating her from poets like Elizabeth Barrett
Browning and Christina Rossetti, link her to them as well as to other
Irish women poets, for they create new images of women and new fe-
male voices.

Strong's next volume in English, *Sarah, in Passing*, did not appear
until 1974, one of the few books by women issued by the most impor-
tant poetry publisher of the time, Dolmen Press. Consisting of a long

sequence (the title poem), and thirty-four other poems, *Sarah, in Passing* illustrates both a growing concern with poetic form[7] and a raised consciousness about the plight of women. Assessing these poems, Brendan Kennelly wrote that Strong's "poems express her own sense of herself as a parental centre of stability and order, but equally vivid is the picture she draws of herself as a scene of conflicting emotions" (1975, 11).

"Sarah, in Passing," a sequence of seventeen poems unified by a woman walking through a number of scenarios, might be seen as a battle of the sexes resolved ultimately by love. In the introductory poem, Sarah, "imagining, assimilating; / seeing much she did / not see, / interpreting what she did / not hear," evokes the poet who, like her persona, moves through life "ingesting scene and situation" (9). The sequence contains both dramatic and lyric poems. Strong uses dialogue, social commentary on men and women, and constant ironic allusions to religious dogma and ritual, especially as these involve images of women, men, and the relationship between the two.

Freedom recurs as a theme, and often, as in "What the Free One Said" (1974, 10), the issue focuses on the role of the church, especially on the power of male clerics:

> O lovely purple bishop
> I see them everywhere, used women
> despicably driven
> accepting the yoke
> of dogmatism
> (a nice woman—another way
> to say a poor uneducated sop).
>
> Mindwashed, they know about swelled thighs
> and calves and bulging veins and piles
> and parts that sag all out of size.
> These things they talk about for miles,
> of prams, of mickeys (shh), of teethings,
> with sly comparings: how much mine does
> that yours does not. Pathetic seethings.
> Their flopmouth child squints in the bus,
> his blibbering lips the desperate cling
> of mother's joy,
> o lovely purple eunuch boy!

7. Strong told me that this grew from her desire to write other kinds of literature, in this case a long poem.

The angry speaker, challenging the image of "nice woman," sees something else: "mindwashed" women whose bodies show the effects of many pregnancies. Their "pathetic seethings" remind us of the women around the table in "When Men Don't Love," but the cause of their problems here lies specifically with celibate priests who, with no sense of what these women go through, still hold out a model of the "nice woman." Another version of this man, a "royal eunuch," shows up in "Temperate Tim" (1974, 19), who visits all the ladies, giving each a few minutes of his time as he moves from house to house, "the prophet of chaste communal love."

Unseen trouble undermines this model of the female, as Sarah sees in "Departure from 13 Cashmere Crescent" (1974, 10–11), where Mrs. Brugh, having lost "all sense / of virtue," fits into neither the mold nor the neighborhood. Sarah finds another problem in Cissie, of the poem "Cecilia" (1974, 11–13), confused about her own identity and what is expected of her:

> They piled kids into me who was never set
> to breed. I am fitter far for exercise asexual,
> sipping the arid juice of mind.
> Sperm does not please me.
> I should have been hermaphrodite.

The anger these women feel goes beyond priests, husbands, and lovers. In "Juxtaposition" (1974, 15), the speaker seeks to make some sense of the male professor in front of her class, feeling that if she questioned him about anything, he would see her as a "bloody eejit woman."

The conflict between men and women appears most clearly in "The Mahonys Observed" and "Mrs. Mahony's Anniversary Thoughts On Her Man." The speaker of these poems verbalizes all her complaints in the first poem (1974, 22):

>   Must I forever
> play pretender, never state, for appearances' protection
>
> that you have packed me with seed I never had the urge
> to need? And must I halleluia for you who tyrannised
> amicably my every year with salutary all-lovingness
>
> which, oddly, never loved helping me on another way?
> My plural womb engorged perennially against the sink;
> my total energy to breeding went, to battered days'
>
> endeavour, nursing, patienting the chaos of the young.

Yet, after she states her case, Mrs. Mahony, on her anniversary, suggests in the second poem (1974, 23–24) something more about her marriage. Speaking of her husband's constancy and faith, she pays tribute:

> It is
> a shrink-tried durable stuff this
> unenchanted cool: catalyst to
> quotidian doubt and treason. I,
> noneuphoric, believe its name is love.

The compensation of love reconciles many of Strong's speakers to the difficulties of their lives and provides an antidote for anger and frustration. Although the vision of this final poem may seem to come too easily, especially given the angry intensity in some of the female voices in *Sarah, in Passing,* it is a key to the volume. The doubt and treason Mrs. Mahony describes surface often in other poems, but she sees the love in her marriage, and especially her husband's faith and "basaltic constancy" (1974, 23), as balancing the frustration she feels. Nevertheless, Mrs. Mahony is determined that people are going to hear about her "furies" and "fevers" (24) whether that makes her a "nice woman" or not.

The furies reappear in the poems in this volume, especially those that express maternal frustration. "Matrilineal" (1974, 29) sets the tone, when the speaker sees her mother's unintentional bequest to her as one she must reject:

> I am remembering it now, ineradicable insisted heritage
> long ever before death, this fear which pulpit caused
> and rostrum: a black-and-white, a priest-and-nun
> delineation of morality where frigid equated chaste,
> where brimstone cancelled love.

Seeing her mother as innately warm, the speaker describes how fear replaced love: "where we should have nourished we / blighted / tight inside our frightened skin."

Madness appears frequently among these women as they struggle to come to terms with the images they have inherited and the expectations they try to live up to. Brontë's Mrs. Rochester makes an appearance in "The Hater's Hymn" (1974, 20), and the speaker in "Response to Munch's *Scream*" (45) admits: "Secretly I am a lunatic." "Dear Doctor" (44) glibly diagnoses his female patient as manic-depressive, not expecting her frenzied return that night when she "threw her heart right at his face."

More often than not, these women's frustration arises from attempts to find some time for themselves within their own homes. So we hear the mother in "Statement to Offspring" (1974, 30) declaring her need for independence and nourishment: "Let me be. There is much / I am starving for. / No muffler I to scarf your / years. I cannot aye be shield." Yet she assures the children, she will not abandon them:

> But test me and I'm there.
> In the meantime, let me burgeon
> whatever else may fruit.
> I have suckled without stint.
>
> Let my statement grate whom will.
> I am no easy choice.
> I never asked to have you
> but having, am entirely true.
>
> Just allow me room.

The heretical admission "I never asked to have you" is one that many mothers might understand but few could ever express. Yet, as the context of this poem suggests, in the grand scheme of things, that is less important than the opening statement of commitment: "Look, I'll never leave you." Motherhood can sometimes seem like slavery, this speaker warns, and mothers are entitled to the same space and nourishment they give to their children. Testing the geography of maternal obligations, Strong argues for new boundaries. Her comments to Rebecca E. Wilson in 1989 seem to be foreshadowed in some of these poems:

> I have very strong views about babies, having had so many myself. I think we should give babies a rest for a while, or certainly the family should be very restricted. . . . I think the human race has gone a bit berserk and it would do us no harm to dry up for a bit and review things. (Somerville-Arjat and Wilson 1990, 114)

The images of mufflers, burgeoning fruit, and feeding in "Statement to Offspring" circumscribe the domestic world of Strong's poetry. The image of a starving mother, the nourisher who needs nourishment, fits into the pattern of eating and ingesting introduced in the opening lines of "Sarah, in Passing," where a woman takes in what she sees around her. Mother and poet are continually linked in the volume, with time and space being crucial nourishment for both. In her version of the image of Ireland as a sow who eats her children, the speaker in "Measuring"

(1974, 31) explains that though she might appear very strange to her offspring, she would like some time for herself:

> I am the sow would like my wallow,
> my snore in the sun.
> Or I would bar the house and read all day:
> be in to none—
> Do not disturb.

Images of eating, digesting, ingesting, and nourishing occur again and again in *Sarah, in Passing*. The opposite of the nourisher, the devourer, appears often as male and phallic. In "Beauty Is in the Eye" (1974, 17–18), one of the poems in the title sequence, the speaker warns an approaching male:

> You would
> devour all that my life has been. Ingest
> reptilian findings in your cellar solitariness
> where damp deliberate you remain barriered
>
> from warm fellows. Whatever you see with
> cold snake's eyes I reject your dart and poke
> of spatulate head your clammy coil
> about my privacies.

The Eve-like speaker here refuses to fall for this devil's tricks, foreseeing that the consequences may be her own destruction, the loss of "privacies."

The invasion of private space also has public manifestations in a poem like "July '69" (1974, 58–59), a commentary on the American arrival on the moon. Describing the moon as female and the American spacemen as having "made her," the speaker sees little cause for celebration:

> All hail the great scientific prick!
> I sink my fangs in my child's corpse
> I roast my frailbone brother's bowels
> I gorge on famine villages.

Atypical of Strong's poetry in that it deals with a specific historical event, "July '69" nonetheless connects with other poems in the volume, developing the contrast between nourishing and devouring. In "Credo"

(1974, 60–61), the speaker maintains that national and international affairs are larger versions of the personal; she describes all of these as "appetites and checks / that flux around the swallowing / demand of predatory devouring 'Me.'" So the Americans' expensive and solo journey to the moon, cause for great international feasting, must be put into perspective; they move into new territory in space while famine and death continue around the world. Toasting a "blended consortium" (59) where all countries would be nourished, the speaker looks with a wary eye on the celebrations for these men on the moon.

Eating also provides the imagery for "After Christmas" (1974, 62), a poem worth looking at closely to see Strong at her best. An elegy for Jonathan Hanaghan, a poet and psychoanalyst who had worked with Strong and others to establish the Runa Press, the poem contrasts the normal with the abnormal in a quiet, subtle exploration of the physical and spiritual effects of grief:

> He mattered in my life for hate and love
> and then he died and I ate turkey dinner.
> The Christmas food being over, followed
> disguise of meats: pie from three days' bits
> chopfolded, helped from cloy with green
> of salads sharp in adverse dressing.
>
> Ten days it took to beat and lemon-cut
> the gorged, the plummy flesh fed cherry
> rimjaws of cake piled to back of tongue
> gone thick with unashamed indulgence. No
> breakfast; stringent efforts towards ascetic
> diet. For pride's sake because of ugly
>
> hips. For soul's sake too or what I think
> is soul, the otherness, the second life
> that, glutton how I may, rides parallel
> invincible, invites me through at points
> of silences to cease, be quiet, to know
> and merge inside the walls of parallelity.
>
> For this I come and still my head past midnight
> the place being quiet, my stomach starved a day.
> In the dark downstairs my daughter who is gypsy
> sings alone, guitars her private winter song

that twists inside my humbled bones. A crying
breaks my vanishing walls. I mourn the man who died.

The contrasts in this poem, between love and hate, birth and death, body and soul, man and woman, mother and daughter, are developed primarily through images of food and the indulgences and denials these involve. The setting details a woman's world: the celebration of Christmas dinner followed by the practical use of leftovers. But the food reminds us of the end of something, as the speaker makes the leftover bits and pieces of Christmas food into a pie. The cake that took ten days to make vanishes, gone like the man who died. The chopfolding, beating, and lemon-cutting echo with suggestions of death's blow, the sharp "adverse dressing" balancing the "cloy" that Christmas represents, a metaphor for death's counterpoint to life. The grief over death mutes the joy of Christmas, and the world the speaker sees reminds her of the "second life" she cannot see. So indulgence gives way to an "ascetic / diet" and "silences."

The understated "For soul's sake too or what I think / is soul, the otherness" suggests an additional problem, when doubt about an afterlife denies her the comfort and nourishment that belief gives others. People's reaction to death and their ultimate loneliness in the face of it when ordinary life must go on surface in different ways, portrayed here by a speaker who starves herself while her daughter "guitars her private winter song." The colloquial matter-of-fact tone of "and then he died and I ate turkey dinner" underlines the significance of the breakthrough that comes in the final lines: "A crying / breaks my vanishing walls." In this poem Strong demonstrates her poetic gifts: her control of stanza form, successful use of enjambment, and ability to draw multiple meaning from word and image to express a woman's complicated response to death.

Two other poems in the volume, "Retarded Child" and "Norms for a Literary Piece," show us a mother coping with adversity, and both have autobiographical overtones. Strong's youngest son, a retarded twin whose sister is not handicapped, suffered from a lack of oxygen at birth; he has remained at home with Strong. His life changed hers significantly, Strong says, emphasizing that experiences like this put others into perspective.

"Retarded Child" (1974, 32–33) catalogues the many feelings of a mother toward this son, including the "comfort" that his handicap was not genetic. His skewed eyes and drooling mouth, the speaker says, she can, in her "foolish time," blame on a doctor. But this "game" does not last long, and the speaker has to face the truth about how she sometimes feels:

> I have wished him dead
> in my coward part.
> My fiery plans
>
> he has cut athwart.
> My blazing drive
> he braked dead stop.

Despite that fact that her son's handicap has "tested her" to "her miser heart," the mother says that she has served "committedly." Strong, who has taken care of her own handicapped child all of his life, creates a speaker whose love is never questioned but whose feelings we understand.

This mother speaks again in "Norms for a Literary Piece" (1974, 35–36) where she demonstrates the difference between literature and life in a description of trying to get some work done:

> I was (readingClarketyping)
> eating a Take-away Special
> from The Great Wall, Main
> Street, Blackrock; hardfried
> egg on top of mixed-up
> dubiosity of rice (all day
> he—impact of Wisdom?—
> crashed my back, jerked
> away from tapping keys
> my hands, trying to spell
> out Clarke on Swift) slices
> of pork, excess of monosodium
> glutamate—an official from
> Swift's Hospital with concern
> for dietetics warned me once
> against that glutamate but I
> like the sound of the name,
> the taste of the sound—

Take-away Chinese food, Jonathan Swift, Austin Clarke, sounds, typewriter, taste, wisdom, words, retarded son all run together as the writer-speaker tries to establish the "norms" of her "mixed up" life and the constraints upon her time and concentration. Food again, "mixed-up /

dubiosity of rice," seems a fitting metaphor for her day, its frenetic pace successfully echoed in a stream of consciousness of run-on lines, run-together words, interrupting phrases, hyphens and parentheses that control the movement of the lines. A mind filled with such stimuli, flying off in different directions, establishes new norms for a literary piece. The child and the home identify the persona as mother; the allusions to Austin Clarke and Jonathan Swift put her in the company of Irish writers.

In another poem, "Substitute for Blueprint" (1974, 41–42), the speaker, alluding to Wordsworth's poetic theories, defines her recollections in tranquility as thoughts before she takes a nap, and "ceaseless making-do." Expressing a woman's response to Wordsworth in "Recollected in Tranquility" (1974, 50), another speaker tries to apply the Romantic poet's theories to her own writing, and ends up describing the lack of tranquility in her response to a man who glibly tells her to throw her work away:

> The man said
> tear it up
>
> like so much
> in my life.
>
> Heighho, he said,
> throwing it all away
>
> with a quick
> drag of smile
>
> that had no happy
> the smile of a man
>
> to contrary
> raw grief.

In these poems, Strong not only challenges some conventional theories about the origin of poetry but also shows how men may not recognize that the sources and methods of a woman's poetry may involve different approaches, problems, and results.

Complicated relationships between a mother and her children recur frequently in *Sarah, in Passing,* when the personae often try to express what they feel they cannot communicate. In "To A Teen-Age Son" (1974, 37–38), a woman takes her child to the ferry, realizing as she returns home that she does not know exactly where he has gone. Seeing the imprint of his body left in the bedclothes, the mother recalls his grumpy answers on the mornings she woke him for school. The poem ends describing the mother's sense of loss, as she quietly meditates on why they had not discussed where he would be:

> Oddly, we had neglected that.
> Because our tie, unlike the trick, is from
> the root where words are not? Needing, however,
> the continuing sign, I was bereft did you not
> write. Always when particulars go from me they
> may not return: there is this fear. So I
> look in rooms, places permeate, hoping shapelessly.

The fearful shapelessness, mitigated at times by shapes the memory stores, is a recurring image—one that both mother and poet share.

In another poem, "Child into Woman" (1974, 39–40), a mother silently addresses a daughter from whom she has grown apart. Her memory gives back spaces and shapes of the past: "you on / the stairs, in the old high / hall; looking out, running / out of spaces to meet me." But time has passed, and the mother has changed: "I did not need to / know the way before, it was / natural to me as breath." In the new relationship, she holds back, even while she recognizes the other's loneliness, not fully understanding or explaining why. The poem ends with a telling image:

> But I could not speak my
> tightened heart nor put a
> shielding care of arms all around
> and safe about you as in
> the past I most instantly would
> have done. Today it would be
> an out-of-place behaviour,
> tabooed by new conditions,
> forbidden by unspoken signs;
> and so I held the urge
> and combed my hair instead
> like one who combs her hair,
> while helplessly deferring
> to the guards that love
>   peculiarly assumes.

Poems like this make us aware of the complexities of relationships between parents and children, and of the feelings not articulated between them. Despite the love that this mother feels for her daughter, a pervasive sadness looms: a "sorrow came then" she says, "and has not / ever really gone." The cause of that sorrow and the failure to overcome it create a change, a barrier between mother and daughter that calls for "new shapes" neither one has been able to find. In such quiet and understated meditations on loss and on silence, Strong is at her best.

Strong's *FLESH . . . the Greatest Sin,* first published in 1980, is, to say the least, a fundamental work in the redefinition of the image of Irish womanhood.[8] A. A. Kelly, in the introduction to *Pillars of the House,* describes its significance and the new direction signaled in Strong's poetry:

> *Sarah, in Passing* (1974) is a volume of poetry mainly about liberation from domestic tyranny. Her *FLESH . . . the Greatest Sin* (1980) is the female equivalent of Patrick Kavanagh's *The Great Hunger.* For Kavanagh "Clay is the word and clay is the flesh"; but for Strong, flesh is "the corruptible mould that grows on bones" and the choice for women in Ireland is between Virgin Nun or Conjugal Rights. . . . Here she speaks for all Irish women. The mental or emotional poverty revealed in this work could be compared to the different aspects of poverty shown by Kavanagh, and there are many links between their two points of view. Man was tied to the soil, and woman to her fertile womb. (23)

Although Kavanagh's poem comes immediately to mind when one reads *FLESH . . . the Greatest Sin,* Strong says that she did not consciously write this poem as a response to *The Great Hunger.* On the other hand, she says that she knew Kavanagh's poem and admits there may have been a "subconscious impetus" at work. As Dillon Johnston demonstrates in *Irish Poetry after Joyce* (1985), there is little likelihood that any Irish poet, male or female, could escape the influence of Kavanagh. In 1980, Mary Maher noted in the *Irish Times* that "Kavanagh's narrative of a rural Irish upbringing is uncompromisingly male, and Ms. Strong's equally could be only female, but there are a lot of common elements: the physical, sensual imagery underneath the bleak and Puritanical ethos, the guilt and confusion and repression" (10).

The Great Hunger (1942) dramatizes the life of Paddy Maguire, archetypal Irish peasant doomed from the beginning by twin evils: Mother Church, as embodied in the local priest, and Mother Maguire, who

---

8. *FLESH . . . the Greatest Sin,* first published by Runa Press in 1980, was revised slightly and published by Attic Press in 1993. For quotations, I have used the Attic edition. John Feeney's review (1980) of a reading from the volume in Monkstown carried the headline "Eithne Gets to Grips with Sin."

"praised the man who made a field his bride" (3). Focusing on a family scenario he perceived in peasant Ireland—domineering mother, bachelor son unable to leave home, and virgin daughter whom marriage and motherhood have passed by—Kavanagh creates a man for whom sexual repression becomes a way of life. While Kavanagh's vision exposed a physical and spiritual hunger in the Irish—and, in doing so, challenged the stereotypes of idyllic peasant life—his is essentially a male vision with Paddy a tragic victim. Paddy's mother appears primarily as a villain with no probing of the causes for her behavior. "She had a venomous drawl / And a wizened face like moth-eaten leatherette" (6), we are told, and we hear her voice only when she orders her son around.

Mary Anne, Paddy's sister, denied her destiny as mother, turns into a bitter wench, a mirror image of her vitriolic mother screaming at children at the door. Though Kavanagh probably thought he was expressing equal sympathy for brother and sister, his images suggest the opposite, and his one-dimensional portraits of shrewish mother and spinster daughter allow for little probing of their characters. At the end of *The Great Hunger,* the curtain comes down and the narrator, unable to "imagine" a happy ending, leaves us with the words: "Silence, silence. The story is done" (33).

Well, not quite. Strong picks it up again years later and shifts the focus, telling a similar story from a woman's point of view. In the updated version, Tom Regan, a tyrant schoolmaster, displaces Paddy Maguire, but he has some of the same problems. Denying the flesh, avoiding temptation, he keeps "a civil distance" from his neighbors (Strong 1993a, 9) and a tight rein on his rage. His is the company of men whose repressed energy seeks outlets: in the mountain, the gun, the bog, and the dog, in card playing, fishing, and pub talk. Like Paddy Maguire, Regan also has a sister, who presides over the household after their mother's death.

Tom's wife, Ellen, a fellow teacher who has learned her own form of denial, soon displaces Mary Anne as homemaker. Ellen's self-image and female identity come from the nuns who have taught her in convent schools, and Strong's images suggest the sources of some of her problems as they depict religious symbols, rituals, and prayers. Mary, the mother of God, is the model for women:

> Ellen was not hungry, getting bread—
> and jam on Sundays; and rosaries were constant diet,
> Hail Mary, Holy Mary. Purest of the pure, Mary:

everyone is to know the awful need for purity.
House of Gold pray for us. Tower of Ivory. (1993a, 15)

A marriage is arranged for Mary Anne, and she is sent to a farm far
from home: "a place where was, oddly, still a blight / of women: old
mother, daft sister, unyoung / furtive husband, mad for a ketch" (1993a,
27). Removed from her childhood home and placed in an inevitable con-
flict with these other newly-displaced women, Mary Anne goes mad and
dies crawling westwards to her former home. "They buried her / in the
east," we are told, in "the husband's cemetery plot: good growing
ground" (28).

Unlike Kavanagh's drama, Strong's has a second act and a resolution
to the conflict. Within a lifeless marriage, Tom and Ellen produce a
daughter, Nance, who inherits her mother's legacy of fear, listening to
the priest preaching on chastity:

> he, from his white removed celibacy, warned:
> girls, who are differently composed, must not rouse,
> must not tempt beyond his strength the weak male;
> a man should be helped to avoid the lightning
> of his nature, not be ignited by idle tantalising.
> Poor pitiable man left helpless
> by Adam's ease with Eve. (1993a, 53)

Nance eventually rejects this image of woman and the fear it inspires,
and her own "fall" leads to a new litany and a resurrection. Instead of the
defeated Paddy Maguire, standing in the doorway with no hope, Strong
leaves us with an image of a woman who must ignore external controls in
favor of internal choices, defining grace as

> some freeing of the web, some opening
> towards new receptivity.
> No dazzling vision
> but a beginning of belief
> in the great importance
> of believing, hoping, loving (1993a, 63)

Such a concept involves the rejection of just about everything Nance
has been taught to believe about herself; most significantly, it depends
neither on the "Conjugal Rights" of men that had trapped her mother
nor on the chastity that the nuns had taught her to value so highly.
According to this poem, integrity, "wholeness," demands that women

define their identity, and control their destinies, beyond these two poles. Love, not fear, prevails. Speaking of this poem and of Nance, Strong explained: "I feel sure that anything at all gained by fear is finally lost. The only real victories are won by love, really, and to me love is a very muscular thing, a battle" (Maher 1980, 10).

A. A. Kelly, quoting Kavanagh's own judgment that *The Great Hunger* lacks "the nobility and repose of great poetry," suggests that Kavanagh and Strong had to "purge" themselves, and that both poems reflect this (1987, 23). *The Great Hunger* is more significant for its startling challenge to conventional thinking than for its success as a poem. The same can be said for *FLESH . . . the Greatest Sin,* especially in the last part, where idea and feeling sometimes do not move beyond direct statement or abstract philosophical meditation. Yet one has to wonder why, with all its weaknesses, Kavanagh's remains one of the best-known poems in Ireland, while few people have even heard of Strong's.[9] A judgment of Kavanagh's, in his *Collected Pruse,* might provide an answer to why women poets were not taken seriously: "Women are wise in their generation and in their instincts, but when they abandon their perceiving bodies for their soon dried-up brains they become intolerable" (1967, 27).[10]

Despite the danger posed by "dried-up brains," Eithne Strong continues to write and, in *My Darling Neighbour* (1985), *Let Live* (1990), and the new poems in *Spatial Nosing* (1993), her volume of selected poems, develops the ideas and feelings of her earlier work, trying to make her poetry "more considered," with a "broader perspective" and "larger reach." "As I write now," she says, "I am more self-critical. I chisel and condense, unlike my earlier poetry which I wrote in a great rush." She feels that her poems in the 1980s are more humorous but also express a great deal of sorrow, particularly since the death of her husband in 1984.

9. Brendan Kennelly, for example, called *The Great Hunger* "one of the most striking and memorable long poems of this century" (1973, 169).

10. The marginalia beside this passage in a copy of Kavanagh's book in the library at University College Dublin at Belfield offer some telling insights into readers' responses to Kavanagh's statement. The comment "Women, we have centuries of ingrained bigotry to overcome" is followed by another that labels Kavanagh an "Idiot." This, in turn, evokes a comment on the comment: "You are the idiot, lady, for not realizing it yourself." Fed up with the debate, another reader objects: "We could do without these fucking commentaries on a book of some merit." I must admit it took all my scholarly integrity to resist the impulse to join the commentators, especially to ask why the third writer automatically assumed the second one was a "lady." But, as an academic, I know better than to deface a book of some "merit."

After the drama and anger of *FLESH . . . the Greatest Sin,* the poems in *My Darling Neighbour* stress the virtue of acceptance, even while they satirize the pretentiousness of modern life. The poets, would-be poets, and critics described in "Values," "Poor Tom," "Library, Section Lit Crit," and "Diameter," or the two women in the hotel lounge playing "One Up," highlight the drawbacks of the unexamined life.

Strong's values and priorities are clear in these poems. The acceptance of vulnerability, the need for forgiveness, the recognition of the pain of others, and the virtue of simplicity in a confusing world come through again and again. The untimely and inexplicable death of a child in "Regatta, West Cork" (1985, 31), where "the crowds saw yachts / . . . and none his / web-slipped drowning head," the "burdened baffled child / taking the absent weight of father, bitter mother" in "Going Home" (25–26), or the young narrator of "Dance to your Daddy" (21–22) are typical of Strong's portraits of innocent victims of the mistakes of others.

In the face of such realities, Strong's response, stated in the title of a poem, is to "Simplify." *My Darling Neighbour* opens with "Necessity for Reverence" (1985, 7), a poem on a potato, whose symbolic significance in Ireland provides a backdrop for a housewife who knows the value of her own work:

O potato that I peel
I am made to know
your raw appeal
insidious, oddly
not blunt nor coarse
as might one
expect from something so
crudely sprung;
in some peculiar fashion
you quietly present
your claim for reverence,
you, cockeyed, swarth
supporter of my family;
I feel a vague design
holds me in curious link
with you whose peel
I strip while the Taoiseach
sits in council.

Blending the personal and the racial, the domestic and the political, the "vague design" that binds many Irish people finds a locus in the "crudely sprung" potato. The reverence that the "raw" potato claims might also be given to the woman who peels it: a supporter of a family, she is as important to this "vague design" as the *Taoiseach,* the leader of the Irish *Dail.* Seeing in seemingly simple things a great deal of meaning, in her best poems Strong makes us aware of values and people we might overlook.

In another poem, "Unions" (1985, 19–20), laundry becomes a metaphor for a marriage and family. As Mrs. Janet Doorly folds her five-year-old sheets, "flakes and fluff" fly in the sunbeams:

> She considered removedly
> the flying motes
> seeing therein atoms
> of Mr. D, herself,
> their shedding young:
> bits of dead Doorly stuff
> inconsequentially floating
> through morning
> keeping company
> with particles
> of scaled commercial sheet.

Ultimately this poem about folding laundry turns into a meditation on loss and the passage of time as

> Mrs D. walked
> in the united atoms
> reflecting fractionally
> on the myriad
> necessary deadnesses
> that proceed
> throughout the living day.

The acceptance of the inevitable that comes through continually in Strong's most recent poems depends often on just getting on, as Mrs. Doorly does, with "usual activity." As the speaker in "Ritual" (1985, 23–24) says, trying to deal with the past in an empty and silent house: "I need an evolved saving ritual that / leads memory to heal: arrived / at middle life we mostly have some wisdom but / forget that we do and are not wise."

As she grows older, Strong's female personae age with her, and in her 1990 volume, *Let Live,* memory and past tense become as important as the voice of a woman in the present trying to make sense out of life in late 1980s Ireland. In "September Song" (37–38), complaining of a stiff neck and poor eyesight, the speaker imagines herself with a new car. Yet she knows that she will still have problems:

> with my new laser view forward
> and my steady rear-view mirror, I'll still
> need boosting, will wish to keep clear
> of all carrier trucks that brute the ground,
> ten-wheel furies to suck you in their violent pull
> and, like some memories, blast a courage mostly fear.

Many of these poems deal with travel, on the continent or across Ireland, moving from the "Bloody Foreland" to the "Beara Peninsula." With a renewed sense of history, they juxtapose past and present, older and younger people. Often the subjects of these poems are searching for something new: the London students in their minibus in "Bloody Foreland" who travel to Donegal; the city people seduced by Achill Island. Many of the poems recall the Irish past and evoke ancient or mythic landscapes: white mares on the shore, or "The Giant's Causeway" (1990, 29) which has "sprung huge from / the imagination of emergent men / to signify a yearned-for power."

Place becomes the repository of memory as well. In "Gaspé to Ottawa" (1990, 18–19), recalling a journey across Canada, the speaker remembers how she watched the river and felt a "leaving" as her companion slept in the car. Recreating the Canadian scene, she notes the difference between what she saw when she traveled and what she remembered later:

> Following us always on the left, repeated flight
> of silver things, flashing an imaginable history—
> silo towers, thin spires, new roofs—their light
> the aluminium glint of Canada.
>
> Its dark, force of northern heights was cobwebbed later
> and queerly sad. The river had said
> what it said. I, remembering now, know nothing better:
> not this nor this . . . and now you are dead.

In poems such as this, written after the death of Strong's husband, time, history (imagined and real), and loneliness are forces to be confronted, inevitably accepted. For the speaker, her companion's sleep in the car foreshadows his coming death; he is described as "not having been able to simulate / a constitution remaining in interested gear." The

irony of memory here, where the speaker recalls wondering whether this
might be their last glimpse of the Canadian landscape, comes back to
haunt her with an answer she had no knowledge of at the time. In eight
understated quatrains, the poem focuses on time passing, moving from
the opening line's "That was Wednesday" to the final and climactic ". . .
and now you are dead." Poems like this, Thomas McCarthy maintains,
"are as good as anything that's been written in Ireland in the last thirty
years" (1990, 93).

The tone of these poems ranges from sad to humorous, and, though
the biting satire of her earlier poems has mellowed, Strong can still make
fun of human foibles. The persona in "Yellow Joke" (1990, 43) describes
her attraction to the ridiculous, "the way it makes / a fatal hole in solem-
nity." The traveler in "Peanut Queenie" (7), tired of endless miles of
scenery and "mannerly enquiry" with friends in their car, tells us: "they
tune into pop radio / and contrary to earlier convictions / you find you
love Peanut Queenie, / The Queen of the Dancing Floor."

Though many of the poems in *Let Live* are lyrics with regular
stanzas, there is a great variety of line length in the poems and a facility
with diction, matching word to meaning and tone. Thus in "Bald"
(1990, 46–47), the run-on, mock-rhetorical description of attempts to
cover a balding head:

> I am always troubled to see
> those unhappy strands compelled
> to freakish length athwart the bone, coerced
> from their natural home, still-active border
> above the ear, or even—unhappier yet—
> dislocated from the innate downward drift
> of poll and dragged across the scalp,
> itself an honourable, often very handsome
> manifestation but now mocked, diminished
> by such grotesque overlay.

With a sharp eye for uncovering human pretensions, Strong also
tries to get beneath the surface and explore the motivations for people's
behavior. Her narratives, like those of "Henrietta, Caleb and Issue"
(1990, 35–36), where parents' plans for their children are thwarted by
the children themselves, or "Hola Verdad!" (39), where a tutor praises
her ability to teach a young man English, often comment on motivations
for people's actions, what the tutor calls "all amusing ballast against /
your inner facts of self-encounter."

In the introduction to *Spatial Nosing* (1993b), Mary O'Donnell sums up Eithne Strong's vision:

> The culture which she observes and partakes of is a man-made one, largely supported by women who either endure the ways of the despot or else forge their own peace by simply getting on with it. That forging is not one of resignation, so much as an energetic re-appraisal of how best a person can live within the constraints of the world as it is apprehended.

O'Donnell also claims that a "poet's relationship with words and her relationship with life are inseparable," a claim substantiated by Strong's work and life.

When asked how she found time to write, teach, and raise nine children, Strong answers: "I stole it from life. I always left something undone." Then she tells you how helpful one of her children was, preparing dinner so Strong could get some time to write. These are the answers of a woman and a writer able to transform what she calls the "chaos" of a domestic life into poetry that insists on the values of home and family, love and forgiveness. It is also a poetry that challenges us to confront the harsh realities of modern life, to look at what we are, and to understand that chaos is not restricted to domestic life. "My family is my community," Strong has said, and the relationship between that community and other communities appears again and again in her poems.

Are hers, as Colum claimed, the "measured sayings" of the Spae-woman? In one sense, yes, as she speaks for herself, for other women— ultimately for many people—in a way Padraic Colum could not have imagined. Very subtly, Strong has used images of women, from witches to furies, from unmarried maidens to crones, to express the multidimensional nature of the female and the complexity of human experience. In the final lines of "Pram" (1990, 61–62), the last poem in *Let Live,* Strong's speaker says: "about keeping / my mouth shut, / I have learned much." We can say that when Strong has opened hers, we have learned much.

Eavan Boland.
Courtesy of *Irish Times*.

3

Eavan Boland

In *A Separate Vision: Isolation in Contemporary Women's Poetry*, Deborah Pope argues that every woman writer has had to "deal with the realization that men write out of experience that is 'universal,' but that her experience is likely to be regarded as trivial and private" (1984, 3). Women poets confront this dilemma in different ways, and in feminist literary criticism, the issue of isolation has been at the center of many debates. Should a woman take a separatist stance, rejecting the attitudes, imagery, and language of a patriarchal tradition, or should she try to work from within, challenging and revising conventional images and ideas to turn the "trivial" and "private" into "universal" and "public"?

Eavan Boland chooses the latter course. In myth, art, literature, and history, she examines how women have been presented over the centuries. Juxtaposing these images with her own experience as woman and writer, her poetry records a process of self-definition that transcends the boundaries of her personal life. Noting how the American poet Elizabeth Bishop wrote from the margin, Boland argues that Bishop in some way defines her country by her absence from it. Bishop's poetry, which illustrates the "complexity of her estrangement" from the American myth, has become, according to Boland, a "new part of the myth" (1988b, 92). As an Irish woman poet, Boland finds herself in a similar position. In an interview with Jody Allen-Randolph, Boland explained: "One of the things women poets have been engaged in—among the other things they've been doing—is revising parts of the poetic self. Re-examining notions of the authority within the poem, and of the poem" (Roche and Allen-Randolph 1993, 128).[1]

Boland published her first volume, *New Territory*, in 1967, when she was twenty-two and fresh out of Trinity College; some of these poems

1. The special issue of *Irish University Review* on Boland contains articles covering all of Boland's poetry, and there is a comprehensive checklist of Boland's work prepared by Allen-Randolph.

were written when she was still a teenager. We hear no identifiable woman's voice in this volume. Boland later described these early poems:

> They were derivative because I asked too few questions of the world around me and myself as a poet. I was Irish; I was a woman. Yet night after night, bent over the table, I wrote in forms explored and sealed by English men hundreds of years before. I saw no contradiction. Inasmuch as I thought about it at all, I believed that ethics and aesthetics could only be guaranteed by the technical encounter. (1987c, 151)

The problem of writing in models developed by English poets has been addressed by Boland's male colleagues as well: several contemporary poets have fused Irish and English language and literary traditions to acknowledge both inheritances.[2] Had she been a man, Boland would still have faced this problem. Her role as woman poet, however, the young Boland failed to recognize, and her male models gave her no sense of how her experience as a woman might affect what she wrote. Despite the title of this volume, Boland covers little new territory, and her poems illustrate quite clearly the literary conventions that so strongly dominated her education and early reading.

The central character in *New Territory* is a version of the epic wanderer who figures so prominently in Western literature. Boland's symbolic explorers range from the Yeats-inspired voyager into mysterious worlds to the traditional religious pilgrim seeking a way to deal with death. Poem after poem celebrates the wisdom and fortitude of conventional male heroes: Isaiah, Oedipus, princes, fathers, sailing men. The seas they must travel, dark and dangerous like the ancient seafarer's, embody those sinister forces all explorers face. In the title poem (1967, 10), the speaker, approaching land, begins to realize:

> Out of the dark man comes to life and into it
> He goes and loves and dies,
> (His element being the dark and not the light of day)
> So the ambitious wit
> Of poets and exploring ships have been his eyes—
> Riding the dark for joy—

Clearly in these lines, Boland sees the poet as an important explorer, an image she develops throughout the volume. She alludes, however, to

2. Austin Clarke's work illustrates the influence of Gaelic prosody, and Seamus Heaney and Paul Muldoon use Irish words, but many other examples can be found. Moya Cannon has also used Irish words in her volume *Oar*.

male poets: opening the volume with an epigraph from Yeats; dedicating poems to contemporaries like Michael Longley, Brendan Kennelly, and Derek Mahon; writing poems on Shakespeare, Yeats, and the Irish poet Egan O'Rahilly. The "ambitious wit" of her poet-explorers is overwhelmingly male.

Boland later began to see these models and mentors in *New Territory* as the natural consequence of the literary tradition in which, as a beginning poet, she tried to carve a niche. As he had for many other young Irish writers, Yeats loomed as mentor, honored in "Yeats in Civil War" (1967, 22) as the poet-explorer of the imagination, despite the turmoil outside his tower:

> Somehow you arranged your escape
> Aboard a spirit-ship which every day
> Hoisted sail out of fire and rape,
> And on that ship your mind was stowaway.
>
> The sun mounted on a wasted place,
> But the wind at every door and turn
> Blew the smell of honey in your face
> Where there was none.
>
> You are its sum, struggling to survive—
> A fantasy of honey your reprieve.

Though still admiring Yeats's work, Boland later rejected the fantasy celebrated in this poem. As she began to see herself as a woman poet, her real world, where honey sat on a kitchen table, replaced her borrowed Yeatsian vision. She had to learn that Yeats's world was not hers, and that this poet, good as he was, could teach her just so much.

In the few poems in *New Territory* that focused on women, Boland adopted the poetic stereotype of women, which, she would later argue, reduced and simplified them. The long final poem in the volume, "The Winning of Etain" (1967, 29–39), clearly presents such a woman. A retelling of the Irish legend of Etain, Fergus, and Aengus, the poem recounts a fairy-tale battle of two men to possess a beautiful woman, ending with Aengus's conquest as he and Etain ride off together: "And Etain from her window knew the prince / For Aengus, and ran to him and took his arm / And mounting up, rode away with him."

A beautiful, passive maiden metamorphosed by Fergus into a dragonfly, Etain epitomizes the dehumanized women that Irish myth and literature often created. Boland never wrote a poem like this again, and her growing realization that such stereotypes betrayed the real women of Ireland was a first step in establishing a new aesthetic. She later said of this process: "I wrote my way into my own identity" (1987c, 151).

One poem in *New Territory* hints of the direction Boland's poetry would soon take. "Athene's Song" (1967, 28) four sestets with a regular rhyme scheme, foreshadows Boland's next volume, *The War Horse,* offering an alternative to male explorers. The poem describes Athene's change from goddess of war to goddess of love, a transformation defined metaphorically as "new music." When Athene (also the goddess of wisdom) plays the pipe of peace, love flourishes, but the noises of war, which drown out this music, force her to drop her pipe. The pipe, not played, "Holds its peace and holds its own."

In mythology, Athene invented the flute, but, because Cupid laughed while she was playing, she threw it from the heavens, and it fell into the hands of mortals. In Boland's poem, the mute pipe suggests not only the muffled music of peace but also the lost voices of women. In a world where the epic warrior prevails, Athene as goddess of war predominates, and her music is silenced: "Beside the water, lost and mute / Lies my pipe and like my mind / Remains unknown, remains unknown."

Unmothered, having sprung from her father's head in full armor, Athene plays his song, her own music unheard. As Jody Allen-Randolph suggests, "the engaging drama of the poem springs from the clash between the 'new music' of Athene's nascent feminist consciousness and her paternal inheritance of boast and gong" (1993, 6). Gradually in Boland's poetry the male troubadours and poets in *New Territory* give way to the woman singer-poet, creating, recreating, and recovering the voices of women.

In *The War Horse* (1975), twenty-five poems reveal another perspective on war. Like the explorer in *New Territory,* Boland's war horse unifies the volume; while the explorer symbolizes different kinds of quests, Boland's war horse embodies all kinds of conflict. Incidents in the Irish-English struggle parallel private family battles that send sisters into opposite camps. Whether between lovers, families, or nations, these wars and quarrels all involve loss and suggest the need for peaceful alternatives.

The title poem (1975, 9–10) evokes the threat of war hanging over Ireland and introduces the political context that other poems, like "Child of Our Time" and "A Soldier's Son," develop. In the title poem, a stray horse represents the menace of war. The speaker first believes that "no great harm is done" when the horse passes her house but soon sees the destroyed flowers and hedge as emblems: "only a crocus its bulbous head / Blown from growth, one of the screamless dead." Whether we read the crocus as a metaphor for the innocent victims of war or for the unnoticed damage war inflicts on the landscape, Boland addresses the ongoing battles in Ireland and the death and destruction the war horse brings.

Boland implies that part of our response to war arises from its glorification in the Western heroic tradition, well known for war stories and horse tales. In "The Greek Experience" (1975, 40–41), the female speaker recounts her fascination with Herodotus, who argued that his time needed iron men, soldiers and fighters. Losing her sense of "wonder" while reading about military adventures, Boland's speaker suggests that Herodotus's pragmatic soldiers might also be seen as confused men. Disillusioned with the warrior hero, the speaker describes a change in attitude towards Herodotus:

> Prepared to be harangued
> And angled by his anecdotes, his school
> Of stories, instead I found that night
> A mind incapable of insight as a mule
>
> Of generation.

The poems in *The War Horse* insist that the failure to see the tragic consequences of the mythic celebration of war persists in contemporary Ireland. The Ulster battles of the early seventies surface in the symbolic war horse, and several poems describe the suffering and conflicts war engenders. "Naoise at Four" (1975, 26–27), one of Boland's most successful poems, underscores the irony of an innocent child whose name recalls a bloody battle in Irish history: "Three brothers die, their three saps / Spill until their split kith / Heals into an Irish myth." Naoise, named for one of these, stands before the speaker, who sees only a child sipping milk from a cup. The old battle evoked by the child's name evolves into a new folk memory, the war in the North dramatized nightly on the television screen. As a godmother entrusted with Naoise's spiritual welfare, the persona urges the child down another path, unlike the one followed by the hero after whom he is named:

> Your father gossips of the wood
> Around your house, a lucky context
> Where values can be learned, fixed,
> A truce with life negotiated
> On terms you yourself can make
> Unlike your luckless namesake.

The wood provides an alternative to the ugly war landscape, a "context" where family love thrives: "your love / Is a closed circuit like your glove / In your mother's." In redirecting the child's gaze from the "sudden Irish fury" dramatized nightly on television screens, this "godmother" posits a world of a negotiated truce and another set of values "learned" and "fixed."[3]

Boland expands the image of the war horse to encompass all kinds of conflict, but her alternatives to war remain constant. In "Botanic Gardens" (1975, 17), lovers, forgetting momentarily their own disputes and the guns in the newspapers, walk among the plants seeded by a foreigner. Forced to live together, the plants have flourished. Boland's images have political connotations, the foreign gardener suggesting the invasions (and the Plantation) of Ireland. The poem suggests that the diverse plants surviving together in the confined space of the botanic gardens might be seen as the natural world's model for peace among warring factions.

But this garden is also a metaphor for marriage, the harmonious coming together of two different people: "Still at night our selves reach to join, / To twine like these trees in peace and stress, / Before the peril of unconsciousness." Love, as a prelude to sleep or a defense against the threat of death, offers peace, even in war. The botanic garden yields what the speaker calls "terms of reference," metaphors for war and peace, both private and public. One has to actively seek alternatives to conflict, the poem suggests, for the noises of all kinds of war often overwhelm the sounds of peace and love. This point, which Boland also made in "Athene's Song" and in "Naoise at Four," becomes an important theme in her future work. Many of these poems depict the value of the gardens and woods where love and peace grow, the landscape the war horse ravages.[4]

---

3. In her revision of the Irish legend of Lir's Son, "Elegy for a Youth Changed to a Swan" (1975, 31), Boland expresses a similar idea when she has Lir teach his exiled son the value of the woods in which he lives:

> That he may see breaking on his breast
> And wings not the waters of his exile,
> Nor the pawn of the wind, the cold crest,
> But branches of the white beam and the maple,
> Boughs of the almond and the laurel.

This, we should note, is the same advice given by his godmother to Naoise, and it is the most persistent theme in *The War Horse*.

4. The comparison of marriage to the botanic gardens becomes part of a larger pattern of poems that link flowers with love. "Cyclist with Cut Branches" (1975, 15), for

The role that women play, often unacknowledged, in understanding the value of this world, Boland makes clear in a love poem that embodies the major images and themes in *The War Horse*. In "Ready for Flight" (1975, 19), the speaker declares her willingness to negotiate peace. Giving us another image of a decimated, war-torn landscape, she offers help:

> And if a runner starts to run to me
> Dispatched by you, crying that all is trampled
> Underfoot, terraces smashed, the entry
> Into holy places rudely sampled,
>
> Then I would come at once my love with love
> Bringing to wasted areas the sight
> Of butterfly and swan and turtle dove
> Their wings ruffled like sails ready for flight.
>
> In such surroundings, after the decease
> Of devils, you and I would live in peace.

"Ready for Flight" illustrates a change from Boland's earlier poem, "The Winning of Etain." Etain, the pawn in the rivalry between Fergus and Aengus, has been replaced with a woman who knows her own strength and value, an "I" who "flies" under her own power. No more the dragonfly created and controlled by the warring Fergus, she is here ready to bring belief in a renewing landscape to the person she loves.

Constructed of highly regular stanzas, the poems in *The War Horse* illustrate Boland's control of traditional form. Rhyming couplets, quatrains, sestets, sonnets, and experiments with iambic pentameter, line length and off-rhymes, all reveal Boland's skill with conventional literary technique. One of the last poems, "Suburban Woman" (1975, 42–44), combines rhyming couplets with a six-line stanza to introduce the images from Boland's own life that become important in the poetry to follow.

An awakening sense of female identity in *The War Horse* underpins the more fully realized female consciousness of Boland's 1980 volume, *In Her Own Image*, ten poems with drawings by Constance Short.[5] Directly

---

example, describes love as analogous to the life cycle of flowers, and the language of the poem ("lethal," "abused," "grief," "decay") reinforces the ever-present image of the war horse. Boland offers the compensation of love to counteract grief and suffering.

5. *In Her Own Image* and *Night Feed* were published by Arlen House. Seven of the original ten poems in *In Her Own Image* and twenty-four of the twenty-seven poems originally published in *Night Feed* have been reprinted in *Selected Poems*. A new edition of *Night Feed* was published by Carcanet in 1994.

confronting images of women in society and in literature, these poems reveal the danger of stereotypes.

Explaining in her prose that hers was no overnight conversion, Boland describes how her marriage, her move to the Dublin suburbs, and the birth of a child all began to affect how and what she wrote. The growing distance between her own life and the women she saw reflected in literature became a central concern:

> The more I looked at these images in Irish poetry, the more uneasy I became. I did not recognize these women. These images could never be a starting point for mine. There was no connection between them and my own poems. How could there be? I was a woman. I stood in an immediate and unambiguous relation to human existences which were only metaphors for male poets. As far as I was concerned, it was the absence of women in the poetic tradition which allowed women in the poems to be simplified. The voice of a woman poet would, I was sure, have precluded such distortion. It did not exist. In the meantime, I could only formulate my rejection of these images as they stood. I did not accept such strategies as my truth. I would not consider them as my poetic inheritance. (1987c, 152–53)

In Her Own Image represents not only Boland's rejection of the old images but also the beginning of attempts to express her own vision of women's lives. Unlike her first volume, these poems do chart new territory, both in subject and in form. Boland describes these poems as "anti-lyric," her response to the constraints she felt the lyric placed on her as a woman (1988a, 40). One of the first things we notice about this volume, after having confronted Constance Short's graphically sexual drawings, is the loosening of stanzaic form. Short-line tercets, reminiscent of the American poet Sylvia Plath,[6] appear in half of the poems. Other poems with four-, five-, or ten-line stanzas employ neither regular meter nor rhyme; two of the poems have no fixed stanza. While not unusual in contemporary poetry, this loosening of form represents a departure for Boland from those conventional models which had dominated her earlier volumes.

The imagery and themes of these poems likewise reflect Boland's willingness to let go, to ignore taboos. The titles reveal their female subject matter: "Anorexic," "Mastectomy," "Menses," "Making-up." The opening poem, "Tirade for the Mimic Muse" (1980, 9–11), announces Boland's intention to unmask a false image of women, especially the fe-

---

6. No doubt the American poets Sylvia Plath and Adrienne Rich had some influence on Boland's thinking and writing. For a valuable comparison of Boland and Rich, see Luftig 1993.

male muse of the male poet: "Your time is up. There's not a stroke, a flick / Can make your crime cosmetic." She pictures the mimic muse as another stereotype, a slut and a whore, done up in trashy makeup masking the realities women face. The speaker addresses this image, asking her to wake up:

> Make your face naked,
> Strip your mind naked,
> Drench your skin in a woman's tears.
> I will wake you from your sluttish sleep.
> I will show you true reflections, terrors.
> You are the Muse of all our mirrors.
> Look in them and weep.

Mirrors and making up recur often in *In Her Own Image* as Boland seeks to uncover many superficial images of women. The last two poems in the volume, "Exhibitionist" and "Making-up," challenge the mimic muse. In Boland's parody of stereotypes (1980, 31–35), a female "exhibitionist" replaces the male fantasy of the slut to make a new aesthetic from the old. A woman's candid appreciation of her own sexuality translates into an artistic striptease that subverts "sculpture, / the old mode" and offers something new: "Into the gutter / of their lust / I burn / the shine / of my flesh." The real woman, in the "flesh," replaces the "trash / and gimmickry / of sex," making herself over in her own image. Moving from darkness into light, she works "from the text," "the old mode" to create something new.[7] The woman in the final poem of the volume, "Making-up" (1980, 36–38), warns: "Take nothing, nothing / at its face value." She suggests that images of women, in culture and in literature, are often as "made up" as the face she puts on in the morning:

> Legendary seas,
> nakedness,
>
> that up and stuck
> lassitude
> of thigh and buttock
> that they prayed to—
>
> it's a trick.
> Myths
> are made by men.

7. I am reminded here of Adrienne Rich's poem, "Diving into the Wreck" (1973, 22–24), which suggests a similar search.

The dangers of mythic images and stereotypes appear in many of these poems. "Anorexic" (1980, 17–18) describes how women, compulsive about thinness, destroy their bodies in a metaphoric witch's ritual. Alluding to Eve, "thin as a rib," the poem suggests that the female anorexic seeks to be sinless, to slip back into Adam's body where she can grow holy again. The anorexic treats her flesh as heretical, her sexuality as sinful. With its references to Eve, to pythons, to bitches and witches, this poem connects the contemporary anorexic to a long line of female ancestors as well as to puritanical visions of female sexuality prevalent in history, literature, and religion.[8]

Metaphors of the female body and of "sculpting" appear in other poems like "Mastectomy" (1980, 19–21), where surgery symbolizes male fantasies that turn the nourishing breast ("What slaked them first") into a "blue-veined / white-domed / home / of wonder / and the wetness / of their dreams." This mutilating unsexing of real women in favor of the whore we see in "Tirade for the Mimic Muse" is the basic image around which the volume revolves.

The effects of such mutilation appear in a different light in "In His Own Image" (1980, 14–15). Unlike the exhibitionist who "sculpts" her own image, this woman is fashioned by a man's brutal fists: "His are a sculptor's hands: / they summon / form from the void, / they bring / me to myself again. / I am a new woman." The image of waking up, which Boland uses often to suggest a liberating enlightenment, is turned upside down here; this woman wakes up to another horror:

> Now I see
> that all I needed
> was a hand
> to mould my mouth,
> to scald my cheek,
> was this concussion
> by whose lights I find
> my self-possession,
> where I grow complete.

Balancing these images of fantasy, brutality, and suffering, Boland also expresses how traditional portrayals of female sexuality might be revised. In "Witching" (1980, 28–30), for example, she imagines the

---

8. Much has been written on puritanical images of female sexuality recently; Elaine Pagels (1988) and Mary Condren (1989) both trace the image back to the early Christian Church.

proverbial hag as producing her own fire, a gift she is willing to give nightly. Refusing to be doused by the intimidation of "nursery lights," the mother in "Witching" proclaims herself a sexual person, not just a breeder. Rather than a witch burned by others, she's a burning witch, proud of her passion.

Boland takes this image one step further in "Solitary" (1980, 23–24), a poem about masturbation. Admitting that she has been taught that "You could die for this" or "The gods could make you blind," the speaker nonetheless takes herself "from spark to blaze." Seeing this experience as sacramental, she presents it as worship of self in "a chapel of unreason." Defying the gods, Christian and otherwise, who make this pleasure sinful, she worships at her own shrine, paying homage, like her sister witch, to her own sexuality. Sylvia Kelly notes that this is more than a poem about masturbation:

> Using the female body as the site where the assumptions of male creativity are internalized, the speaker defiantly states that she herself, and "only" she, knows the true sensual rhythms of her own body. By writing her own sexual experience into the text with the use of graphically visual metaphors she is attempting to force the reader to grasp that the deepest sexual experience is for the speaker a private moment. (51)

In an interview with Rebecca E. Wilson, Boland says that she thinks *In Her Own Image* might be misunderstood, and she explains her purpose:

> I wrote it with a puritan perspective, but it was taken to be a confession of a number of diseases which I had and neuroses which I was clearly giving evidence of! There are certain areas that are degraded because they are silent. They need to be re-experienced and re-examined. Their darker energies need to be looked at. (Somerville Arjat and Wilson 1990, 82)

Set beside the "darker energies" in *In Her Own Image,* the poems in *Night Feed* (1982; new edition, 1994b), many of which were written at the same time, are more traditional lyrics and different in tone. As Boland (1986) has written, her marriage and two daughters, born in 1965 and 1977, added both a new focus to her life and another dimension to her poetry.

Van Eyck's painting *Giovanni Arnolfini and His Bride* (1434) supplies a backdrop for the volume and the major image for the poem, "Domestic Interior" (1994b, 20). A self-portrait of Van Eyck reflected in the convex mirror at the center of the painting, and the inscription above the mirror, "Johannes de Eyck fuit hic," both suggesting the presence of the artist in the work, parallel Boland's role as poet describing in *Night Feed* her own domestic interiors.

In the painting the mirror also reflects the bride and groom, who stand hand in hand for a formal portrait. As the speaker in the poem compares herself to this woman, the difference between art and life becomes clear. The bride painted by Van Eyck, "by whose edict she will stay / burnished, fertile, / on her wedding day," reinforces the contrast with the speaker, who sees herself as an imperfect "woman in her varnishes" who "won't improve in the light." Nevertheless, the poem suggests, a married couple can often create a way of life "that is its own witness," and has its own significance:

> Put the kettle on, shut the blind.
> Home is a sleeping child,
> an open mind
>
> and our effects,
> shrugged and settled
> in the sort of light
> jugs and kettles
> grow important by.

In *Night Feed*, Boland shows how images of women in art, often idealized, must be set beside others, like the one seen outside a window in "The Muse Mother" (1994b, 14): "a mother hunkering, / her busy hand / worrying a child's face, / working a nappy liner / over his sticky, loud / round of a mouth." To complement Van Eyck's portrait, Boland's speaker would like to "paint" an image of this woman:

> If I could only decline her—
> lost noun
> out of context,
> stray figure of speech—
> from this rainy street
>
> again to her roots,
> she might teach me
> a new language:

This new language, defined in the final lines of the poem, will turn the speaker into a "sybil / . . . able to speak at last / my mother tongue." Mother Muse becomes here both image and imagemaker, the poet-mother herself.

The pervasive tone of *In Her Own Image* is developed by the assertive woman trying to uncover her own female identity; the speakers in *Night Feed* grow more meditative, introduced by the hushed voices of night feedings and maternal whisperings. The first six poems, written in four, five, and seven short-line stanzas, typical of the poems in the volume, describe a very complex bonding between mother and infant and manifest how Boland's own experience of motherhood has universal meaning. Set at very specific hours of dawn and twilight, when mother and child come together alone, these poems focus on the passage of time, when beginnings foreshadow endings and the relationship between birth and death is revealed. The connection between mother and child has sacramental value, a lullaby becomes a "Hymn" (1994b, 8), as these shared moments sanctify an ordinary interior, and the value of motherhood is made clear:

> Here is the star
> of my nativity:
> a nursery lamp
> in a suburb window
>
> behind which
> is boiled glass, a bottle
> and a baby all
> hisses like a kettle.

Night feedings, recovering for the mother the closeness of the child in the womb, bring with them, however, a melancholy "undersong," as she realizes how quickly the child will grow and mother and child begin "the long fall from grace." Nevertheless, "Before Spring" (1994b, 12) tells us, the mother will enjoy her "seedlings": "Sweet child / asleep in your cot, / Little seed-head, / there is time yet."

As she has done in many of her poems, Boland often turns to images of flowers and woods to embody feelings; the life cycle in the natural world reminds her speakers of the limitations of maternal joy. In "Endings" (1994b, 19), a mother anticipates loss, drawing a parallel between her baby daughter and the apple trees outside her window:

> If I lean
> I can see
> what it is the branches end in:
>
> The leaf.
> The reach.

>The blossom.
>The abandon.

Images of dawn and twilight, 4 A.M. feedings, and the short life of the apple blossom all reinforce the passage of time and the value of the moments mother and child share. The inevitability of future partings makes these moments precious—suspends time, as it were—while mother and child, "By the mercy / of the nursery light / . . . are one more and / inseparable again."

In these poems Boland shows how the intensity of a woman's experience as mother can suggest much about the universal meaning of love, life, and death. Describing herself as an "indoor nature poet," Boland says: "And my lexicon was the kettle and the steam, and the machine in the corner and the kitchen, and the baby's bottle. These were parts of my world. Not to write about them would have been artificial" (Roche and Allen-Randolph 1993, 124).

Revising the image or rewriting the convention, however, is not easy with a home and children. The speaker in "The New Pastoral" (1994b, 25) proclaiming that she is no shepherdess, wonders if she can make a poem out of sprouts, lamb's knuckles, bacon flitch, and such. The ironic contrast between art and life emerges again as the woman tries to solve this problem. To build his world, the speaker maintains, early man had flint and a wheel; she has only the objects in her kitchen. But there is a world and a poem in any kitchen, and this woman with a "non-stop / switch and tick" will create her own pastoral out of the "chance sights" she sees.

In "Tirade for the Epic Muse" (1982, original edition, 43), Boland reinforces this idea, turning from pastoral to epic as she invites the male-created muse of the war epic into her kitchen:

>They've done with you. Your eyes are dunced.
>Your mouth's a bone. You switch and tic.
>In my kitchen, in my epic
>Wretch find peace. You won't notice
>My machines. They mist and wink.
>But how they'll know you for their own!

Washing machines replace war machines as the muse takes refuge in the poet's kitchen, where they can work on what another poem calls "Patch-work."[9]

---

9. Boland has talked and written about the shift from woman as subject to woman as author of poetry. In the *American Poetry Review,* she discusses the simplification of Irish

In the last poem in *Night Feed*, "A Ballad of Beauty and Time" (1994b, 39–40), Boland concentrates on traditional images of female beauty, a recurring theme carried over from *In Her Own Image* and related to that volume's dedicatory poem, "Domestic Interior." In this ballad, the speaker has reached a point where makeup no longer hides the effects of aging. She visits a sculptor, seeking to restore her face and body, only to be told that he can only "seam the line"; "It wouldn't do for you," he says, "your quarrel's with the weave." Disappointed, she sets out again, to the studio of another sculptor who will turn her into a statue. Finally recognizing the falseness of the image she wants to project, and arguing that "Beauty is not truth," the woman challenges an established aesthetic:

> "It's all very well
> when you have bronzed a woman—
> pinioned her and finned
> wings on either shoulder.
> Anyone can see
> she won't get any older.
> What good is that to me?"

Challenging Keats's famous declaration that "'Beauty is truth, truth beauty,'—that is all / Ye know on earth, and all ye need to know," Boland returns again to the contrast between life and the artist's image of that life, emphasizing how much heavier the burden of "beauty" weighs on women. Attempts to thwart the effects of time, or to meet some standard of beauty, lead women to try to sustain youth, a frustrating effort doomed to failure. In this poem only the woman and the artist who are willing to accept the "honest flaw" and "let it stand" tell the truth.

Merging woman as portrait with woman as painter, image with imagemaker, in "Fruit on a Straight-Sided Tray" (1994b, 16), Boland imagines the relationship between mother and child as an artistic still life:

> When the painter takes the straight-sided tray
> and arranges late melons with grapes and lemons,
> the true subject is the space between them:
>
> in which repose the pleasure of these ovals
> is seen to be an assembly of possibilities;
> a deliberate collection of cross purposes.
> Gross blues and purples. Yellow and the shadow of bloom—

---

women in literature and argues that now "those emblems are no longer silent. They have acquired voices. They have turned from poems into poets" (1990a, 32).

The room smells of metal polish. The afternoon sun
brings light but no heat and no distraction from

the study of absences, the science of relationships
in which the abstraction is made actual: such as
fruit on a straight-sided tray; a homely arrangement.

This is the geometry of the visible, physical tryst
between substances

This "science of relationships," whether in the painter's arrangement
of fruit on a tray or in the "tryst" between mother and child, is a valuable
coming together of "substances" within the infinite space in which we all
live. The repose of the fruit provides the artist with not only "an assem-
bly of possibilities" but also "a deliberate collection of cross purposes."
Comparing this "arrangement" to that between mother and child, Bo-
land imagines both as compensation for the "equation that kills": "you
are my child and between us are / spaces. Distances. Growing to
infinities."

The first six poems in *Night Feed*, where we might picture the
mother and child as "ovals" in a painting suspending time only momen-
tarily, echo here. In "Fruit on a Straight-Sided Tray," a mother again sees
time as limited, her child's body as the "destiny" of her own, with inevi-
table "spaces," "distances," and "infinities" between them. In this poem,
as in others in *Night Feed*, Boland witnesses the value of art and of moth-
erhood, as she insists on the truth and beauty of a "homely arrangement"
and the "still life" of a domestic interior.

By the time she came to publish *The Journey*,[10] Boland had spoken
and written often about the Irish woman writer. In essays and interviews,
as well as in workshops where women could gather to discuss their writ-
ing,[11] Boland drew attention to the need to break the silence of women
in modern Irish poetry. In her prose she examined the problems of the
Irish woman poet from many perspectives: the lack of a visible female
tradition in Anglo-Irish poetry; the established aesthetic that developed

10. *The Journey* was first published by Gallery Press in 1982. It was republished by
Carcanet Press and Arlen House in *The Journey and Other Poems* in 1986 and in a revised
form in *Outside History: Selected Poems, 1980–1990* by Norton. For quotations, I have used
the Norton edition.

11. For many years Boland has supported and participated in these workshops, argu-
ing that they are often the only places where some women get encouragement for their
work. See her essay "In Defense of Workshops" in *Poetry Ireland Review* (1991).

from male visions and assumptions; and what she calls "simplified and reduced" images of women (1987c, 152). As her prose shows, one of Boland's greatest frustrations involves the distance between her own experience as a woman and the images she saw in literature. In *The Journey* Boland focuses on the problems she articulates in her prose, continuing to explore the issues of identity and imagemaking.

The long title poem, "The Journey" (1990c, 93–96), sets the tone as a mother-persona, watching over her children, falls asleep and dreams of the wailing children described in book 6, the underworld scene, of the *Aeneid*. In Boland's poem, unlike Virgil's, the dreamer identifies with the anxiety of grieving women who must confront the terror of their children's death. Though the scene she sees seems to be "beyond speech, beyond song," the speaker resolves to "at least be their witness," and her guide, Sappho, encourages her: "remember it, you will remember it." Waking up from this nightmare, the speaker tells us, with relief, "my children / slept the last dark out safely and I wept."

"The Journey" describes the fears of women with sick children, their ultimate powerlessness in the face of an infant's death. Like the male pilgrims (Dante, for example) led through the underworld by male guides, the speaker here follows Sappho, her female literary mentor. "The Journey" begins as a poem to an antibiotic, the modern medicine that could have prevented the death of the infants in the *Aeneid*. Yet the contemporary woman speaker, whose children may be safe because of antibiotics, still understands the fear and the loss her female ancestors had to face. Although describing mythic woman, Boland explains that she also had in mind the women in Ireland's past: "The woman I imagined—if the statistics are anything to go by—must have lost her children in that underworld, just as I came to possess mine through the seasons of my neighborhood" (1990d, 109). Alluding here both to Virgil's underworld and to the myth of Ceres, Boland shifts the spotlight to the way in which women might imagine these tragedies.

Though dominant in the title poem, mythic revision represents only one approach in *The Journey and Other Poems*. The ordinary details of women's lives are celebrated in many other poems. Boland often portrays the ways in which women in the present relate to those of the past. So we have a poem about quilting, "The Unlived Life" (1990c, 91–92), in which a woman learns from her neighbor how to make a template:

> "You start out with jest so much caliker"—
> Eliza Calvert Hall of Kentucky said—
> "that's the predestination

> but when it comes to cuttin' out
> the quilt, why, you're free to choose".

These two women, brought together by their children and the details of quilting, evoke an image of foremothers:

> Suddenly I could see us
> calicoed, overawed, dressed in cotton
> at the railroad crossing, watching
> the flange-wheeled, steam-driven, iron omen
> of another life passing, passing

The woman's art of quilting, inherited by Eliza Calvert Hall, who passes it on to her neighbor, brings these women together as ethnic, geographical, and historical boundaries collapse. Again, Boland witnesses women's experience, women's voices, and women's art, remembering "the unlived life."

Boland's attempts to express the voices of women, to create alternative speakers to those heard most often in Irish poetry, can be seen in a poem like "The Oral Tradition" (1990c, 75–77). A poet recounts an incident after a reading, when "only half-wondering / what becomes of words," she overhears one woman telling another a story:

> "She could feel it coming"—
> one of them was saying—
> "all the way there,
> across the fields at evening
> and no one there, God help her"

Before we know it, we, like the poet, are caught up in this story, listening to all the details:

> "and she had on a skirt
> of cross-woven linen
> and the little one
> kept pulling at it.
> It was nearly night . . ."
> . . . .
> ". . . when she lay down
> and gave birth to him
> in an open meadow.
> What a child that was
> to be born without a blemish!"

The fascination of this miracle birth comes through in the women's dialogue, a "musical sub-text" to the language of the rest of the poem. The poet, "not seeing out" and "only half-listening," suddenly hears another kind of language, this story of a great-grandmother and a summer birth handed down in a woman's oral history. The poet here discovers "the oral song / avid as superstition, / layered like an amber in / the wreck of language / and the remnants of a nation." On the train "journey" home, she goes back enlightened about the value of different kinds of language, and "a sense / suddenly of truth, / its resonance." We have in this poem a song within a song, in which the story of the birth of a child brings together the poet-persona, the two women speakers, a great-grandmother, and a reader in a beautiful weaving together—like a skirt of cross-woven linen—of different kinds of words. The speaker's "half-wondering / what becomes of words" resonates with understatement as Boland emphasizes the need to record women's words and what they may signify.

In *Writing a Woman's Life,* Carolyn Heilbrun argues that new stories will not "find their way into texts if they do not begin in oral exchanges among women in groups hearing and talking to one another" (1988, 46).[12] Boland's "The Oral Tradition" is as much an argument for the need to listen to the stories women tell, as it is for not denying the voice of the female poet. "Their talk was a gesture, / an outstretched hand" (76), the speaker tells us, connecting the poet with other women, and present with past. The outstretched hand also links this poem to "The Journey," where the poet Sappho shares with the speaker her insight and the significance of the scene before her. Life and art, the real and the "artifice," intersect in the shared lives of women.

While these remembrances record the value of chance meetings between women, other poems in the volume describe Boland's journey into her own past to remember, recover, or discover the women in her family history. The opening poem, "I Remember" (1990c, 100), depicts a significant moment in her own childhood when the "mystery" of the artist's imagemaking first struck her. Boland's mother, Frances Kelly, was an artist, and the poem describes her paintings in the drawing room of their

12. Heilbrun's study, focused primarily on biography and autobiography, considers the relationship between a woman's life and her poetry. Looking at Adrienne Rich's work, Heilbrun suggests that Rich has revolutionized autobiography, and that her "most fundamental struggle was to recognize herself as a poet, and to mean by this that the quality of what she felt impelled to say in poetry was not diminished because it was thought to be female, political, and offensive" (1988, 66). I think we can trace a similar struggle through Boland's work.

postwar London home.[13] Recalling how the face of the person who had come up the stairs in the morning eventually took shape on her mother's canvas, the speaker describes her wonder at the image still there after the sitter had gone. As a nine-year-old, she felt "the need to touch, to handle, to dismantle it, / the mystery" in order to understand the relationship between the person she had seen and the image composed on canvas. As the first poem in this volume, "I Remember" stands as tribute to Boland's own mother's work and her influence in awakening her daughter's artistic vision and impulse. But the poem also witnesses the work of women artists, as Boland carries out Sappho's advice in "The Journey": "remember it, you will remember it."

Poems like "I Remember" record autobiographical details etched in memory; other poems lament the lost facts and details of women's lives. In "Fever" (1990c, 87–88), Boland memorializes the life of her grandmother who died in a fever ward, younger than Boland was as she wrote the poem and leaving five orphan daughters behind:

> Names, shadows, visitations, hints
> and a half-sense of half-lives remain.
> And nothing else, nothing more unless
>
> I re-construct the soaked-through midnights;
> vigils; the histories I never learned
> to predict the lyric of; and re-construct
> risk; as if silence could become rage,
>
> as if what we lost is a contagion
> that breaks out in what cannot be
> shaken out from words or beaten out
> from meaning and survives to weaken
>
> what is given, what is certain
> and burns away everything but this
> exact moment of delirium when
> someone cries out someone's name.

This is probably Boland's most direct statement of intent. The fever that killed her grandmother represents a lost history, which erupts, weakening "the given" and "the certain," that legacy of the Irish past that

13. Paintings by Boland's mother, Frances Kelly, hang in the National Gallery of Ireland. Her father, F. H. Boland, was a diplomat in London, where Boland spent her early years.

often ignores the lives of women like her grandmother. Insisting that the poet can witness, can imagine, Boland makes these women more than "names, shadows, visitations" and brings them, like their mythic counterparts, out of a shadowy world. The grandmother's fever also reminds us of the sick children in "The Journey." In *The Journey* history, story, myth, and daily life are closely woven together by image and idea.

Embarking on this trip into history and myth, Boland addresses the issue of nationhood as it affects Irish women. Her stance, with its added emphasis on gender, differs from that of her male colleagues who also struggle to confront Ireland's social and political problems. In her essay *The Woman Poet in a National Tradition,* Boland argues that Irish poets, in making women "figments of national expression" (1987c, 155), evaded the real women of the past. She makes it clear that she has committed herself to trying to change this: "The real women with their hungers, their angers, endured a long struggle and a terrible subsistence. Those women are in all our pasts. We are the heirs of their survival. They exist in history and in family archives as specters and victims, memories and ghosts. Their suffering is our common possession" (155).

In "Tirade for the Lyric Muse" (1987b, 55–56), Boland describes her goal: "Listen. / Bend your darned head. / Turn your good ear. / Share my music." With the metaphor of music, Boland takes us back again to one of her early poems and the image of Athene's silent pipe, reminding us of the many images in her work evoking the silent voices of women. No longer willing to ignore what the lyric muse's "songs left out," Boland creates a new kind of music in the female voices in her poems. Firmly committed, in "Envoi" (1990c, 97), to a muse who will remain "until the song is proven," in *The Journey and Other Poems* Boland has become, in a way that the personae in her first volume could never have imagined, a poet-explorer in "new territory."

In a special supplement in the *American Poetry Review* devoted to her work, Boland discusses the poems in her 1990 volume, *Outside History,*[14] stressing again the need to examine how women became identified with nationhood, "emerging in Irish poetry as fictive queens and national sibyls" (1990a, 33). Analyzing what happened, Boland argues:

> Irish poems simplified women most at the point of intersection between womanhood and Irishness. The further the Irish poem drew away from the idea of Ireland, the more real and persuasive became the images of

14. *Outside History* was published by Carcanet in 1990 and as part of *Outside History: Selected Poems, 1980–1990* by Norton in 1990. For quotations, I have used the Norton edition.

women. Once the pendulum swung back the simplifications started
again. The idea of the defeated nation being reborn as a triumphant
woman was central to a certain kind of Irish poem. Dark Rosaleen.
Cathleen ni Houlihan. The nation as woman; the woman as national
muse. (33)

Boland maintains that though few Irish poets accepted the politics of
nationalism, they continued to "deploy the emblems and enchantments
of its culture" (33).

Faced with this dilemma, Boland speaks of her alienation, of a cor-
rupt image obscuring the real suffering women endured in the history of
the nation. Posing this as an aesthetic and ethical issue, she defines her
own goal as woman poet, one that explains the twelve-poem sequence
"Outside History," the middle section of the volume of the same title.
The poems in the first section of the book, "Object Lessons," and those
in the final section, "Distances," develop the central themes and images
of this middle sequence.

The tone of these poems might best be described as elegiac; a deep-
ening sense of loss, of time and of people, grows from its emphasis on
personal and national hardship. Typically, Boland merges the two, show-
ing us how womanhood and Irishness might be more truthfully linked.
The opening poem of the sequence, "The Achill Woman" (1990c, 35–
36), recalls a memory from a college vacation. Boland describes a woman
who brought water to the Achill cottage where she was staying: "She has
a tea towel around her waist—perhaps this is one image that has become
all the images I have of her—she wears an old cardigan and her hands are
blushing with cold as she puts down the bucket" (1990a, 32).

The Achill woman's importance in the poem depends upon a con-
trast. Describing herself in the *American Poetry Review* as reading the
Court poets of the Silver Age, "In token of the need to do better"
(1990a, 32), Boland remembers this woman as the first person to talk to
her about the famine. Unaware at the time of the irony of reading poems
of the oppressor's culture, Boland says that she still "sensed a power in
the encounter. I knew, without having words for it, that she came from a
past which affected me" (32). This is the past outside history, recorded
in the final lines of the poem, where the speaker tries to come to terms
with her memory:

> but nothing now can change the way I went
> indoors, chilled by the wind
> and made a fire

and took down my book
and opened it and failed to comprehend

the harmonies of servitude,
the grace music gives to flattery
and language borrows from ambition—

and how I fell asleep
oblivious to

the planets clouding over in the skies,
the slow decline of the Spring moon,
the songs crying out their ironies.

In one sense the sleep symbolizes the persona's unenlightened state: her failure to realize the connection between the ambitious and flattering language of the English court poets and the "songs" of the Achill woman. Continuing a theme expressed in poems like "The Oral Tradition," Boland stresses the need to look and listen outside recorded history to understand the complexities of a personal or national past.

Such encounters lie in every person's past, unrecorded moments that influence much of what we are. Such moments among women unify this sequence, reinforcing the title of one poem, "We Are Human History. We Are Not Natural History." Not restricted to Irish history, these moments nonetheless enlighten us about the Irish past. In the poem "In Exile" (1990c, 46), a young girl's experience of hearing German girls talking comes back as a memory, linking Germany with Ireland, and language with truth: "syllables in which pain was / radical, integral; and with what sense of injury / the language angled for an unhurt kingdom—." Another speaker, in "We Are Always Too Late" (1990c, 47), "re-visiting" a scene in a New England café where she saw a woman weeping, "re-enacts" that scene, imagining herself trying to show the woman the beauty of the snow falling outside the window:

I raise one hand. I am pointing to
those trees, I am showing her our need for these
beautiful upstagings of
what we suffer by
what survives. And she never even sees me.

The lost connection, enacted in imagination after the event, relates not only to the Achill woman and the German girls, but to all lost opportunities. In the broadest historical context, this means failing to acknowledge the suffering of Irish women; the title "We Are Always Too Late" refers to both personal and national responses.

A prevailing image in this sequence, a wound that does not heal, appears in "The Making of an Irish Goddess" (1990c, 38–39). Alluding to Ceres, who lost her daughter to Pluto, the speaker imagines the goddess looking back to "a seasonless, unscarred earth." Reminding us of the woman in Boland's earlier poem "Domestic Interior," she lives in time, with a body "neither young now nor fertile, / and with the marks of childbirth / still on it." Trying to articulate her feelings, this new Ceres recasts the mother's loss and redefines the myth:

> myth is the wound we leave
> in the time we have—
>
> which in my case is this
> March evening
> at the foothills of the Dublin mountains,
> across which the lights have changed all day,
>
> holding up my hand
> sickle-shaped, to my eyes
> to pick out
> my own daughter from
> all the other children in the distance;
>
> her back turned to me.

Transferring Ceres' suffering over the loss of her daughter to a Dublin mother who anticipates such a loss, the speaker links her own feelings to those of the mythic woman. But she also identifies with Father Time, for the hand shading her eyes is shaped like his sickle. This Irish goddess, seeking an "accurate inscription" of her fear and loss, sets it within history.

Explaining the source for scenes like the one in this poem, Boland writes that as she looked for her daughters in a summer twilight, she felt a connection to the past and to other women, a sense of timelessness:

Then I would feel all the sweet, unliterate melancholy of women who must have stood as I did, throughout continents and centuries, feeling the timelessness of that particular instant and the cruel time underneath its surface. They must have measured their children, as I did, against the seasons; they too must have looked at the hedges and rowan trees, the

height and the color of their berries, as an index of the coming loss.
(1990d, 105–106)

The last two poems in "Outside History," lamenting the lost voices
of the past, again relate to Boland's own life, as she tries to see public
significance in personal history. "What We Lost" (1990c, 48–49) pic-
tures the speaker's mother and grandmother in a country scene, as the
grandmother "settles and begins her story." Lest we miss the significance
of this scene, the speaker tells us:

> Believe it, what we lost is here in this room
> on this veiled evening.
> The woman finishes. The story ends.
> The child, who is my mother, gets up, moves away.
>
> In the winter air, unheard, unshared,
> the moment happens, hangs fire, leads nowhere.
> The light will fail and the room darken,
> the child fall asleep and the story be forgotten.

As the voices fall silent, the tableau freezes, unless someone can call it
back:

> The dumb-show of legend has become language,
> is becoming silence and who will know that once
>
> words were possibilities and disappointments,
> were scented closets filled with love-letters
> and memories and lavender hemmed into muslin,
> stored in sachets, aired in bed-linen;

This poem embodies many of Boland's recurring themes and images:
the cottons, linens, and silks that figure so prominently in her poems; the
woman working in the kitchen, child at her side; the need to bring
women out of silence and shadow. While emphasizing what is lost and
"unshared," however, the poem also gives us an imaginative vision of
what might have been, in its evocation of a quiet, winter afternoon:

> She is a countrywoman.
> Behind her cupboard doors she hangs sprigged,
> stove-dried lavender in muslin.
> Her letters and mementoes and memories
>
> are packed in satin at the back with
> gaberdine and worsted and

the cambric she has made into bodices;
the good tobacco silk for Sunday Mass.

She is sewing in the kitchen.
The sugar-feel of flax is in her hands.
Dusk. And the candles brought in then.
One by one. And the quiet sweat of wax.

The language and rhythm of these lines create the hushed dusk of an old kitchen; the repetition and rhyming in such phrases as "the sugar feel of flax," "the quiet sweat of wax," show Boland's talent for fitting words to tone and mood. Though the grandmother's story, like her letters, mementoes, and memories, is lost, the "dumb-show of legend" comes alive. Like the "tones of cotton / tautened into bodices, subtly shaped by breathing," these women live again in the words of the poem.

"What We Lost" brings us ultimately to the title poem, "Outside History" (1990c, 50), where a poet-speaker expresses the unifying theme of the sequence. Noting that the stars are outside history, she says that, nevertheless, under them we find that we are mortal and human. So women must choose where they will locate themselves:

out of myth into history I move to be
part of that ordeal
whose darkness is

only now reaching me from those fields,
those rivers, those roads clotted as
firmaments with the dead.

How slowly they die
as we kneel beside them, whisper in their ear.
And we are too late. We are always too late.

Typical of Boland, this poem, as part of the sequence, works on several levels: loss covers the spectrum from family to race, from missed opportunity to unacknowledged suffering. While more than one of these poems say that "we are always too late," the poems themselves suggest otherwise, as they show not only what is gone but also what survives. From memory and imagination Boland brings moments outside history into poetry.

On first reading, the other two sections of the volume, "Object Lessons" and "Distances," may seem only loosely related to "Outside History," but similar ideas and images link them. In "Object Lessons," ordinary objects and incidents become the basis for recovering moments of personal and public history in poems R. T. Smith describes as an "insurrection against traditional male iconography" (1993, 96). These object lessons cover a spectrum, from young child and convent student to mature women, from lovers to mothers and wives, from coffee mugs to black lace fans and Irish silver. Many of the poems focus on artifacts revealing the past, but their importance carries over to the present. In "The Shadow Doll" (1990c, 26), the glass-domed porcelain model a Victorian dressmaker clothed in the bride's wedding dress, "survives its occasion" to remind another bride of how enclosed her world is becoming, and to suggest what the role of wife has often meant in Ireland: "Under glass, under wraps, it stays / even now, after all, discreet about / visits, fevers, quickenings and lusts."

The past outside history inspires and instructs, becomes the source of image and imagemaking in poems like "The Rooms of Other Women Poets" (1990c, 20–21), where the speaker identifies with literary ancestors by recreating their rooms:

> The early summer, its covenant, its grace,
> is everywhere: even shadows have leaves.
>
> Somewhere you are writing or have written in
> a room you came to as I come to this
>
> room with honeyed corners, the interior sunless,
> the windows shut but clear so I can see
>
> the bay windbreak, the laburnum hang fire, feel
> the ache of things ending in the jasmine darkening early.

In this poem Boland transforms the oppressive enclosed space of the shadow doll's glass dome into a sunless room with closed windows. But it becomes a room of one's own where, through the magic of a symbolic literary lamp, the woman poet brings light to a dusky world. "I sometimes think / I see that gesture in the way you use language," the speaker tells the female poets whose rooms she imagines, identifying with them as she brings them out of darkness and into history.

While "Object Lessons" focuses on artifacts, the third section of *Outside History*, "Distances," records memories. A carousel in the park, scenes from a family kitchen, hanging curtains, power cuts—all seen from a distance—become emblems and defining experiences, images for the poet and lessons from history. In "Our Origins Are in the Sea" (1990c, 60), a granddaughter tries to picture the grandfather she never knew who drowned in the Bay of Biscay; in "Contingencies" (1990c, 58), an adult remembers not only the sweet voices of the women in her childhood but also their "crisis bright words": "'Stop that.' 'Wait till I get you.' / 'Dry those tears.'"

Looking at things from a distance, however, to see what "A Different Light" (1990c, 63) calls a "neighbourhood on the verge of definition," Boland's personae pass beyond the boundaries of personal memory. The final poem, "Distances" (1990c, 69), describes a winter morning with the sounds of the old ballad, "I Wish I Was in Carrickfergus," drifting from the radio. As the speaker remembers a day in the coastal town described in the song, the poem highlights the difference between her experiences and those of the "handsome rover" in the song.

Recalling the market place with linen, "tacky apples and a glass and wire hill / of spectacles on a metal tray," she views Carrickfergus less nostalgically. She imagines herself and her love in the town:

> We would walk the streets in
>
> the scentless afternoon of a ballad measure,
> longing to be able
> to tell each other that the starched lace and linen of
>
> adult handkerchiefs scraped your face and left your tears
> falling; how the apples were mush inside the crisp sugar
>
> shell and the spectacles out of focus.

Reacting to the sentimental ballad, Boland warns again of the danger of a romanticized vision of place and of a past potentially as out of focus as the spectacles on the tray. The clash between the image we get from songs, what she calls the "perfect music," and the reality of Carrickfergus as a "basalt and sandstone / coastal town," is central to this poem. Over and over again in *Outside History,* as she has done in earlier poems, Boland returns to the issue of "fiction" and the ways in which what we take to be truth might be fiction while what we imagine as fiction could very well be true.

A valuable way to read *Outside History,* and indeed much of Boland's other poetry, is to see it as the construction or re-creation of a past, whether that involves personal memory or imagination, her own history or Ireland's. The fine line she walks between fidelity to her own experience and the imaginative fictionalizing of human experience creates tension in her poetry and transforms the details of daily life into art. That this is both an aesthetic and ethical issue Boland makes clear:

> All good poetry depends on an ethical relation between imagination and image. Images are not ornaments; they are truths. When I read about Cathleen ni Houlihan or the Old Woman of the Roads or Dark Rosaleen I felt that a necessary ethical relation was in danger of being violated over and over again; that a merely ornamental relation between imagination and image was being handed on from poet to poet. . . . No poetic imagination can afford to regard an image as a temporary aesthetic manoeuvre. Once the image is distorted the truth is demeaned. (1990a, 38)

In an age that questions the possibility that we can know what is "true," and in which much poetic theory challenges the idea that literature has any ethical function, Boland argues for both ethics and truth, and her starting point is the image. Reacting to what she calls an alienating "rhetoric of imagery" (1990a, 32), Boland set out to construct another set of images, with a different history and a different voice, maintaining that "in poetry in particular and women's writing in general, the private witness is often all there is to go on" (33). In Boland's journey from *New Territory* to *Outside History,* the private witness crossed into the public domain.

No one guarantees, however, that the public welcomes a newcomer. A review of *Outside History* in the April 21, 1991 issue of the *New York Times Book Review* illustrates the problems a poet like Boland still faces.[15] Missing the meaning of a good number of the poems, William Logan writes: "For Ms. Boland, the kitchen is a mortuary, but in poem after poem the kitchen and the garden remain scenes of her bloodless anger. When a poet is so self-divided, so drawn to the realms she despises, it should not be surprising if her poetry suffers division too, here between prose and the poetic" (22).

Logan's review is punctuated with the loaded language and judgments women poets are sometimes subjected to: Boland is "domestic but not domesticated"; her volume "slants against" Irish culture; she attempts to write by "force of personality"; she writes "poems of quiet desperation in the kitchen" that "do not form an original esthetic." Echo-

15. While I focus on Logan's review, he is not alone in this type of response to Boland's subjects and themes (see, for example, Hutcheson, 1989).

ing gender stereotypes, Logan says that Boland's memories are "mere retrospection"; that the "dainty melancholies" of some poems "seem crewel work"; that "she becomes a darling of the sure particular." Ultimately, Logan anoints Boland the "bard of fabric," complaining that "in one stretch of 10 pages we find silk, lace, crepe de Chine, cotton, linen, damask, gaberdine, synthetics, calico and dimity, some of them two or three times." Only when she stops being this kind of bard, he argues, is she "truest to her own culture."

The stereotyping and devaluing of experience these judgments reveal ("crewel work" a pun for the craft of "dainty" hands) contribute to Logan's shortsightedness. An enlightened critic would do more than count images of fabric and might see these as a pattern of imagery, as metaphors drawn from and expressing a woman's experience. Reading the poems more carefully, one must question Logan's judgment that Boland writes a "passionless household poem" or that for her the kitchen is a "mortuary." Oversimplifying complex feelings and concluding that Boland is "self-divided," Logan overlooks the fact that in these poems, Boland is true to *her* own culture, revealing images that should not be dismissed as trivial.

Typical of the problem is Logan's judgment of the poem "Object Lessons," which he reduces to: "When a mug breaks, a love affair is over." The poem deals with a hunting scene on the mug, a "pastoral" vision of a "lady smiling as the huntsman kissed her." Its breaking symbolizes an enlightened loss of innocence, which had been foreshadowed by "veiled warnings" that this image was bound to shatter. The "thrush's never- / to-be-finished / aria" recalls Keats's nightingale, the coffee mug brings to mind his Grecian urn, as this poem offers an alternative vision aimed at puncturing romantic illusions and challenging the imagery of the romance. Despite giving Boland credit for "virtuoso details" and a "gift for the graven phrase," Logan does not follow where these lead. The difference between the romanticized image on the cup and the speaker's own experience is at the heart of this poem, and one of the unifying themes of *Outside History*.

Seeing a close relationship between the aesthetic and the ethical, Boland often combines her images with direct statement. In some poems this approach works better than in others, and critics should note when it does not succeed. But her poetry also needs to be judged for language, tone, image, sound, pattern, idea. Describing the poetry as divided because the poet is "self-divided," or because she is "so drawn to the realms she despises," Logan misinterprets both the poet and the poetry.

For all the emphasis on Boland as a new and different voice, she is in many ways a very traditional poet, a judgment that I do not think she would object to. She has the same suspicions about the limitations of art that Yeats had; she returns in *Outside History* to the conventional forms she had left behind in *In Her Own Image*. As her body of work grows, Boland continues to demonstrate her talent with conventional poetic technique. In couplets, tercets, quatrains, she experiments with line length (alternating short and long), internal and end rhymes, caesura and enjambment. Her success with sound patterns, with assonance and alliteration, comes through in stanzas like those in "We Were Neutral in the War" (1990c, 23–24), where she describes the experiences of a woman, using the images of stitchery and preserves:

> you walked by the moonlit river and stopped
> and looked down. A glamorous circumference is
> spinning on your needle, is
> that moon in satin water making
>
> the same peremptory demands on
> the waves of the Irish sea and as each
> salt-window opens to reveal
> a weather of agates, you will stitch that in
>
> with the orchard colours of the first preserves
> you make from the garden. You move the jars from
> the pantry to the windowsill where
> you can see them: winter jewels.

Over and over again Boland has said that women must be given an equal voice and an equal hearing, that their experience reflects human experience, universal and not trivial. Declaring herself a feminist but not a separatist, she works within the tradition to add the voice of the woman poet to the more dominant male voice in Irish literature. There is a metaphor for such addition in her poem "An Old Steel Engraving" (1990c, 45), which alludes to an artist's rendering of a patriot who breaks a fall with his hand. A speaker tells us to look "at the stillness of unfinished action in / afternoon heat, at the spaces on the page. They widen / to include us."

And who is this "us"? On a universal level it is all readers as we approach any image, adding our own experience to what we see, imagining what had happened. On the historical level, it is the Irish who need to broaden their vision of the past to acknowledge where women fit. On the most specific level, the "us" includes an Irish woman poet, like the other women poets she had imagined, sitting in a room, filling in the spaces on her page.

Adrienne Rich's 1971 essay, "When We Dead Awaken: Writing as Re-Vision" (Rich 1979, 33–49), comes to mind here. The ghosts that reappear in Boland's poems, the shadows she often seeks to illuminate, the artists' images she examines "widen to include" us all, even those outside "history." Boland correctly predicts the effects of such revising, suggesting that when "the history of poetry in our time is written—I have no doubt about this—women poets will be seen to have re-written not just the poem, not just the image. They won't just have re-balanced elements within the poem. They will have altered the cartography of the poem. The map will look different" (Roche and Allen-Randolph 1993, 130).

Eiléan Ní Chuilleanáin.
Courtesy of The Gallery Press.

4

Eiléan Ní Chuilleanáin

In her introduction to *Irish Women: Image and Achievement* (1985), a book of essays by Irish women scholars, Eiléan Ní Chuilleanáin argues strongly for the need to examine the image of Irish women from two perspectives. One, which she calls the social and historical, gives us images of women created by men. The other comes from women "as they liberate themselves, through achievement in their work, and through their vision and insight as artists, from servitude to an image that has been imposed from without" (1). Half of this book covers the work of women artists and writers, and Ní Chuilleanáin explains its goal: "Looking at women's performance in the arts we search, on the one hand, for authentic expression of what woman have felt and thought, and at the same time we pay tribute to their achievement in taking us beyond what any ordinary person has managed to articulate"(8). Suggesting the broad implications of such a goal, Ní Chuilleanáin explains that when the woman artist creates an authentic image of herself, she arrives at a more comprehensive view of the whole of human experience, exploring what has been missed by the male perspective.

While this emphasis on women artists was relatively new for Ní Chuilleanáin, she had long been interested in the cause of Irish writers, especially poets. Her writer mother, Eilis Dillon, and professor father, Cormac Ó'Chuilleanáin, provided early academic and creative stimuli for their daughter's later life.[1] After reading history and literature at the university in Cork, Ní Chuilleanáin moved on to Renaissance literature at Oxford before returning to a teaching position at Trinity. Since the 1970s, while continuing to teach, Ní Chuilleanáin has been active in Irish poetry circles, especially as coeditor of *Cyphers,* a journal she founded

---

1. Eilis Dillon is known for her novels and children's stories; Cormac Ó'Chuilleanáin was a professor of Irish at University College Cork. Both were associated with the Republican cause. Eiléan Ní Chuilleanáin is also the stepdaughter of the writer and critic Vivien Mercier.

in 1975 with the writers Leland Bardwell, Pearce Hutchinson, and her future husband, Macdara Woods.

Ní Chuilleanáin's own history as a writer illustrates that she did not always see herself as a woman poet; indeed, her early work in *Acts and Monuments* (1972) gives little hint of her female identity. Discussing this, Ní Chuilleanáin once explained that she had a problem articulating a female voice: "My early poems concealed this behind various asexual masks. To say 'I' in a poem is hard for me."[2] Gradually, as Ní Chuilleanáin began to create female figures in her poetry, a more distinctive voice appeared, and in *Site of Ambush,* twenty-two poems published in 1975, a definable female persona emerges in some of the poems. The 1977 publication of the first edition of *The Second Voyage,* a selection and new arrangement of thirty-seven poems previously published in *Acts and Monuments* and *Site of Ambush,* reveals the ways in which Ní Chuilleanáin began to challenge established values and models for human behavior based solely on male experience.

The poems that open and close *The Second Voyage,* "The Lady's Tower" and "A Gentleman's Bedroom," present a study in contrast. First published in *Site of Ambush* in 1975, "The Lady's Tower" marked an important turning point in her poetry, Ní Chuilleanáin says, because of its explicit identification of the central figure of the poem as female.[3] Set beside "A Gentleman's Bedroom," which explores the world of male privilege, "The Lady's Tower" expresses a woman's view of her world.

Ní Chuilleanáin suggests that "The Lady's Tower" be read as a feminist's riposte to Yeats's tower, Thoor Ballylee, a major symbol in his later poetry. To understand what she means, we need to see Yeats's restored Norman tower as primarily a male domain. Constructed as a fortress against early invasions, it became for the poet an oasis in the swirling chaos of the Irish civil wars of the 1920s. In Yeats's volume *The Tower,* an aging and frustrated poet ponders the choices he has made, alternately defending his commitment to the artistic life and then questioning, when soldiers appear at his door, the "envy in his thoughts." Admitting that his days are "dragon-ridden," Yeats's speaker juxtaposes the images of war, from swords to rough men-at-arms, with those of art to express the tension he feels. Women are the subject of some of these poems: seductive legendary beauties who drove men to their death; the Maud Gonne

---

2. On Ní Chuilleanáin, see Browne 1985.

3. All comments and quotations in this chapter by Ní Chuilleanáin, unless otherwise attributed, are from conversations I had with her in Dublin and in the United States in 1988, 1990, 1991, and 1992.

of "Among School Children"; the helpless Leda raped by Zeus; or, in "Meditations in Time of Civil War," Yeats's own wife, for whom he "chose the house / And decked and altered it" (Yeats 1990, 210).[4]

With Yeats's symbol in mind, we note a very different image and tone when we turn to Ní Chuilleanáin's poem. In "The Lady's Tower" (1986, 11), a woman describes her surroundings, emphasizing how the tower merges with the landscape: it "leans / Back to the cliff"; the "thatch / Converses with the sky"; the "grey wall / Slices downward and meets / A sliding flooded stream." Overgrown quarry brambles brush the speaker's hair as she opens the kitchen door, and the natural world even intrudes into her bedroom: "And up the tall stairs my bed is made / Even with a sycamore root / At my small square window." The lady accepts this intrusion, absorbing nature's energy and movement, listening to the changing pace of the stream as she cooks. Attuned to the rhythmic activity around her, she feels it even while she sleeps:

> All night I lie sheeted, my broom chases down treads
> Delighted spirals of dust: the yellow duster glides
> Over shelves, around knobs: bristle stroking flagstone
> Dancing with the spiders around the kitchen in the dark
> While cats climb the tower and the river fills
> A spoonful of light on the cellar walls below.

Lacking the self-conscious ambivalence of Yeats's poet-speaker, and seeing her tower as integrated with the landscape, the lady enjoys herself in an overtly domestic and natural environment. This is a home, not a battleground, where a woman describes the ordinary details of her kitchen and her bedroom; it is not a retreat filled with the ghosts of the past or warring demons outside the door. Her imagination, like that of Yeats's speaker, is at work, but her tower reverberates with dream visions in which housework gets done as the woman sleeps. In her witch's world, swinging brooms and gliding dusters consort with dancing spiders, climbing cats, a flowing river, and a "spoonful of moonlight." Unlike Yeats, who in the opening poem of the *The Tower* declares his intention to sail to Byzantium, escaping to the artistic world of golden birds, Ní Chuilleanáin's lady stays put, the punt outside her tower, "floating freely / Bobs square-ended, the rope dead-level."

Using one of her most unique and consistent poetic techniques—a shifting angle of vision as the perceiving eye looks up, down, in, out, and

4. In many cases, Yeats is drawing on established images of women in legends and myths.

over—Ní Chuilleanáin suggests her persona's relationship with the world around her. The speaker sees herself in a moving and shifting natural world in which she actively participates.

On another level these images have sexual connotations: the hollow tower leaning back to the cliff, thatch conversing with sky, evokes images of female genitalia, with hints of one of the ways in which women participate in the rhythms and cycles of the natural world. A challenge to Yeats's Leda, victim of the powerful and "indifferent" Zeus who descends upon her "helpless breast," the lady in the tower "converses with spread sky." James McElroy, in commenting on some reviewers' "superficial treatment" of Ní Chuilleanáin's poetry, including the failure to note the sexual imagery, suggests that we might see Ní Chuilleanáin's tower "as an aperture: a poetic opening where writers can begin to organize, protest, and feminize a self-image" (1989, 191).[5]

Exploiting the stereotypes of the evil and threatening female witch or the passive female vessel, Ní Chuilleanáin gives us an image of a woman who enjoys herself and the natural world around her. She is neither helpless victim nor romantic seductress who drives men mad. As such, she is an alternative to the "ladies" who populate Yeats's landscape in "The Tower": the mad Mrs. French who drove her "serving-man" to cut off an insolent farmer's ear; the peasant girl, remembered in song, whose beauty causes a man's drowning; or the legendary Helen who "has all living hearts betrayed" (Yeats 1990, 200–206). Displacing these images of women created by the male imagination, Ní Chuilleanáin's lady in the tower offers a less romanticized and more positive vision of women. She is also an alternative to Mother Ireland, a social and cultural icon identified with the effects of invasions on Irish history and the Irish landscape.[6] Significantly, Ní Chuilleanáin's speaker lies "sheeted" and tells us about her own pleasures and dreams.

Ní Chuilleanáin juxtaposes this view of female experience with one presented in the final poem, "A Gentleman's Bedroom" (1986, 68). In "The Lady's Tower," the interaction between lady and landscape provides a source of continuous energy. The imagery of the final poem suggests just the opposite, where a barrier separates the gentleman from the outer world:

5. McElroy also compares this poem to Medbh McGuckian's "The Soil-Map" (191–92).

6. A video entitled *Mother Ireland*, produced by Derry Film and Video, documents several women's responses to this image, including those of Nell McCafferty and Margaret Mac Curtain. The relationship between the image and Irish nationalism is highlighted in the film. Edna O'Brien's *Mother Ireland* (1976) offers an interesting autobiographical response to the image.

> The house sits silent,
> The shiny linoleum
> Would creak if you stepped on it.
> Outside it is still raining
> But the birds have begun to sing.

In the opening poem the activity and noise of the natural world permeate the lady's tower; in the final poem the gentleman's house is silent while the birds sing outside. The imagery of the gentleman's bedroom alerts us to his distance from the world around him. Everything in his room sits carefully arranged, geometrically perfect:

> Opening the door, all walls point at once to the bed
> Huge red silk in a quarter of the room
> Knots drowning in deep mahogany
> And uniform blue volumes shelved at hand.
>
> And a desk calendar, a fountain pen,
> A weighty table-lighter in green marble,
> A cigar box, empty but dusted,
> A framed young woman in a white dress
> Indicate the future from the cold mantel.

The connotations of these objects—from the emptiness of the dusted cigar box and the heaviness of bed and table lighter to the "framed" young woman in the white dress—illustrate, in the words of Clair Wills (1987), a "male need to fix, measure and control objects" that is "represented as a fear of flux."[7] The desk calendar, a way in which he marks time, suggests that the future, like the woman, is under the gentleman's control.

In contrast to the woman in "The Lady's Tower," who sees the natural world flowing toward her, the gentleman, looking out from his high window, sees a dead landscape moving away from him:

> Those long retreating shades,
> A river of roofs inclining
> In the valley side. Gables and stacks
> And spires, with trees tucked between them:
> All graveyard shapes
> Viewed from his high windowpane.

7. Wills notes Ní Chuilleanáin's contrast between fluidity and rigidity.

The image in the opening poem, the receptive tower leaning back to converse with the sky, is reversed here: the gentleman, above the landscape and peering down, cuts himself off from the outside world and sees only dead shapes below him. His perspective in the bedroom indicates not only his failure to interact with the natural world but also his need to dominate (an intepretation that the image of the framed woman on his mantle reinforces).

One step takes us back to Yeats, his tower, and his image of Leda (or of Maud Gonne), and we begin to understand what Ní Chuilleanáin means when she says that women writers and artists often express images different from the "social and historical" image of Irish womanhood created by men. The static, geometric precision of the gentleman's room leads us to contrast it with the lady's bedroom, where the "square window" is "made even," counterbalanced perhaps, by the random sycamore root growing in from the outside world. In the gentleman's bedroom everything remains squared, angled, and dead.

How far we can generalize about these two poems as representative of a distinction Ní Chuilleanáin makes between men and women is debatable. We might, for example, see them as less concerned with gender and more with different types of people and life-styles, or with class. The plush furnishings of the male bedroom certainly demand that we consider the implications of the term *gentleman,* especially in light of the less luxurious surroundings the lady enjoys. But we must also see Ní Chuilleanáin's ironic use of the word *lady,* because the image she creates challenges the conventional vision of what a lady is, especially as a poet like Yeats presents it. In examining the ladies and gentlemen here, we must take into account both gender and class, as well as the images and connotations suggested by the terms *lady* and *gentleman.*

Ní Chuilleanáin herself has said that the poem grew from a "fantasy" of what her father's bedroom might have looked like before he married. Cormac Ó'Chuilleanáin, the only son in a family of seven, did not marry until he was thirty-eight. Before this, Ní Chuilleanáin says, he was "minded by women" who had their own ideas of what a gentleman likes, arranging and caring for his room as they thought he would like it to be. Because Ní Chuilleanáin has said that she had a happy childhood, we have no reason to believe that a difficult relationship with her father, or with her aunts, led the poet to imagine such a room. What then is Ní Chuilleanáin up to?

While we must be careful about reading a poem in the light of information we have about what inspired it, such material helps us to understand that underlying the contrast between the lady in the tower and the gentleman in the bedroom are issues of inherited roles that men and women often accept without question in Ireland. The male in the Irish household often assumes the dominant status, and the role of the Irish woman, as sister or wife, has frequently been to devote herself entirely to the happiness and care of men and children. Jenny Beale, in *Women in Ireland: Voices of Change,* describes the structure:

> The woman of the family was expected to be wife, mother and home-maker. In practice, of course, many women did not accept a secondary position in the family but were strong and assertive individuals who took pride in themselves and their achievements. But the role of women in the ideal family was defined by both Church and political leaders as a strictly home-based existence—so much so that it too was written into the Constitution. (1987, 7)[8]

Even unmarried people, as we see in "The Gentleman's Bedroom," accepted their predestined roles, sisters as caretakers for brothers. With this in mind, we might reconsider how revolutionary Ní Chuilleanáin's image of the "lady" in the tower is—dependent on and minding no one but herself, in control of her own life.

Reinforcing this reading of the poem is the contrast presented by the penultimate poem in the volume, "Wash" (1986, 67). Asked about this poem, Ní Chuilleanáin explained that she had once contemplated a series of poems about household tasks of which this would be a part. She also notes that she was thinking about a woman whose husband had committed suicide, thus the opening image:

> Wash man out of the earth; sheer off
> The human shell.
> Twenty feet down there's close cold earth
> So clean.

Left behind when her husband dies, the wife now must separate herself from him. Ní Chuilleanáin's images are specifically sexual, suggesting not only death, but the consequences of intercourse:

> Wash the man out of the woman:
> The strange sweat from her skin, the ashes from her hair.
> Stretch her to dry in the sun
> The blue marks on her breast will fade.

---

8. Beale's study charts the growth of the women's movement in recent years and covers topics including gender roles, marriage, sexuality, careers, education, and religion.

Standing in a squalid room, the woman in the poem washes water from a
fish, trying to make it clean, for she and the world are not yet "clean as
the cat." This woman's openness to the world, symbolized by sexual pen-
etration, leaves her vulnerable. A very unsentimental view of woman-
hood and, indeed, of sexuality, "Wash" emphasizes the effects of all kinds
of consummation, and the difficulty a woman may have "washing" a man
out of her body and her life.

With its emphasis on suffering, "Wash" recapitulates the theme and
voice of many of Ní Chuilleanáin's poems in *The Second Voyage*. The
complicated vision that emerges from this poem insists that marriage and
the relationships between men and women can be happy but are often
fraught with difficulties. Its tone differs greatly from that in "The Lady's
Tower," where a relationship with a man is not depicted, and where the
speaker is seen in a world of her own devising. But "Wash" should also
be read in the light of "A Gentleman's Bedroom," where the woman on
the mantel is about to begin a life ("the future") that the woman in
"Wash" has just ended. If we place these images beside Yeats's women,
whose relationship to men, including Yeats himself, is of prime impor-
tance, we realize how different a vision Ní Chuilleanáin gives us of
women's lives.

Other poems in *The Second Voyage* also lead us to probe cultural
images of men and women, especially as these apply to mythic and reli-
gious heroes. The titles of the volumes in which some of these poems
were originally published, *Acts and Monuments, Site of Ambush,* and *The
Second Voyage,* alert us to Ní Chulilleanáin's questioning of traditional
heroic action. *Acts and Monuments* ironically calls to mind John Foxe's
Acts and Monuments of these Latter and Perillous Days (1563), an English
clergyman's record of the Protestant martyrs of the Reformation who
were willing to die for a religious cause. The title poem in *Site of Ambush*
focuses on an incident in which overly confidant soldiers are ambushed.
In *The Second Voyage,* Odysseus, the Greek hero renowned for overcom-
ing overwhelming obstacles, appears as a confused man who questions
his own actions.

In the title poem of *The Second Voyage* (1986, 26–27), Ní Chuillea-
náin imagines a frustrated Odysseus railing against the uncontrollable
sea. The epic hero, looking down at the waves as "he rammed / The oar
between their jaws," wishes he could name each wave as "Adam named
the beasts." This quest to control nature through force of will underpins
Odysseus's attempt to tame the "Unfenced valleys of the ocean." Repeat-
ing the imagery of "A Gentleman's Bedroom," Ní Chuilleanáin presents
a male hero impelled by the desire to measure and control the uncontrol-

lable, to put boundaries around that which challenges him, even while he dreams of another kind of journey and memories of home. The phallic connotations of the oar that he "rams" between the jaws of each wave illustrate the underlying metaphors of sexual domination that run through some of these poems.

At the same time, Odysseus longs for the land, where water flows through the landscape:

> He considered the water-lilies, and thought about fountains
> Spraying as wide as willows in empty squares,
> The sugarstick of water clattering into the kettle,
> The flat lakes bisecting the rushes. He remembered spiders
>   and frogs
> Housekeeping at the roadside in brown trickles floored with mud
> Horsetroughs, the black canal, pale swans at dark:
> His face grew damp with tears that tasted
> Like his own sweat or the insults of the sea.

In these images water becomes not a force to conquer, but an element flowing through all things. The images of the land that cause Odysseus's tears recall the scene described in "The Lady's Tower" where we also see water penetrating the house: in the damp of the walls, in the kettle, and in the stream that meets the tower's gray wall. The lady's spiders appear likewise in Odysseus's memory; he has left them behind to travel on the sea. His moving boat creates an ironic contrast to the punt tied up outside the lady's tower.

Ní Chuilleanáin has said that when she wrote this poem, she imagined herself as Odysseus: "I read these things at such an early age, and identified with the moving figure who is Odysseus; everybody else is to some extent static."[9] Odysseus needed the strength of will to get home, she says, but he wanted to get home in order to change. In her poem, Ní Chuilleanáin explains, she was concerned with "scale": "the sea has got this large scale and you want something that has been humanized. I think that a lot of domestic actions are more humanized, what might appear to be very ordinary actions are important because they are on the right scale." In imagining a different Odysseus, Ní Chuilleanáin shifts the emphasis from conventional heroic action, and our final vision is of a man

---

9. In this conversation with me in 1990, Ní Chuilleanáin described characters working on what she called the "life plan" in the epic, distinguishing this from the "task" which I discuss later in this chapter.

caught in a trap: "His face grew damp with tears that tasted / Like his own sweat or the insults of the sea."[10]

Like Eavan Boland in *The War Horse*, Ní Chuilleanáin highlights the destructive underside of traditional heroic adventuring, focusing more on the divided mind of the hero than on his ultimate victory. Images of flowers, kettles, and spiders, as well as the "housekeeping" and "domestic actions" Ní Chuilleanáin sees as humanizing, are common not only to these two poets but also to many other women writing today. Some feminists, like the psychologist Carol Gilligan, explain these shared images by distinguishing typical female values, which have been subordinated to more dominant male values centered on the competitive adventurer winning against all odds.[11]

In another poem in *The Second Voyage*, "Odysseus Meets the Ghosts of the Women" (1986, 25), Ní Chuilleanáin again dramatizes the darker side of the epic adventure. Alluding to the underworld scene in the *Odyssey*, Ní Chuilleanáin pictures the hero as he meets a group of women:

> He saw the daughters, wives
> Mothers of heroes or upstanding kings
> The longhaired goldbound women who had died
> Of pestilence, famine, in slavery
> And still queens but they did not know
> His face, even Anticleia
> His own mother. He asked her how she died
> But she passed by his elbow, her eyes asleep.

Ní Chuilleanáin describes how the women reject Odysseus; she shifts the focus, as Eavan Boland does in "The Journey," to the suffering of the women associated with epic heroes. Even though they turn away, Odysseus tries to force his will upon these women, pursuing them as he does the waves:

> The hunter still followed
> Airy victims, and labour
> Afflicted even here the cramped shoulders—
> The habit of distress.

10. The warriors in another poem, "The Persians" (1986, 28–29), realize that men cannot "flog the sea," but "By now their lives were nothing / But flowing away from them, breath blood and sweat." In these poems Ní Chuilleanáin challenges the presumptions, and illustrates the limitations, of warriors who struggle against all odds to "win."

11. See Gilligan 1982. Her argument has been the subject of much debate.

Armed with sword, Odysseus tries to engage the women; their rebuff drives him to the safety of his ship with their voices, "A hiss like thunder," breaking on him. Seeming less heroic than confused, Odysseus loses this battle to the ghosts, those women who emerge from the shadows to assert their influence on him.

Like the scene in the *Odyssey* from which it is taken (Odysseus's "habit of distress" is a direct quotation from Pope's translation), this poem emphasizes the transitory nature of fame, the lesson learned in the underworld. But with its images of neglected women who died of pestilence and famine, whose lives had been subordinated to men's ("goldbound women" echoing the image of the framed woman on the cold mantel in "A Gentleman's Bedroom"), and its final allusion to the kidnapped Persephone, "Odysseus Meets the Ghosts of the Women" insists on making the female "victims" as significant as the embattled male hero. As Alicia Ostriker maintains, this change is typical of women's poetry where "the core of revisionist mythmaking . . . lies in the challenge to and correction of gender stereotypes embodied in myth" (1985, 318).[12]

It is useful to keep Ostriker's point in mind when we read *The Second Voyage,* especially with poems like "The Absent Girl," whose relationship to the ghostly women in Odysseus' underworld may not be obvious. The young girl's vacant face and conspicuous silence illustrate a problem women face, what Ní Chuilleanáin has described as "the experience of being invisible." The girl, sitting at a courtroom window, face against the glass while "night presses on the window-panes," lives in a world of shadows, an emblem of her powerlessness. The opposite of the lady in the tower, she withdraws from the life around her:

> She can feel the glass cold
> But with no time for pain
> Searches for a memory lost with muscle and blood—
> She misses her ligaments and the marrow of her bones.

As ghostly as the women Odysseus meets, the absent girl wraps herself in silence, retreating into the grayness of her underworld: "Her skin is shadowed / Where once the early sunlight blazed." In talking about this poem, Ní Chuilleanáin comments on the problem of the female "inclined to be absent," suggesting that the poem should be read as more than just an image of one young girl. Like "Odysseus Meets the Ghosts of the Women," it focuses on the invisibility of women.

In the world of folklore, where nature's force often humbles even the

12. Ostriker also develops this point in her book, *Stealing the Language* (1986).

most courageous, Ní Chuilleanáin finds an alternative to the classical hero. The world of folklore gives similar status to male and female, she feels, but ultimately grants less power and value to the human will. Ní Chuilleanáin describes folk tales as "fatalistic in an optimistic way." Success in folklore often depends on luck, and "tasks" are allotted to both men and women. Seeking to direct attention away from the person and toward an action, Ní Chuilleanáin often alludes to legends in which the performance of a task provides a way to deal with forces beyond an individual's control.

We can see this in the poem "Ransom" (1986, 44), where the speaker, like Odysseus, sets out on a journey to appease an anonymous power, one we might equate with the mythic gods, or more generally with the destructive side of nature. However, this journey differs from the classical hero's quest. The poem begins:

> The payment always has to be in kind;
> Easy to forget, travelling in safety,
> Until the demand comes in.
>
> Do not think him unkind, but begin
> To search for the stuff he will accept

As the speaker (identified neither as male nor as female) describes a journey to find the proper sacrifice, we see a contrast to Odysseus's battle with the sea:

> I left home early
> Walking up the stony bed
> Of a shallow river, meaning to collect
> The breast-feathers of thousands of little birds
> To thatch a house and barn.
> It was a fine morning, the fields
> Spreading out on each side
> At the beginning of a story,
> Steam rising off the river,
> I was unarmed, the only bird
> A lark singing out of reach:
> I looked forward to the journey.

This is the type of journey Odysseus would like to take; he says in "The Second Voyage": "I'll face the rising ground and walk away / From tidal waters, up riverbeds / Where herons parcel out the miles of stream." Neither angry, frustrated, nor sad, as Odysseus is, the speaker in "Ransom" goes unarmed (there will be no battle), up the riverbed. The gifts of nature bring peace ("It was a fine morning"), in contrast to Odysseus's "habit of distress." This journey, the poem tells us, is the "beginning of a story," a tale which, in the context of *The Second Voyage,* illustrates another way to deal with the mysteries and challenges of human experience.

Several other poems in *The Second Voyage* reinforce this contrast, many of them developing the water imagery so prevalent in Ní Chuilleanáin's work. In the poem "Site of Ambush" (1986, 14–21) she turns to a modern scene but a new version of the old battles, and water imagery is again significant. Set in the Irish civil wars of the 1920s, "Site of Ambush" describes a scenario in which soldiers in an overturned lorry die upside down in a stream. Their deaths inspire a meditation on the endless flow of the water in which they lie. Against this force, whose "currents yield return to none," Ní Chuilleanáin pictures the soldiers before they die, planning and confident of their success. Her description of their strategy reminds us of Odysseus's futile attempts at control and of the mathematical precision of "A Gentleman's Bedroom":

> The enemy commanders synchronised their heartbeats:
> Seven forty-five by the sun.
> At ten the soldiers were climbing into lorries,
> Asthmatic engines drawing breaths in even shifts.
> The others were fretting over guns
> Counting up ammunition and money.
> At eleven they lay in wait at the cross
> With over an hour to go.

The landscape recoils from the death of the soldiers and an innocent child killed with them: the path twists away, grass grips the wall under gray clouds, and frightened birds fly off as the moment of death approaches. Again, Ní Chuilleanáin highlights the separation of these men from the natural world around them—their guns, lorries, and watches giving them a false sense of power. Their military calculations and the attempts to control life and death are contrasted to the timeless flow of the stream, which eventually passes indifferently over their dead bodies.

Tracing this water back to glacial origins, Ní Chuilleanáin sees a prophetic warning of human limitations, which the soldiers fail to heed, and she ironically presents it in the mythic image of the whirlpool the fictive Odysseus was able to escape: "You are the twining gulf Charybdis / Whose currents yield return to none." Ní Chuilleanáin's insistence that the challenger often loses questions the conventional happy ending and the epic hero's success.

Continually linking water with the fate of what one section calls "Voyagers" (including heroes like Maelduin and Odysseus), "Site of Ambush" emphasizes the limitations of human skill by describing how the natural world so quickly absorbs the wreckage of human life:

> They all looked the same face down there:
> Water too thick and deep to see.
> They were separated for good.
> It was cold, their teeth shrilling.
> They slept like falling hay in waves.
> Shells candied their skin; the water
> Lay heavy and they could not rise but coiled
> By scythefuls limply in ranks.
> A long winter stacks their bodies
> And words above their stillness hang from hooks
> In skeins, like dark nets drying,
> Flapping against the stream.
> A watch vibrates alone in the filtering light;
> Flitters of hair wave at the sun.

The watch, ticking off human minutes, symbolizes vain attempts at mastery, and this site of a military disaster yields an emblem for nature's ultimately greater ambush: that harsh force which the speaker in "Ransom" respects and tries to appease. Believing themselves in control of their fate and their future, these soldiers die at the mercy of the folkloric "wolf that will swallow down both sun and moon." The poem warns against the celebration of traditional heroism; the best-laid plans guarantee little against fate's overwhelming blind ambushes.

"Site of Ambush" ends with an ironic phoenix-like vision of resurrection as the innocent child killed in the ambush comes back from a "sleep":

> —troubling for a minute the patient republic
> Of the spider and the fly
> On the edge of the aspic stream
> Above the frail shadows of wreckage

Significantly, the young boy killed returns as a girl; she enters a world where a saint's hand spreads under the nesting wren, a symbol of the peacemaking man who respects the "patient republic" of spider and fly.[13] In the context of the Irish civil wars, which were fought over the estab-

13. The Irish saint who fits this image is Brendan.

lishment of an Irish "Republic," Ní Chuilleanáin brings into focus the continuing problem of the Troubles in Ireland, questioning the value of military strategy and the confidence of the male soldiers. We might look at this poem as another response to Yeats and to poems like his "Meditations in Time of Civil War."

The earth is female here: "Symmetrical breasts of hills criss-crossed." Ní Chuilleanáin has said that the returning girl represents the idea that you do not get back what you lost: the boy is not recovered; he is replaced in the natural cycle of death and rebirth. In Ní Chuilleanáin's scenario, the saint's "arms began to sag," we are told, "But did not give way." In the restored landscape, the peacemaking male saint, the earth goddess, and the young girl displace the soldiers to symbolize another set of values.[14]

The final images in "Site of Ambush" stress the timeless world of the spider and the "patient republic" of the stream, evoking again the setting of "The Lady's Tower." Recurring images in Ní Chuilleanáin's poetry, they represent one face of a natural cycle whose other face reduces human life to "a clean sweep of clay." Against this force the military ambush, timed down to the minute, appears as futile as Odysseus's attempt to name the waves as he beats them down one by one.

Ní Chuilleanáin says that she does not always see her figures as male or female and that they may be different aspects of herself. On one level, then, we can look at some of her poems as gender neutral, exploring attitudes and behaviors traditionally defined as masculine or feminine and blurring conventionally accepted distinctions between the sexes, much as Medbh McGuckian does. On the other hand, she has, as a poet, given women a status they have rarely received in modern Irish literature. Her female characters, Ní Chuilleanáin notes, are often isolated and in motion, doing something that theoretically might be considered dangerous. Not passive, they often act on their own, moving beyond stereotypes.

The speaker in "Lucina Schynning in Silence of the Nicht" (1986, 12), for example, comes out of her house, after three days of rain, to immerse herself in cold water. Alluding to the opening line in William Dunbar's poem, "The Birth of Antichrist" (1932, 70–71), where the speaker dreams of a horrible battle between the forces of good and evil,[15]

14. Parallels can be drawn between this poem and those of Eavan Boland (for example, *The War Horse*).

15. In Dunbar's poem, Fortune appears to the persona in a dream and offers a vision of the struggle between the forces of God and the devil.

Ní Chuilleanáin's poem presents a different response to the vicissitudes of fortune. Rejecting the temptation to challenge the darker implications that water suggests (the three days of rain a symbolic deluge), she turns away: "Behind me the waves of darkness lay." Keeping still, rather than journeying, this heroine finds not only the water in which she can bathe but also a world she might otherwise have missed:

> Sheepdogs embraced me; the grasshopper
> Returned with lark and bee.
> I looked down between hedges of high thorn and saw
> The hare, absorbed, sitting still
> In the middle of the track: I heard
> Again the chirp of the stream running.

The speaker bathes in moonlit channels created in the landscape, attuned, like her counterpart in "The Lady's Tower," to the movement and the sound of the running stream. She compares her "relaxed" self to the mosaic beasts on the floors of the chapels Oliver Cromwell destroyed; the moonlight shines down on her as it had on them when the chapel roofs collapsed. The warrior Cromwell, a type of Antichrist, also represents a deluge, waves of darkness spreading as he battled across the countryside, imposing his will on both people and landscape. The persona here identifies with the mosaic beasts who outlast the warrior, just as she enjoys her kinship with the grasshopper, the hare (like herself "sitting still"), the lark, and the bee. We should note here that she has achieved the peace Odysseus longs for in "The Second Voyage."

In many of the poems in *The Second Voyage,* especially those first published in *Acts and Monuments,* water symbolizes the vastness and destructiveness of nature, and the images describe the foolhardiness of failing to comprehend the limitations of human action. The speaker in "Ferryboat" (1986, 34), for example, remarks that "Once at sea, everything is changed" and notes how the chained tables and chairs acknowledge the possibility of drowning. A "death's-head in a lifejacket grins" as it carries its warning: "In case you should find yourself gasping / In a flooded corridor or lost between cold waves." Even the great burial monuments will disappear, Ní Chuilleanáin says, as she imagines the destruction of the Etruscan tombs in "House of the Dead" (1986, 43).

Ní Chuilleanáin reiterates this message in the female voice of "Ardnaturais" (1986, 31),[16] where a woman realizes how quietly water reveals its destructive force:

16. *Ardnaturais,* Irish for "place of pilgrimage," is also the site of a ship explosion.

Warm death for a jellyfish, lost
Ten legs in a crinoline; the furred bee
Slants down from the cliff field, straying
Over salted rocks. The water
Searches the branching algae and my hair
Spreads out like John the Baptist's in a dish.
Shouldering under, I feel fear
As I see them plain: the soft anemone,
Bladdered weed, the crouching spiked urchin, rooted
In one clutch of pebbles, their long strands
Shivering under the light.

Alone in the sea: a shallow breath held stiffly:
My shadow lies
Dark and hard like time
Across the rolling shining stones.

Substituting her hair for John the Baptist's sacrificed head, this speaker sees her shadow across the stones, the water a reminder of her impotence in the face of death. Like a delicate sea flower, "rooted in one clutch of pebbles," she symbolizes the frailty of human life, anchored tenuously against nature's overwhelming power, symbolized by the water. Unlike Odysseus, this woman sees "No pounding historical waves, / No sandribbed invasions" or "violent ebb," just the sea's quiet reminder of its power. Like the speaker in "Lucina," she immerses herself in the water, though here her insight forces her to hold her breath "stiffly" as she floats alone in the sea.

If we recall the imagery of the dead soldiers in "Site of Ambush," we notice the ironic contrast Ní Chuilleanáin sets up. Had the soldiers understood, as this speaker does, the message of the stream, they might have had less faith in their own power and future. The image of their bodies floating dead in the stream is recalled here, where the bather's shadow falls "Dark and hard like time / Across the rolling shining stones." A metaphor for death, the shadow is a warning. The minutes that the soldiers in "Site of Ambush" ticked off, believing they controlled both fate and time, are meaningless as the shadows of their dead bodies fall across the stream. Reinforcing this contrast is the image of John the Baptist. Comparing herself to him, the female speaker assumes the right to voice her "revelation," one we might see as different from the road to salvation, that second voyage, which St. John foretold.

Because Ní Chuilleanáin allows her image to carry her message, it is sometimes difficult to see how she challenges stereotypes and traditional myths. Nonetheless, the poems in *The Second Voyage* question the value of celebrated concepts of hero and heroism, introduce images of courageous and independent women or confused and frightened men, and create figures who subvert conventional presumptions about gender. In the poem, "Swineherd" (1986, 22), for example, a man dreams of what he will do when he retires: "I intend to learn how to make coffee, at least as well / As the Portuguese lay-sister in the kitchen / And polish the brass fenders every day." As this man, like Odysseus in "The Second Voyage," reduces things to what Ní Chuilleanáin calls the "human scale," he envies the work and life more often associated with a woman's world.

By ignoring assumptions associated with gender, Ní Chuilleanáin suggests that we might conceive androgynous heroes like the ship's pilot she imagines in "Lost Star" (1986, 42):

> The lonely pilot guides
> The lost star, its passengers the crowd
> Of innocents exiled in winter.
> Sometimes, letting the vessel drift
> Into danger, he pauses
> To feed them at his miraculous breast.

The pilot of the lost star-vessel here is neither the epic Odysseus, nor the "crouching" Noah depicted in the poem "Survivors," but an imagined androgynous figure whose maternal breasts provide the nourishment to keep the passengers going, especially when they must inevitably confront danger. Explaining the androgynous figure in twentieth-century women's writing, Judith Kegan Gardiner maintains that such images do not "reflect authorial confusion about gender identity." As she explains, "the problems of female identity presented in women's poetry and prose are rarely difficulties in knowing one's gender; more frequently, they are difficulties in learning how to respond to social roles for what being female means in our culture" (1982, 189).[17]

On the other hand, the woman speaker in "Ardnaturais," as well as those in "The Lady's Tower," "Lucina Schynning in Silence of the Nicht," and "Cypher," marks the emergence in Ní Chuilleanáin's poetry of a clearly identifiable female "I." Though there are poems in which the

17. Another critic, Mary Jacobus, sees androgyny as an "essentially Utopian vision of undivided consciousness" and writes that the "gesture towards androgyny is millennial, like all dreams of another language or mode of being; but its effect is to remove the area of debate . . . from biological determination to the field of signs; from gender to representation ('words' not 'things')" (1989, 61). Ní Chuilleanáin's creation of the androgynous figure may arise from such a motivation.

"I" recounts experiences from Ní Chuilleanáin's own life ("Night Jour-
neys," "Early Recollections," "Going Back to Oxford"), she avoids what
she calls the "intrusive I," in which the poet and the voice are closely
linked. Her statement in the introduction to *Irish Women: Image and
Achievement* explains the value of these female speakers: "if the history of
women's fate and women's actions cannot create new people it can make
available a wider variety of exemplars, able to instruct or to inspire as
well as to equip with information" (1985, 3).

We can see one of those exemplars at the beginning of the eighteen-
poem sequence *The Rose-Geranium*.[18] The opening poem, "Like One
Borne Away in a Dance and Veiled" (1991, 48) alludes to Spenser's
Amoretti, in which a woman is carried off on her wedding night to a
world of frightening eroticism, from which her true love cannot rescue
her. Ní Chuilleanáin adapts this image to another purpose to suggest
how captive a woman feels when she learns that the body is affected by
"the laws that rule / The acorn's fall and the erosion of tall cliffs."

In this poem Ní Chuilleanáin again uses the image of the tower, but
the setting differs greatly from that in "The Lady's Tower." While the
speaker dreams of a high house and shining floors, she sees before her a
tower on which a fungus feeds, a building being torn down. A metaphor
for the human body, the tower ultimately collapses:

> And the day the building fell into the street
> And blood fell and bodies folded and spun
> The prisoner had company:
>
> X-ray bones of snow.
> Rivers grinding south,
> Planes of ice bleeding at the edges downstream.

One has only to recall the contrasting scenery and tone in "The Lady's
Tower" to see how much a sense of disaster colors both this opening
poem and the others in the sequence. With its allusion to Spenser's
poem, where the woman is borne away against her will, this poem
stresses not only the power of fate but also the loneliness of the woman
who must confront it. Many of the poems in this sequence have either a
female speaker or subject, illustrating Ní Chuilleanáin's more frequent

18. This sequence was published with six other poems (including the thirteen-poem
sequence *Cork*) by Gallery Press in 1981. Revised, *The Rose-Geranium* is part 2 of *The
Magdalene Sermon and Earlier Poems* (1991).

use of the female "I" and "she," but this voice is of a woman cut off from the world that surrounds her.

Images of light and darkness recur in these poems. Describing herself and a lover in bed at night, a woman in the poem "Overmantel" (1991, 56) sees them below the light:

> (Breast high, if one stood,
> Night napped the bookshelves
> And a dying light floated
> Above us, never reaching
> Us, our arrested embrace)

A shaft of light touches the glass over the hearth in this room but does not reach the couple. For the female speaker the room remains shadowy and cold until morning.

Ní Chuilleanáin has said that these poems deal with the failure of communication between men and women, a statement the above poem makes clear. Even when we see them together in the sequence, couples waste time in such rituals as a shared examination of conscience before confession. The imagined "M. et Mme van Gramberen" in the poem "Willaupuis" (1991, 50) sit one afternoon in a small enclosure, in "the windmill's afternoon shadow," quarreling over their sins for confession, "Prepared and calm in case one thought / Struck them both." In the context of the rest of the volume, this couple symbolizes the failure of such activities to offer any help for the problems Ní Chuilleanáin's characters face.

In the volume of poems *The Magdalene Sermon*,[19] female speakers and women are the focus of most of the poems. From a hill-town mother to the "Permafrost Woman," Ní Chuilleanáin populates this landscape with her variations of the female: mythic earth goddesses, the butcher's daughter, sisters who preserve their brother's room exactly as it was the day he died, a mother who watches her child sleep. The title alludes to Mary Magdalene, who, according to legend, became a preacher in Marseilles after the death of Christ.

Deliberately subordinating the better-known sinner to Magdalene the patron saint of preachers, Ní Chuilleanáin turns her into a symbol for the female voice. Alluding to paintings that depict the saint with long red

---

19. Published as *The Magdalene Sermon* by Gallery Press in 1989 and, with *The Rose Geranium*, as *The Magdalene Sermon and Earlier Poems* by Wake Forest University Press in 1991. *The Magdalene Sermon* was shortlisted for the *Irish Times*/Aer Lingus Poetry Prize.

hair draped to cover her body,[20] Ní Chuilleanáin imagines her in "St. Mary Magdalene Preaching at Marseilles" (1991, 33):

> Now at the end of her life she is all hair—
> A cataract flowing and freezing—and a voice
> Breaking loose from the red hair,
> The secret shroud of her skin:
> A voice glittering in the wilderness.
> She preaches in the city, she wanders
> Late in the evening through shaded squares.

Imagining Magdalene alone, out of the shadow of Christ, Ní Chuilleanáin paints her as an ordinary woman:

> The hairs on the back of her wrists begin to lie down
> And she breathes evenly, her elbows leaning
> On a smooth wall. Down there in the piazza,
> The boys are skimming on toy carts, warped
> On their stomachs, like breathless fish.

Looking beyond the city to the outlying marshes, Magdalene sees the waterweeds, "collapsed like hair / At the turn of the tide," which become a metaphor for the "turn" in her life: "They wait for the right time, then / Flip all together their thousands of sepia feet." Grounding Magdalene in the natural world, as she does so many of her female figures, Ní Chuilleanáin pictures her as an awakening voice, a new life emerging from the "secret shroud of her skin." As such, she is the prototype for the voices of other women we hear throughout *The Magdalene Sermon*.

In "The Informant" (1991, 36), for example, an old widow tells folk tales to a young man who later listens to her voice on tape. Like an Irish sybil, she describes a death she has seen:

> "The locks
> Forced upward, a shift of air
> Pulled over the head. The face bent
> And the eyes winced, like craning
> To look in the core of a furnace.

20. Ní Chuilleanáin told me that she had seen a St. Mary Magdalene attributed to Botticelli at the Philadelphia Museum of Art. In a review of *The Magdalene Sermon* in the *Irish Literary Supplement,* Jonathan Allison notes: "Usually her poems encapsulate a telling scene from a larger untold narrative, and aptly many of the poems have titles like those of paintings: 'River, with Boats,' 'St. Mary Magdalene Preaching in Marseilles,' 'Fallen Tree in a Churchyard'" (1991, 14).

> The man unravelled
> Back to a snag, a dark thread."

The contrast between this woman's surroundings ("fuchsias, a henhouse, the sea") and the fantastic stories that she tells reinforces the contrast between the young man's questions and the informant's answers. Her "own fairy-cakes, baked that morning" counterpoint his tape recorder. In a poem like this, Ní Chuilleanáin implies that such a woman, the Irish equivalent of Mary Magdalene preaching, has much to teach us. With her lore of folk and fairies, the informant has her own way of confronting and explaining the mysteries of birth and death.

Other poems in *The Magdalene Sermon* feature female speakers: in "Recovery" (1991, 25), coming to life again after an illness; in "London" (22), trying to console a friend who feels that her life is over:

> At fifty, she misses the breast
> That grew in her thirteenth year
> And was removed last month. She misses
> The small car she drove through the seaside town
> And along cliffs for miles. In London
> She will not take the tube, is afraid of taxis.

We hear many versions of the female voice: in "The Italian Kitchen" (24), the woman who settles comfortably into her home in Italy: "I've brought blankets and firewood; we live here now"; in "Looking at the Fall" (20), the mother who warns her child about the danger of waterfalls:

> Look, don't touch, she said to the reaching child.
> Across her eye a shadow fell like a door closing upstream,
> A lock slipping, a high stack of water
> Loosed, spinning down, to slam them out of breath.

As is typical of Ní Chuilleanáin's poetry, water often suggests danger, and mariners and fish show up in some of the poems. In "Balloon" (1991, 21), a young boy leaves a courtroom with a balloon, which floats around him later as he sleeps. As the air currents sweep the balloon through the room, Ní Chuilleanáin imagines the scene where "A big strange fish gleams, filling the child's bed."[21] In "River, with Boats" (23), we see a woman in bed, beside a window. At high tide:

21. Ní Chuilleanáin and her husband, the poet Macdara Woods, adopted a son, and the legal proceedings provide the background for this poem. The fish image also appears in

The window is blocked
By the one framed eye
Of a tethered coaster
Swaying and tugging and flapping with the wind,
And the faces of the mariners
Crowd at the glass like fishes.

In addition to its female speakers, *The Magdalene Sermon* also recognizes the silent women who have lived in the shadow of better-known men, the "invisible" women Ní Chuilleanáin has written about before. The volume is dedicated to Patrick Kavanagh's wife, Katherine, who died in 1989, and pays tribute, in "So She Looked, in that Company," to writer John Jordan's mother,[22] who sits in quiet dignity until his wake is over:

Seeing her there
I know at once who she must be.
She does not move while
The pale figures out of the anthologies
In their coarse shirts are paraded
To tell their hesitant stories
Twisting the grammar of their exotic speech.

Many of these poems highlight a woman's loss. "J'ai Mal à nos Dents" (1991, 29) depicts the life of a nun who has surrendered herself to her community; Sister Mary Anthony so buried her own self that to the dentist she complained, "I have a pain in our teeth." But in old age, when she left the convent to care for her sister Nora: "They handed her back her body, / Its voices and its death." In another poem, "Consolation" (30–31), a wife tries to uncover the cause of her husband's death, questioning a blow he told her he received when he was robbed. She is ignored, not only by the police but also at the hospital, as she stands silent and helpless. The understated lines and incisive imagery describe her tragedy:

The hospital basement is vaulted and pillared:
A wide crypt, old and clean. The nun sits down
To rifle a desk for the right form of receipt.

"St. Mary Magdalene Preaching at Marseilles" (1991, 33), where Magdalene sees young boys playing below her "on their stomachs, like breathless fish." The traditional identification of the fish with Christ adds irony to the image.

22. John Jordan was also the editor of *Poetry Ireland Review*.

"It was just as if he waited for the priest to come."
"He was quite collected, he spoke sensibly."
She hears the words, the repeated story:
There was no assassination, the fire in his brain
Came only from the red of the dyed cloth.
There was a pillared space when he was dying,
A voice and a response. It was not a hunt and a blow.

Bones moving, landscapes coming alive, voices speaking all appear in the poem, "Pygmalion's Image" (1991, 9), where the statue created by Pygmalion is linked with Medusa and both are associated with an awakening female landscape:

Not only her stone face, laid back staring in the ferns,
But everything the scoop of the valley contains begins to move
(And beyond the horizon the trucks beat the highway.)

A tree inflates gently on the curve of the hill;
An insect crashes on the carved eyelid;
Grass blows westward from the roots,
As the wind knifes under her skin and ruffles it like a book.

The crisp hair is real, wriggling like snakes;
A rustle of veins, tick of blood in the throat;
The lines of the face tangle and catch, and
A green leaf of language comes twisting out of her mouth.

As in her other poems, Ní Chuilleanáin draws on the myths from which these images derive, exploring the frightening responses the images suggest. The head of Medusa, cut off by Perseus, "begins to move," like the statue of Galatea, which in Ovid's story undermined Pygmalion's efforts to avoid women and never marry. In alluding to such stories, Ní Chuilleanáin, as she does with the image of Mary Magdalene, attempts to take these women beyond the status of emblems and symbols created by men, to give them a "life" and a voice of their own.

She also connects them with the female figures in "A Voice" and "Permafrost Woman." In the first poem (1991, 27) a man follows the sound of a voice who invites him: "You may come in- / You are already in." The poem draws on conventional images of earth mothers, female scapegoats, wailing women, and siren voices as a frightened voyager searches for the "humming" voice, the "muscle that called up the sound." Moving beyond the surface, the traveler follows the voice:

> In the bed of the stream
> She lies in her bones—
> Wide bearing hips and square
> Elbows. Around them lodged,
> Gravegoods of horsehair and an ebony peg.
>
> "What sort of ornament is this?
> What sort of mutilation? Where's
> The muscle that called up the sound,
> The tug of hair and the turned cheek?"
> The sign persists, in the ridged fingerbone.
>
> And he hears her voice, a wail of strings.

The "bearing hips," the peg, and "the ridged fingerbone" suggest the details of a domestic life as the earth goddess metamorphoses into a housewife and mother. While the invitation "You may come in" conveys a sexual meaning, it also suggests an entrance into a world where the female voice has been muted—what the poem calls a "sort of mutilation." The exposure of the male voyager to this voice, and ultimately to more complex and multidimensional images of women, ties this poem to many others in the volume.

In "Permafrost Woman" (1991, 15), Ní Chuilleanáin creates another female figure and female voice, this one more threatening and dangerous to a male traveler who confronts a landscape energized by female sexuality:

> Now, that face he coursed
> Beyond all the lapping
> Voices, through linear deserts
>
> Unfolds among peaks
> Of frozen sea, the wave
> Coiling upward its wrinkled grace.
>
> Dumb cliffs tell their story, split and reveal
> Fathomed straits. The body opens its locks.

As he discovers the effect of this unlocking body:

> The traveller feels
> His hair bend at the fresh weight
> Of snow, the wind is an intimate fist

> Brushing back strands: he stares at the wide mouth, packed
> With grinding ash: the landslide of his first dream.

These prototypic females evoke some traditional images in Irish culture, from the ancient female earth deities to the *sheela-na-gig,* a figure found in ancient stone carvings who prominently displays her sexual organs. Imagining these women as more natural and ultimately less threatening than they have often been pictured to be, Ní Chuilleanáin concentrates on conventional social and artistic images, challenging the ways in which women have been imagined and perceived.

Many of the poems in *The Magdalene Sermon* center on language and women moving out of silence, the emergence of what, in "St. Mary Magdalene Preaching at Marseilles" (1991, 33), Ní Chuilleanáin calls a voice "glittering in the wilderness." This new voice appropriates the Baptist's role as preacher of the word of God (John the Baptist was identified as a "voice crying in the wilderness") and thus gives to women a role traditionally restricted to males. All of the women and women speakers are ultimately connected by the poet, another carrier of the word, whom we might also see as a new version of Pygmalion's image: "the wind knifes under her skin and ruffles it like a book," and a "green leaf of language comes twisting out of her mouth."

In *The Magdalene Sermon,* Ní Chuilleanáin creates a complex female "I." Her reservations about this pronoun in her earlier poems have been replaced by a confident voice exploring and revising images of women from the past and creating voices of women in the present who reveal their deepest feelings and fears. She combines lyric and dramatic voices with experiments in dialogue, sometimes dramatizing contrasting voices and attitudes through italics and quotation marks. Her subjects range from mythic to contemporary women, and from mothers and grandmothers to the young girl, "Chrissie," whom Ní Chuilleanáin has described as a female version of the young men in *Lord of the Flies.*

In *The Magdalene Sermon,* Ní Chuilleanáin continues to illustrate her unique talent for rendering tenuous relationships among people in the most evocative images. In "The Hill-Town" (1991, 17), for example, she pictures a husband and wife who live apart but near to each other and dramatizes their lives in their daughter's view of her mother coming up the hill:

> She turns to salt the boiling water
> As her mother begins to climb, dark blue in the blue shade,

Past the shut doors and the open windows,
Their sounds of knife and glass.
She crosses into the sun before passing
The blank shutters of the glazier's house.

He is in there, has heard her step and
Paused, with the sharp tool in his hand.
He stands, his fingers pressed against the looking-glass
Like a man trying to hold up a falling building
That is not even a reflection now.

The images of houses, (the "steep rift," "blank shutters," "a falling building") carry the weight of feeling here, suggesting the sadness of a family split and a relationship gone bad.[23] As is typical of this volume, the spotlight falls on the wife and mother, seen at the beginning of the poem coming from the bus at night, and at the end in her daughter's memories of past mornings:

She remembers lying in the wide bed, three years old,
The sound of water and the gas going silent,
And the morning was in the white sieve of the curtain
Where a shadow moved, her mother's body, wet patches
Blotting the stretched cloth, shining like dawn.

As in so many of her poems, from the earliest in *The Second Voyage,* Ní Chuilleanáin pictures the woman here coming out of darkness ("dark blue in the blue shade") and into light ("crosses into the sun"). This is one of her most consistent images, distilled in the final lines above, where the shadow of the mother's body appears to the young child, "shining like dawn." Behind this image lies a clear message about the need to bring women and the lives of women into the light.

In her introduction to *Irish Women: Image and Achievement,* Ní Chuilleanáin discusses the importance of images:

Human beings make use of images as exemplars to learn about life, to achieve maturity and to launch themselves towards the objects of their life's struggle. They identify and they are intimidated or they are inspired. Sexual identity in particular and the outlook on life, life considered as a series of possibilities, that accompanies sexual identification seem to be sharply conditioned by the available patterns of behaviour seen as inextricably connected with one or other sex. (1985, 3)

23. Ní Chuilleanáin says she had in mind the divorce referendum when she wrote this poem.

If we apply this thinking to her poems, we can see that Ní Chuilleanáin wants to supplement "available patterns" with alternative images. Degendering the hero, she challenges traditional concepts of heroism and demonstrates the value of simple actions and the human scale. While her numerous images of water, travelers, and pilgrims remind us of the deepest human fears and needs, her images also catalogue the importance of the ordinary and the domestic, what she calls the humanizing: kitchens, bacon slicers, housekeeping, and balloons provide new metaphors for human experiences and emotions.

Increasingly in her poetry, woman speaking has become a central theme. Women have moved out of silence and shadow, out of a subordinate role to men, to speak about the human condition. In the first poem in *The Second Voyage,* Ní Chuilleanáin imagined an image of a lady's tower to complement Yeats's tower. Since that time she has created many other female figures and speakers, using her voice to broaden the horizons of Irish poetry and bridge what she has identified in her book of essays as the gap between the Irish woman's image through history and "what many Irish women have actually experienced." Like Eavan Boland, who speaks of the same gap, Ní Chuilleanáin sees poetry as one way to reflect the "authentic expression of what women have felt and thought."

Medbh McGuckian.
Courtesy of The Gallery Press.

5

Medbh McGuckian

Medbh McGuckian's poetry has elicited a great deal of interest since the publication of her first major volume, *The Flower Master,* in 1982.[1] Born in Northern Ireland, she was the first woman to be recognized among the "Northern Voices," the Ulster poets who came to prominence in the 1970s. Chosen as first woman poet-in-residence at Queens University in Belfast, McGuckian has been described both as "the most *white-hot* Irish poet since Yeats" (1990, 210) and as a writer whose work "cheerfully and explicitly ignores the risk of choking on its own exclusivity" (1992, 20). By 1991, McGuckian had published three other volumes: *Venus and the Rain* (1984), *On Ballycastle Beach* (1988), and *Marconi's Cottage* (1991). In another volume, *Two Women, Two Shores* (1989), McGuckian's poems are collected with those of the Irish-American poet Nuala Archer.[2]

From the beginning McGuckian's work sparked a variety of critical responses.[3] Reviewers praised the striking quality of her imagery, generally agreeing that her poems had something to do with "womanliness." Struck by the associative nature of her images, readers also found her poetry discursive, oblique, and, in some cases, incomprehensible. McGuckian had given them ample fuel for this fire with her very dense and complicated style.

In a 1982 review in *Encounter,* Alan Jenkins summed up some of the problems he saw in *The Flower Master:* "discontinuities of sense; sudden changes of grammatical subject and tense, shifts in personal pronoun and

1. Two earlier publications, *Single Ladies* and *Portrait of Joanna,* were issued in 1980.

2. Nuala Archer's other works, both published in Ireland, include *Whale on the Line* (1981) and *The Hour of Pan/Amá* (1992). Born in the United States of Irish parents, Archer has also lived in Ireland and Latin and Central America. Her extensive travels are reflected in the varied settings and experimental techniques of her latest poems.

3. *The Flower Master* won both the Rooney Prize and the Alice Hunt Bartlett Award.

the consequent indeterminacy of the speaking voice; startling juxtapositions and ellipses; the subverting of expectations set up by the apparent direction of a sentence; qualifying or elaborating phrases proliferating endlessly" (57). Jenkins expressed an ambivalence toward McGuckian's work echoed by other readers; calling some of her poems "stunning," he also accused her of "rhetorical posturing." In a fall 1992 review of *Marconi's Cottage* in the *Irish Literary Supplement,* Denis Flannery demonstrates a similar impatience with McGuckian's work when he argues that "the language and the self are omnivorous in their relation to the world around them" and that the poetry "manages to be self-obsessed while refusing to be intimate" (21).

Concentrating almost exclusively on style, Jenkins, as well as some other readers, failed to recognize the connections between idea and style in McGuckian's poetry. This is not to say that every one of McGuckian's poems works, nor is it to downplay the difficulty that confronts the reader. But if we are to understand the "idiosyncrasies" of a poet labeled both "original" and "brilliant" by readers who also admit to sometimes being baffled by her poems, we might start with the assumption that she is writing as a woman about women's experience. Every McGuckian poem embodies, directly or indirectly, the conflicts and ambivalences of a woman poet trying to understand the multiple facets of her life, and McGuckian's language and style must be examined in light of this.

Reading McGuckian's poetry, it is helpful to draw on feminist literary theory and descriptions of "womanwriting" and *écriture féminine*. McGuckian herself encouraged such a reading when she suggested, in an interview with Kathleen McCracken in the *Irish Literary Supplement,* that her poetry has "its own logic which may be opposite of men's"; that, because language has been devitalized, "poetry must dismantle the letters" (McGuckian 1990, 20). The charge of solipsism leveled against McGuckian may arise from our failure to consider that her experiments move beyond conventional definitions of poetic voice, language, and self.

Hélène Cixous's description of "invention" sheds some light on McGuckian's approach: "there is no invention possible, whether it be philosophical or poetic, without there being in the inventing subject an abundance of the other, of variety: separate-people, thought-people, whole populations issuing from the unconscious, and in each suddenly animated desert the springing up of selves one didn't know" (1989, 103). Though Cixous maintains that female writing cannot be *"theorized, enclosed, coded"* (109), McGuckian presents an interesting illustration of the way in which poetry may reveal the "invention" Cixoux describes.

Multiple layers of meaning and numerous associations suggest both a deconstructed language and a deconstructed self.

If Eiléan Ní Chuilleanáin struggled to create an "I" in her poetry, McGuckian suffers from the opposite problem: at times there are so many *I*s and *you*s addressed that we have trouble knowing who is who. Likewise, McGuckian's *he*s and *she*s seem to defy our attempts to keep the genders separate and in place. We should note, however, that these are all personal pronouns, and the *person* is what McGuckian is trying to redefine. Her pronouns often fracture selfhood into many components: her personae see in themselves both the conventional feminine and masculine, and they have multiple and variable personalities. Refusing to be limited by a fixed "I," McGuckian's poetry demands that we go with her into new territory, even if, as Kate Newmann suggests, "just as you are about to read the compass the needle disappears" (1992, 173).

In describing the characteristics of *écriture féminine,* Luce Irigaray, like Cixous and Julia Kristeva, connects language with sexuality. Describing what she defines as "womanspeak," Irigaray, a psychoanalyst drawing on the work of Derrida and Lacan, sees woman's language as decentered, irrational, and nonlinear, unlike the logocentric, hierarchical expression of patriarchy. In "When Our Two Lips Speak Together," Irigaray describes woman as remaining "in flux, never congealing or solidifying" (1985, 215), and argues that women must invent a language that expresses their difference: "Stretching out, never ceasing to unfold ourselves, we have so many different voices to invent in order to express all of us everywhere, even in our gaps, that all the time there is will not be enough" (213).

McGuckian's imagery reflects such different voices, as well as the "cracks," "faults," and "flux" Irigaray describes. Multiple figures continually appear and disappear in McGuckian's poems. Sisters, female and male lovers, husbands and wives, parents and children come together and separate, are born and die, in the landscape of McGuckian's world. Speakers move in and out of shadow and mist, confront the day and hide in the night. Ghosts, mirrors and looking glasses, dream sisters, and phantom lovers materialize and dissolve. Weather, the elements, planets, houses, flowers, and ships take on gender to embody McGuckian's themes. One speaker's assertion in "Prie-Dieu" (1984, 29), that "This oblique trance is my natural / Way of speaking" and another's claim in "Aviary" (1984, 21) that "my longer and longer sentences / Prove me wholly female" signal that McGuckian's style may indeed be a challenge to logocentric thinking and conventional grammar and syntax.

Difficulty arises from the multiple meanings emanating from Mc-Guckian's words and images, especially her personal pronouns. While the "I" and the "you" in a poem like "From the Dressing-Room" (1984, 14) are described as a woman and a man, numerous *I*s and *you*s materialize to complicate matters. Sometimes the speaker apologizes for her "surrenders" to a "you" she addresses, as in "The Sofa" (1982, 19):

> . . . If you were friend enough
> To believe me, I was about to start writing
> At any moment; my mind was savagely made up,
> Like a serious sofa moved
> Under a north window. My heart, alas,
>
> Is not the calmest of places.

Temptations, referred to as "disasters," "surrenders," "loss" (and evoking suggestions of seduction by a lover) undercut her commitment to start writing. In the final lines, the speaker, focusing on the personal pronoun "I," imagines "herself" as a missing actor: "A curtain rising wonders where I am, / My books sleep, pretending to forget me." Ironically, McGuckian has written a poem about not writing a poem, and her speaker embodies both the "you" and the "me" (displacing the missing "I"), with the final stage metaphor reinforcing the different roles she plays.

As Catherine Byron says, McGuckian's "'I' is never to be taken for granted . . . it is always to be understood afresh in each poem, as is her 'you'" (1988, 16).[4] Multiple meanings emanate from McGuckian's pronouns; "I" and "you," "he" or "she" can be read on many levels. Complicated experimentation with personal pronouns, what Jenkins calls the

---

4. Byron also notes the originality of McGuckian's work as she compares her to Emily Dickinson, a woman poet misunderstood in her time:

> the image-areas she draws on are astonishingly similar to Emily Dickinson's: the house, the room, its windows and its furnishings; snow, and the voyaged-over sea; exotic places, exotic (and native) flowers; extremes of pain and love expressed in terms of the tension between male and female; light, whiteness, the colour blue. The list could continue, and be refined. But what is perhaps most striking is the way in which the McGuckian voice speaks from this nexus of images with the dizzying swings of reference and the syntactical high-wire acts so reminiscent of her predecessor. (1988, 16–17)

Although time, nations, and distance separate these two poets, the similarities Byron describes point to the value of exploring the ways in which women poets not only relate to one another but also circumscribe a world different from that of male poets.

"indeterminacy of the speaking voice," is indeed difficult to follow. However, when we recognize how McGuckian's pronouns and images express the complex interaction among her multiple figures (those "different voices" Irigaray describes), we marvel at both the originality and success of her achievement.

In an essay on "Postmodern McGuckian," Thomas Docherty associates McGuckian not only with feminist poetics, but also with postmodern literary techniques:[5] "Often it is difficult to locate any single position from which the poem can be spoken. In philosophical terms, we have a kind of a 'blank phenomenology': the relation between the speaking Subject or 'I' and the Object of its intention is mobile or fluid. It reads as if the space afforded the 'I' is vacant: instead of a stable 'persona,' all we have is a potential of personality, a voice which cannot yet be identified" (1992, 192). Suggesting the effects of this "blank phenomenology," Docherty maintains that McGuckian "is always—temporally and temperamentally—at odds with herself: the poems chart a dislocation in their speaker, who always occupies some different temporal moment from the moment actually being described in the poem" (201–202).

McGuckian's numerous speakers appear in many guises, as writers, lovers, wives, mothers, and the mediation among and between them is at the heart of most of her poems. We see, for example, the housewife and mother in "Power-Cut" (1982, 47) showing how her multiple lives overtake one another as day dissolves into night in her kitchen:

> My dishes on the draining-board
> Lie at an even keel, the baby lowered
> Into his lobster-pot pen; my sponge
> Disintegrates in water like a bird's nest,
> A permanent wave gone west.
> These plotted holes of days my keep-net shades,
> Soluble as refuse in canals; the old flame
> Of the candle sweats in the night, its hump
> A dowager's with bones running thin:
> The door-butler lets the strangers in.

Reading McGuckian, we become familiar with opening and closing doors, one scene dissolving as another comes into focus. McGuckian's images here detail aspects of a woman's life: babies, dishes, nests, the permanent wave. For this mother, however, the disappearance of day life

5. James McElroy (1989) takes a similar theoretical approach.

has ominous overtones. The baby in his "lobster-pot pen" suggests the sacrifice of one part of her life for another; the disintegrating sponge and the "holes of days" as "Soluble as refuse in canals" reinforce how one life dissolves into another.

The images in this poem depict different states in which this unstable persona exists: the domestic day world of sink, sponge, and baby, and the imaginative night world of the poet, identified with the flame of the sweating candle. Intruding strangers recur in McGuckian's poetry, and passages from night to day, day to night, season to season, waking to sleep describe the movement from one state to another.

In McGuckian's poems mothers are juxtaposed with lovers, and love-making has many dimensions: the union between lovers can be an image for the intercourse between man and woman or between a speaking "I" and an "other" voice within the self. In "To the Nightingale" (1984, 13), McGuckian writes:

> I remember our first night in this grey
> And paunchy house; you were still slightly
> In love with me, and dreamt of having
> A grown son, your body in the semi-gloom
> Turning my dead layers into something
> Resembling a rhyme. That smart and
> Cheerful rain almost beat the hearing
> Out of me, and yet I heard my name
> Pronounced in a whisper as a June day
> Will force itself into every room.

Our first reading of these lines suggests a woman describing love-making and her lover's wish for a son. But the title, "To the Night-ingale," refers us to Keats, and the body and voice helping to create "something / Resembling a rhyme" take on another meaning as McGuckian compares the intercourse between poet and muse to that between man and woman. The "you" addressed is not another person, but another voice within the speaker, one struggling to be heard; the consummation of "you" and "I" will create the child/poem. When we understand this, the initial confusion over pronouns is cleared up and we can see McGuckian revising Keats: "To the nightingale it made no differ-ence / Of course, that you tossed about an hour, / Two hours, till what was left of your future / Began." Embedded in these lines also is another kind of intercourse, between poet and poet, as McGuckian's female speaker consorts with the male Romantic poet who inspired the poem.[6]

6. The struggle involved in this union with the muse recurs in many poems. In

In her early poems there is less experimentation with pronouns, but McGuckian's images have a logic of their own. One of the most startling aspects of her first volume, *The Flower Master,* is its focus on sexuality and the ways in which gender lines are sometimes blurred. Like Eavan Boland in *In Her Own Image,* McGuckian continually stresses the sexual nature of the subjects and speakers of these poems, and her flower images suggest both sex and gender roles. "Womanliness" is highlighted in McGuckian's "Tulips" (1982, 10); the flowers, the poem tells us, close up at night, declaring their independence from sun and rain:

> such present-mindedness
> To double-lock in tiers as whistle-tight,
> Or catch up on sleep with cantilevered
> Palms cupping elbows. It's their independence
> Tempts them to this grocery of soul.

In this poem, as well as in many others, McGuckian gives the sun and the rain male qualities. The speaker sees the "lovelessness" of the light that opens the tulips as a "deeper sort / Of illness than the womanliness / Of tulips," for the controlling sun (a flower master) undermines their independence. Like their human female counterparts, and like fictional governesses, tulips can also be "carried away."

The flowers in another poem, "Gentians" (1982, 25), can be contrasted to the tulips in one respect:

> No insects
> Visit them, nor do their ovaries swell,
> Yet every night in Tibet their seeds

"Ode to a Poetess" (1984, 11–12), McGuckian makes it clear that although Keats is in the background, she is seeing the problem from a woman's point of view:

> Now you are in a poem of your own cold
> Making, on your second fret, your life knit
> Like a bird's, when amid the singing
> Of the Sparrow Hills, you yourself could not sing.
> It is ten o'clock, I am thinking of those
> Eyes of yours as of something just alighted
> On the earth, the why that had to be in them.
> What they ask of women is less their bed,
> Or an hour between two trains, than to be almost gone,

the woman "almost gone" (a postmodernist reading might also describe her as "almost there") is the most pervasive motif in McGuckian's poetry. Michael O'Neill in a review of *Venus and the Rain* argues that in "Ode to a Poetess" McGuckian "insists mockingly on the absence of the 'male principle' from the poem" (1984, 63).

> Are membraned by the snow, their roots
> Are bathed by the passage of melt-water;
> They tease like sullen spinsters
> The dewfall of summer limes.

The gentians' spinsterly qualities fascinate the speaker; their "independence" links them to the tulips. Clearly suggesting female sexual organs ("something precious / Deep inside, that beard of camel-hair in the throat"), the androgynous gentians also exhibit male characteristics: "their watery husbands' knots." Not subject to the mastery of the day sun, as are the tulips, the gentians reproduce at night, without swollen ovaries. We do not have too far to go with a theory of correspondences to see the links McGuckian makes between the natural and the human worlds. The relationships between women and men, female and male lovers, reproduction and motherhood are all embodied in these images. Questions of mastery, of dependence and independence, and of gender constructions, continually arise.[7]

Sometimes, as in "The Swing" (1982, 31), McGuckian turns to mythological images to suggest the potential consequences of sexual activity:

> Each evening the Egyptian goddess
> Swallowed the sun, her innocent
> Collective pleasure, never minding his violent temper,
> His copious emissions, how he sprinkled
> The lawn of space till it became
> A deadly freckled junkyard.

These lines describe the stars in the night sky as emissions of the sun, but in the sexual intercourse they suggest there is another meaning. Freckles evoke the image of children, and "deadly" and "junkyard" both hint at

7. The ambivalence McGuckian's women speakers feel toward sexual desire, the sharing of the self, and the potential for swelling ovaries, recurs as a theme in the volume. In "Ducks and Drakes" (1982, 20), for example, a woman acknowledges how she freely gives herself to a man, declaring: "Not . . . / That I needed persuading / Even my frowns were beautiful, my tenable / Emotions largely playing with themselves, / To be laid like a table set for breakfast." The final lines of the poem reinforce the mixed emotions a woman may have about intercourse and childbearing. In another poem, "The Dowry Murder" (1982, 38), the speaker, very conscious of her sexual desire, imagines "a last kiss, your clutch on my ordinary stem, / Then your head falling off into a drawer." McGuckian has said that she intended here not only the traditional linking of intercourse and death but also the mixed feelings that a woman might have toward the object of her desires.

the latent consequences of the sun's "copious emissions" and the god-dess's "innocent" pleasures.

The image of an "invisible child" at the end of the poem, recalling the "deadly freckled junkyard" of the earlier lines, creates a deliberate ambiguity. The strange weather, the drought, and the Egyptian goddess in the opening lines identify a speaker very much concerned with the relationship between lovemaking and childbearing, with the conse-quences of her actions and decisions. The title image of the swing, sug-gesting movement back and forth, reinforces the ambivalence we hear in the speaker's voice and illustrates McGuckian's repeated use of images of suspension between states of mind or action.

This potentially precarious side of lovemaking and childbearing, however, is offset by a more affirmative one, described by other speakers in *The Flower Master*. The mother-to-be in "The Sunbench" (1982, 32), for example, meditates on the value of motherhood. The speaker explains to the child in her womb what she has given:

> This is not the hardness of a single night,
> A rib that I could clearly do without. It is
> The room where you have eaten daily,
> Shaking free like a hosting tree, the garden
> Shaking off the night's weak appetite,
> The sunbench brown and draining into fallow.

The male's part in this creation, whether the phallic "hardness of a single night" or the expendable rib Adam supposedly gave Eve in another gar-den, is slighted here in favor of the longer and more difficult female work of sheltering the child in a "room" in the mother's body/house. As the hosting tree, this speaker, another flower master, recognizes that her "control" as host is temporary.

The role of gardener (or flower master) has not traditionally been assigned to women, as a poem like "The Heiress" (1982, 50) reveals. Commenting on the "husbandry" that the fields before her reveal, the speaker acknowledges the "delicate adam work." Explaining that she has recently delivered a son, she stresses the value of Eve work, though she notes that "the birth / Of an heiress means the gobbling of land." Chal-lenging her role, this heiress, who has been told to stay out of the fields, nevertheless walks along the beach, dropping acorns among the shrubbery.

McGuckian has said that she had Mary Queen of Scots in mind when she wrote this poem, which lends a historical dimension to the volume's focus on mastery and control of the land and to questionable issues of heirs, ownership, and gender in English and Northern Irish history. At the same time, the poem suggests the ways in which women have been denied not only the right to own property but also comparable acknowledgment for their work as wives and mothers. The adjective "unruly" can be applied both to Mary Queen of Scots, who also "lighter of a son" found herself involved in the "gobbling of land,"[8] and to all women who try to move beyond and reimagine the domestic life and subordinate roles defined for them.

Much of the conflict expressed by the speakers in *The Flower Master* grows from their movement into spheres other than lover and mother. The most frequent of these involves the woman as artist. Over and over again, McGuckian pictures women as makers and subjects of works of art. "Some women save their sanity with needles. / I complicate my life with studies / Of my favourite rabbit's head," announces the speaker in "Mr McGregor's Garden" (1982, 14). Ticking off the creatures in her garden, she also describes the "fungi," the "dry-rot," the "slimy veil" under some flowers. Most curious is her hedgehog who, moving out of Beatrix Potter's world, turns into a male version of a harried housewife: "very cross if interrupted, / And returns with a hundred respirations / To the minute, weak and nervous when he wakens, / Busy with his laundry." Suggesting that her studies might reveal much about herself (and also about Beatrix Potter), this speaker is one of many artists and poets in *The Flower Master* for whom art is both an escape from their more mundane lives and a form of self-expression.

"The Seed-Picture" (1982, 23) is a good example of such a poem and a fine illustration of the ways in which McGuckian fuses the different image patterns in *The Flower Master*. The female artist here "masters" flowers in the portrait she creates from seeds. The poem begins with the barest outlines of a narrative:

> This is my portrait of Joanna—since the split
> The children come to me like a dumb-waiter,
> And I wonder where to put them, beautiful seeds
> With no immediate application. . . .

Working from the image of children as seeds that need nurturing, the speaker tries to create a seed picture of Joanna. Maintaining that seeds have their own "vocabulary," sometimes expressing more than one in-

8. Mary Queen of Scots was forced to abdicate in favor of her son, James VI of Scotland, and was later executed.

tends, the speaker tells us that she can only "guide" them. Still she questions what she is doing:

> Was it such self-indulgence to enclose her
> In the border of a grandmother's sampler,
> Bonding all the seeds in one continuous skin,
> The sky resolved to a cloud the length of a man?
> To use tan linseed for the trees, spiky
> Sunflower for leaves, bright lentils
> For the window, patna stars
> For the floral blouse? Her hair
> Is made of hook-shaped marigold, gold
> Of pleasure for her lips, like raspberry grain.
> The eyelids oatmeal, the irises
> Of Dutch blue maw, black rape
> For the pupils, millet
> For the vicious beige circles underneath.
> The single pearl barley
> That sleeps around her dullness
> Till it catches light, makes women
> Feel their age, and sigh for liberation.

In this portrait, words and images allude to a potential narrative: the "Dead flower heads where insects shack" might be a metaphor for a home; the artist's attempt to attach the seeds "by the spine to a perfect bedding" an ironic commentary on the marriage bed after the "split." Adjectives and nouns reverberate with multiple meaning: the more negative "tear-drop apple," "pocked peach," "wrinkled pepper-corns," "black rape," and "vicious" circles underneath Joanna's eyes counterpoint the more positive "gold / Of pleasure for her lips" and "irises / Of Dutch blue maw." The image of the "sky resolved to a cloud the length of a man" suggests that we read the poem as a portrait of a woman's life with husband and children.

On another level, however, the poem deals with the speaker's artistic work, and McGuckian's use of the term "vocabulary" encourages us to broaden the definition of artist to include writers, who "guide" words. Likewise, McGuckian's tendency to fragment the poetic voice leads us to read the images and pronouns as different sides of one woman. With her question "Was it self-indulgence . . .?" McGuckian returns to her theme of the conflicts women writers and artists confront, and it is not hard to imagine the two women here as wife/mother and artist/poet, with the artist/poet worried about abandoning her domestic and maternal duties.

The poem opens with the maker of the seed picture anxious about Joanna's children ("I wonder where to put them") and closes with an image of women who, recognizing the "dullness" of Joanna's life, "sigh for liberation." Making a seed picture, "Bonding all the seeds in one continuous skin," like creating a child, can bring "light" to a woman's life, but it can also lead to stress as she juggles the roles of mother and artist.

Highlighting the value of women artists whose subject is women, whether in folk-art seed pictures or "portrait" poems, "The Seed-Picture" is one of McGuckian's finest poems. The speaker explains that the seed work has opened "new spectrums of activity," but it seems also to have created problems. Her question about whether such work is self-indulgent gets directly to the heart of the matter: over and over again, women in *The Flower Master* ask how they can balance the traditional life of a woman, with all of its attendant expectations, with the artist's career.

On the other hand, as Susan Porter demonstrates, the mother and the poet in "The Seed-Picture" share similar experiences:

> In all senses of seed, then, and particularly as it connotes children, the work involved is partly guiding and partly knowing that what one guides is ultimately beyond any "author's" control and contains within it from the beginning elements that were not subject to her desires or intentions. The woman who is also a poet is prepared by her experience in the female world of "children," "home," "jumbled garages," "seed-work" for the realization that words and arrangements of words, too, "capture / More than we can plan" and carry within them the seeds of many and varied meanings. (1989, 97)[9]

As Georgia O'Keeffe's *The White Trumpet Flower,* on the cover of some editions of *The Flower Master,* suggests correlations between the sexual connotations in O'Keeffe's paintings and McGuckian's poems, the illustration on the cover of *Venus and the Rain,* Jan Toorop's 1892 work *The Younger Generation,* leads us into McGuckian's second volume. Noted for his symbolism, the Dutch painter experimented with surrealism in the 1890s. Some of his scenes of Dutch fishing villages, *The Younger Generation* among them, include nursing mothers and melancholy women.

In the illustration on the cover of *Venus and the Rain* (1984), a young woman stands in a doorway opening into a garden, where mysterious figures appear in shadowy foliage. Creating a multiple perspective,

---

9. See also Beer 1992, which draws on Sara Ruddick's *Maternal Thinking: Towards a Politics of Peace* to examine McGuckian's work.

Toorop places the hinges on what seems to be the wrong side of the door, so that we are not sure whether it is opening in or out: the door appears to open on one side as it closes on the other. The young woman's face is indistinct; we cannot see what lies behind the door at which she is standing; and the elaborate facade appears to be both attached, and at a right angle, to the door. In the disconcerting garden outside the door, railroad tracks and a warning light frame a scene in which a tree spirit hovers above a child sitting in a chair. Toorop experiments here with the modernist's technique of simultaneity: planes and worlds interpenetrate as he blends detailed linear, representational images with the more ambiguous, fantastic, and shadowy curves of the garden. Foreground and background are not clearly delineated, and the demarcation between house and garden, represented by the door, is deliberately blurred.

This illustration gives us several visual clues to the landscape McGuckian creates in *Venus and the Rain*. As we have seen in *The Flower Master,* her women move from one realm to another in an often frustrating attempt to live several different kinds of lives, and houses, doors, and rooms are prominent images. Like the almost faceless woman standing in the doorway in Toorop's picture, McGuckian's speakers are often suspended between worlds; at times, they speak of disappearing or "rising out." While there is a danger in reading too much into the relationship between the cover illustration and the poems, much of McGuckian's imagery encourages us to do so. Houses, doors, gardens, trains, and infants show up frequently in these poems.

Outside the door the blending of the ordinary with the fantastic expresses the fusion of the mundane and the mysterious we often see in the lives of McGuckian's personae. The tracks, like McGuckian's staircases, suggest the journey from one of these worlds to the other, and the warning lights hint of the problems involved in such transformations. Toorop's work reinforces a point McGuckian demonstrates: that images, whether in poetry or the visual arts, can illustrate the multidimensional lives women lead, so that what first appear to be strange associations among these images are not necessarily so. Toorop's modernist technique, in which he connects images to one another in an associative, nonrepresentational way, is similar to McGuckian's; both fuse seemingly unrelated images into an artistic and symbolic whole.

In *Venus and the Rain* rooms appear and disappear, doors open and close, and windows reflect both in and out. McGuckian's subjects move from one part of the house to another, locking and unlocking doors as they go. Houses expand: some are tethered; others cannot be anchored.

And McGuckian's gardens, like Toorop's, can be frightening places: they are "ragged" in one poem, "desolate" in another, and in a third, emblems of change and death where "once you have seen a crocus in the act / Of giving way to the night, your life / No longer lives you."

In talking about *Venus and the Rain,* McGuckian has said that when she was writing these poems she was at home "going crazy," and "stuck in the house with babies."[10] Given these circumstances, we can understand why images of houses appear so often. But McGuckian's images have additional meanings, and the confinement and expansion of houses, the shifting of boundaries within them, quite often reflect the woman writer's struggle with words. Such is the case in "Isba Song" (1984, 23), in which the speaker sits at a desk:

> Beyond the edge of the desk, the Victorian dark
> Inhabits childhood, youth-seeking, death-seeking,
> Bringing almost too much meaning to my life,
> Who might have been content with one storey,
> And the turned-outwards windows of the isba.

An isba, a note to the poem explains, is a Russian one-story dwelling, and the writer here, with "two hands free," meditates on what lies beyond the edges of the desk, beyond the "turned-outwards" windows. She tells us she has heard in the darkness the voice of another woman who had been eager "to divide her song." We soon realize that "storey" refers not only to the levels of a dwelling but also to the many "stories" a poem might express, and that the windows, like Toorop's door, turn both inwards and outwards.

The two subjects here, an "I" and a "her," are separate but fused: one lives beyond the perimeters of the desk, the other sits as the locus of everything beyond the desk, but there is interaction and sharing between them, a shifting of boundaries, as it were.[11] A part of this "other" voice ("the first syllable of her name") survives in the woman at the desk, who sees the effect of borrowing as "a gentler terrain within a wilder one," or "as wood might learn to understand / The borrowings of water, or pottery capitulate / Its dry colours."

The wild, the dark, or the fluid coming into form evokes images of the artist creating (the wood to be sculpted, the wet pot before it is

10. These comments and others in this chapter not otherwise attributed are from conversations I had with McGuckian in 1990 in the United States and in 1992 and 1994 in Ireland.

11. We might see these as versions of Cixous's "separate people" mentioned earlier, "the springing up of selves one didn't know."

dried) and connect directly to the speaker whose desk is the locus of the darkness that surrounds her. In the final lines she describes the value of listening to this other voice, drawing on the multiple connotations of "I" and "me," as McGuckian often does: "Otherwise I might have well / Ignored the ground that shone for me, that did enough / To make itself rebound from me, out of which I was made."

Positioned between the darkness beyond the desk and the light that shone for her, the woman at the desk is another version of McGuckian's metamorphosing persona.[12] The woman in the darkness, willing to "divide her song," is essentially a maternal figure and the final image is one of birth. Phrases like "death-seeking" and "mournful locus" and "almost too much meaning to my life" suggest that there is also a darkness of mood, a gloominess that must be challenged for the poetic voice to emerge. These phrases can also be connected to the process of writing, illustrating that "invention" of different voices to "speak all of us" that Luce Irigaray describes as "womanwriting."

Venus, the volume's presiding deity, has both mythological and planetary significance: McGuckian alludes to the goddess of love who rose from the sea, but Venus is also the second planet from the sun, shrouded by thick clouds and distinguished by a unique backwards rotation.

In the opening poem, "Venus and the Sun" (1984, 9), McGuckian turns to astronomy for her imagery. "I am the sun's toy—," the planet complains, yet it also claims to have its own influence: "because I go against / The grain I feel the brush of my authority." Orbiting the sun, Venus follows a fixed path within the solar system; nevertheless, because it rotates backwards, it has its own "authority." The planet's role in the interplay of gravitational forces is described in the opening lines:

> The scented flames of the sun throw me,
> Telling me how to move—I tell them
> How to bend the light of shifting stars:
> I order their curved wash so the moon
> Will not escape, so rocks and seas
> Will stretch their elbows under her.

These images remind us of the power of the sun in *The Flower Master,* especially in the way it undercuts the independence of the tulips.

12. Eileen Cahill, offering a valuable reading of McGuckian's "middle voice," a "position of greyness" that "allows McGuckian to interrogate oppositions" (1994, 266), points to a number of poems in which this "grayness" is a central image.

Frustrated by the restrictions of orbiting within a solar system, Venus contrasts its role to that of the stars, who are "still at large" and can fly apart from one another. Venus describes the sun as a "traplight" and imagines the sun and moon as opposites, positing a murky middle ground where its own influence lies.

From one perspective McGuckian's astronomy can be read as modeling a woman's struggle to balance dependence and independence, to be connected to others but maintain a course of her own. Her "direction,"˙ or freedom of movement, is often controlled by the roles she plays, like orbiting a man, reflecting the light of the "brighter" star. Yet this Venus stresses her own unique identity, the force of her backwards rotation and its influence upon the other planets in the system. The conflict between these roles provides the source for much of the imagery and many of the themes in *Venus and the Rain*.

Venus in her mythological role as goddess of love inhabits many of these poems, highlighting as they do the sexual lives of their speakers. The relationship between sexuality and art is stressed in poems like "The Sitting" (1984, 15):

> My half-sister comes to me to be painted:
> She is posing furtively, like a letter being
> Pushed under a door, making a tunnel with her
> Hands over her dull-rose dress. Yet her coppery
> Head is as bright as a net of lemons, I am
> Painting it hair by hair as if she had not
> Disowned it, or forsaken those unsparkling
> Eyes as blue may be sifted from the surface
> Of a cloud; and she questions my brisk
> Brushwork, the note of positive red
> In the kissed mouth I have given her,

Familiar with McGuckian's imagery, we can read the half-sister as one of the speaker's selves, what the poem calls "something half-opened." In *Venus and the Rain,* openings and apertures are associated continually with Venus: on one level, they allude to Venus emerging from the sea; on another, they suggest female sexual organs; on a third, they express the artist's ability to open up hidden parts of herself. Pictured here as "a letter being / Pushed under a door," the "half-sister" sits reluctantly, prudishly, with her hands forming a tunnel over her "dull-rose dress." She is more comfortable with "sea-studies" (the unseen, unformed, nonsexual Venus) than with the colorful and sensual image ("coppery," "blue," "red") the painter creates. This poem may delineate the difficulties of a woman painting herself, analogous to a woman poet writing about herself.

Venus and the Rain is packed with "doubles": two sisters inhabiting one house, sister planets, ghosts, mirrors, Alice and Alice in the Looking Glass. The narratives of these poems interweave the complex situations of speakers with multiple lives: a woman who longs for union with her husband but demands a life of her own; a mother who describes both the joys and the burdens of bearing and raising children; a poet who consummates her relationship with her muse. These figures sometimes have both traditional male and traditional female qualities, for McGuckian's images often challenge conventional gender distinctions in search of a middle ground.

Images of intercourse, conception, birth and rebirth multiply in this volume; generation and regeneration occur in the speakers' sexual, maternal, and poetic lives. Significantly, McGuckian links poems about pregnancy with those about writing poems—the difficult process of creation expressing different versions of similar experiences. McGuckian's personae take us through stages of fertility—from intercourse, with lover or with muse, through the difficulties of carrying to term (both baby and poem), to the release that birth represents.

If we listen carefully to the numerous women's voices, we discover that fertility has advantages and disadvantages; it is both pleasurable and burdensome, attractive and dangerous. "The inhabitants of Venus / Are constantly in love, and always writing verses—," the speaker in "A Day with Her" (1984, 48) tells us, and therein lies their problem. Like the planet that orbits backwards within the gravitational boundaries of the solar system, they seek both union and separation. The movement from one state to another is imagined in "The Rising Out" (1984, 35) as both a death and a birth:

> My dream sister has gone into my blood
> To kill the poet in me before Easter. Such
> A tender visit, when I move my palaces,
> The roots of my shadow almost split in two,
> Like the heartbeat of my own child, . . .

Children in this volume are a source of both pleasure and anxiety for the woman writer. The speaker in "Sabbath Park" (1984, 54–55) describes her guilt, portraying herself as both mother and temperamental child:

> Broody
> As a seven-month's child, I upset
> The obsolete drawing-room that still seems
> Affronted by people having just gone,
> By astonishing Louisa with my sonnets,
> Almost a hostage in the dream
> Of her mother's hands

The domestic world of children, houses, and furniture here provides, as it does for most of McGuckian's work, the background for a poem about writing poems, and the mother's gift of her sonnets to her daughter—an ironic sharing with a child who is hostage to her mother's dream—expresses clearly the conflict and ambivalence of many of McGuckian's speakers.

But other speakers describe the advantages of motherhood, as in the beautiful poem "Confinement" (1984, 42), in which a mother and a child are alone in "a half-unpeopled / household":

> Child in the center of the dark parquet,
> Sleepy, glassed-in child, my fair copy,
> While you were sailing your boat in the bay,
> I saw you pass along the terrace twice,
> Flying in the same direction as the epidemic
> Of leaves in the hall. Our half-unpeopled
> Household, convalescent from the summer's leap,
> That indiscreetly drew the damp from walls,
> And coaxed our neighbour, the forest, into this
> Sorority, how could I share with you, unpruned
> And woebegone? A swan bearing your shape
> Re-entered the river imagery of my arms.

In this short poem McGuckian brings together many of the ideas and images of the other poems in *Venus and the Rain*. Developing the imagery of boundaries, which recurs throughout the volume, this poem portrays a mother confined to the house with her "fair copy," who is positioned in the center of a dark floor. If we associate the mother here with the female grayness so prominent in the rest of the volume, the child is a point of light to which her eyes are drawn. This light-shadow motif connects "Confinement" to the sun-Venus imagery in other poems, the image of confinement echoing, for example, the "traplight" of the sun in "Venus and the Sun."

The child's circular "Flying" around the terrace reminds us, likewise, of the planetary images in "Venus and the Sun" and other poems.

McGuckian illustrates the interdependence of mother and child while demonstrating their individuality: the child's world is glassed in, separating mother from child; but in flying around the terrace, the child also orbits its mother. The mother's question "how could I share with you?" makes this "confinement" ironic by revealing her love for her child, the "unpruned" and "woebegone" offspring transformed into the beautiful swan. The final image of the swan reentering the river, the child moving into the mother's arms, is a beautiful expression of the opening up of self, as mother embraces child in a simple act of love, counterpointing the confinement suggested by the title. The swan, an animal sacred to Venus, also alludes to the goddess of love.

If we look back to the earlier poem, "Isba Song," we can read "Confinement" in still another way and see the child and mother as a variation of the interacting women. Like the one woman who borrows from another willing to "divide her song" in the earlier poem, the mother and child in "Confinement" are united at the end. The repetition of the central image in both poems not only links the mother with the writer but also suggests the way in which numerous components of a woman's life flow into one another. The river imagery of the mother's arms in "Confinement" echoes the "two hands free" of the writer in "Isba Song"; the conversion from woebegone child to swan expresses the transformation of personal experience into poem, the "glassed-in child, my fair copy" described in the opening lines. As I suggested earlier, every McGuckian poem directly or indirectly deals with multiple roles women play.

McGuckian's 1988 volume *On Ballycastle Beach* covers similar ground but also signals a new direction for the poet. Recurring images of houses, alter egos, colors, and weather accrue new meanings as McGuckian continues the self-explorations begun in her earlier poems. But the title alerts us that we are moving into a more specific regional landscape, Ballycastle being the birthplace of both McGuckian and her father,[13] and into the murky territory of the "Northern" question. While this is not immediately clear from an initial reading of the poems, *On Ballycastle Beach* merges the personal with the political to embody a woman poet's commentary on the problems in her homeland. Because the volume is so dense with images and so packed with ideas, McGuckian's political message becomes part of a larger framework constructed from a very broad definition of "home." Issues of time, territory,

13. *On Ballycastle Beach* is dedicated to McGuckian's father, Hugh Albert Mc-Caughan, and her son, Hugh Oisin. *Venus and the Rain* is dedicated to her mother, Margaret Fergus, and her mother-in-law, Mary McAuley.

gender, language, and art emerge from images of homes, dreams, rivers and fountains, children, mothers, ships, and colors. Repeated readings yield new connections as McGuckian continually breaks down and redefines boundaries.

Again, the cover illustration on some editions, a Postimpressionistic Jack B. Yeats painting of a person standing on a beach dwarfed by a merging sea and sky, is closely related to poems McGuckian calls her "seascapes." In the painting the lines between sea and sky, and between sea and land, are not clearly delineated, and Yeats blends colors into one another as numerous shades of blue, enhanced with white, black, yellow, red, and other colors, create the image we see. The barest outlines of a human shape define a person standing on the shore, with feet in the water. The more we look at this illustration, the more the boundaries separating the natural elements from one another, and the human figure from nature, tend to disappear.[14]

This illustration relates to the poems in many ways. On the most obvious level, it alludes to personal territory and to Ballycastle as a birthplace from which the poet moves away but to which she is still anchored. It also represents a place in Northern Ireland, shores to which English ships sailed hundreds of years ago, drawing new boundaries not only between England and Ulster but also between Northern Ireland and the Republic. As what one poem calls "a child of the North," McGuckian sees the effects of such boundaries, and the poems deal with several dimensions of the personal and social realities of the Northern landscape. Numerous images of water and boats emphasize Ballycastle as a place from which one can leave and to which one can return. In the opening poem, "What Does 'Early' Mean?" (1988, 11), a house across the way evokes images of "ships and their wind-blown ways," and in the final and title poem, a ship comes into harbor. Between these two, McGuckian takes us on a journey but never leaves "home."

Yeats's painting also reinforces McGuckian's colors, one of the most intriguing and difficult of her image patterns. When asked what blue means in her poems, McGuckian has said that readers should look at the context in which the blue appears. A poem like "Scenes from A Brothel" (1988, 48–49) illustrates what she means more specifically:

14. Yeats's fusion and blending of colors, the blurring of lines in the painting, reinforce themes in the volume as well. The blue of the sea and the sky is actually a combination of colors. Sea, sky, and beach interpenetrate and, while we see them as separate, the boundaries between them are not always clearly defined. From a knowledge of McGuckian's earlier poetry, in which boundaries are continually shifting, we can see parallels between the two artists' work. For more on Jack B. Yeats, see White 1971.

Any colour lasts a second, three or four
Minutes at most—and can never be repeated.
So few words for so many colours.
This blue, this blue, an enfeebled red,
The child of old parents.
Though it is immutable, it has no more lustre
Than the moon in its first quarter,
Or the wall above the coat-stand.

The paradox of transient immutability is a key to much of what McGuckian writes about in *On Ballycastle Beach,* and she gives colors as many meanings as she creates contexts for them. There are warm colors—reds, golds, and browns—and they are associated with many things, including but not restricted to the sun, dying leaves, blood and bloodshed, men, wind, dreams, death. The coolness of blue appears in images of skies and water but is also often associated with women and with art: "Blue Vase," "The Blue She Brings with Her," "Woman with Blue-Ringed Bowl."

That these properties of color also apply to words is confirmed, not only by the speaker in "Scenes from a Brothel," who complains that there are "so few words for so many colours," but also by the frustrated poets who speak, like the one imagining herself as a disintegrating painting in "Through the Round Window" (1988, 52):

I feel the room being torn to pieces, till no black
Is connected to any other black, my yellow
Pencil, my green table, can never be lit again.
Each poem in my alchemist's cupboard
That was an act of astonishment has a life
Of roughly six weeks, less than half a winter
Even in the child's sense of a week. . . .

The passage of time, and our attempts to capture, stop, or control it, appear in many of the poems in *On Ballycastle Beach.* In her explorations into the nature and limitations of time, McGuckian covers a broad spectrum of topics, ranging from Ireland's history to a vision of her own mother's death, and she ties them together in the volume in remarkable ways. Although the speaker in "Through the Round Window" describes how quickly, like color, the "act of astonishment" fades, many of the other poems in the volume focus on the staying power of art. Like many other poets, including Jack B. Yeats's brother, McGuckian presents art as one of our few defenses against the ravages of time and death, even if it does not always provide the reassurances we need.

As a tribute to that staying power, McGuckian turns to the Romantic poets, and to imaginative dream landscapes that outlast the dreamer.[15] In "Coleridge" (1988, 34), boundaries of time and space collapse as a contemporary Irish woman poet meets her nineteenth-century male counterpart:

> In a dream he fled the house
> At the Y of three streets
> To where a roof of bloom lay hidden
> In the affectation of the night,
> As only the future can be. Very tightly,
> Like a seam, she nursed the gradients
> Of his poetry in her head,
> She got used to its movements like
> A glass bell being struck
> With a padded hammer.
> It was her own fogs and fragrances
> That crawled into the verse, the
> Impression of cold braids finding
> Radiant escape, as if each stanza
> Were a lamp that burned between
> Their beds, or they were writing
>
> Their poems in a place of birth together

McGuckian's equation of the birth of a poem with that of a baby turns Coleridge into a female, who having "fled the house" discovers "some word that grew with him as a child's / Arm or leg." We recognize in this image a persona we see in many of McGuckian's poems, one who finds in the night, away from the duties of mother and housewife, her poetic self. In separate beds, an allusion also to their own respective English and Irish birthplaces, these two poets nevertheless merge as his English lines echo through her head to be transformed by her Irish "fogs and fragrances." Like many other poems in *On Ballycastle Beach*, "Coleridge" touches on questions of language and borrowings, how the Northern Irish female poet might change the language of the English male poet. Ultimately, this poem brings into focus one of the larger

---

15. Calvin Bedient maintains that McGuckian is not "Catholic Ireland's daughter, after all—or not enough; when it comes to push and shove, she's the heir, however captious, of the Romantics" (1990, 196).

themes of the volume: the way in which poetry and art in general can transcend political, historical, and geographical boundaries.

In another, more overtly political poem, "Little House, Big House" (1988, 33), McGuckian again uses the images of houses and rooms to picture the way in which art can break down boundaries. Alluding to the big houses inhabited by English settlers, and the small homes of the Irish cottagers, the speaker imagines a different kind of house, where

> On the ground floor, one room opens into another,
> And a small Matisse in the inglenook
> Without its wood fire is stroked by light
> From north and south.

Here the house becomes an image for Ireland, described in the opening lines as "half-people, each with his separate sky." But as the lines quoted above remind us, the same sun shines both north and south. If the Matisse painting, which represents the world beyond borders, replaces the fire in the inglenook, which suggests the conflict in Ireland, the light from both parts of Ireland can shine upon it.

The speaker in this poem shows how such an image affects her:

> That started all the feelings
> That had slept till then, I came out
> From behind the tea-pot to find myself
> Cooled by a new arrangement of doorways

From earlier poems, we are familiar with McGuckian's shifting doorways, but in this volume the opening and closing of doors expands to include the borders of Ireland. Thinking about the house's "minstrel's gallery," the speaker looks beneath the "tangled" house to its foundation: "our blood / Is always older than we will ever be."

Many of the images McGuckian used in earlier poems to suggest a fractured self appear in this volume as metaphors for a divided Ireland, or for the troubled relationship between Ireland and England. Throughout the volume, the green, white, and gold of the flag of the Republic, and the blue, red, and white of the British flag, also have political significance.[16]

16. In an interview with Susan Shaw Sailer conducted in Belfast in 1990 (1993a) McGuckian said that the poems "The Dream-Language of Fergus" and "A Dream in Three Colours" were both political poems, the first concerned with her son learning English, not Irish, the second with her wish that "we could all be English and all Irish and all Europeans."

A reappearing woman on a beach is part of a larger pattern of imagery involving ships and travel.[17] These images sometimes suggest a "flight," like the earls described in "The Bird Auction" (1988, 50), whose leaving helped to create many of the troubles Northern Ireland has suffered. But they have other implications as well. In modern times many of Ulster's better-known poets have left, overwhelmed by the violence around them. In this context the meaning of home, and McGuckian's role as the best-known of Northern Ireland's women poets, takes on added significance, for the value she continually gives to house and home becomes a political statement as well. McGuckian has said that she was often tempted to leave but chose to stay because of family connections, roots, and a sense of belonging (1993a).

"But none of my removals," says the speaker in the aptly-titled "Girls in the Plural" (1988, 42), "Was in any sense a flight," contrasting herself to those "boys," earls or poets, who have deserted Northern Ireland in its troubles. As Clair Wills says in her review of *On Ballycastle Beach,* "This is no mere abstract argument—other poets, such as Seamus Heaney and Paul Muldoon, in the grand tradition of Irish writers, *have* left Northern Ireland." Quoting other lines from the volume, Wills explains that "McGuckian's abiding obsession with seeds, and her association of the womb with the growth of both words and children, suggest the possibility of a new type of 'plantation'" (1988, 915). Even if she stays home, the McGuckian persona explains in "Four O'Clock, Summer Street" (1988, 31), her rooms can fly, given the right color: "I kept insisting / On robin's egg blue tiles around the fireplace / Which gives a room a kind of flying-heartedness."

That McGuckian sees a difference between men and women on this issue is confirmed by the images in "For a Young Matron" (1988, 41):

> An aeroplane unlike
> A womb claims its space

17. These women include the mythic figures Grainne and Pomona. Though there are several ships, and even some airplanes, they do not sail or fly. McGuckian's "First Letters from a Steamer" (1988, 28) is a poem about a steamy spring that comes after four perfect springs. As the sea this season "turns on / Another light," the speaker learns, on her own voyage of discovery, how to borrow some sunlight to get through foggy days. Likewise, in "Lighthouse with Dead Leaves" (1988, 32), the speaker never leaves the house, even though "All wounds began to glow, / And lighthouses sprang to mind." This woman sets out on the kind of journey we are used to in McGuckian's poetry: "I have locked my bedroom door from the inside, / And do not expect it to be mutilated. / My garb is chosen for a dry journey."

And takes it with it.
It says, Once it wasn't like this.

But wood grows
Like the heart worn thin
Within us, or the original
Spirit of October.

The frustrated young matron speaking is a poet in the top floor of a house (which can "grow" from wood), listening to a "he" who asks her:

Why not forget this word,
He asks. It's edgeless,
Echoless, it is stretched so,
You cannot become its passenger.

But McGuckian's women, especially her poets, do travel on words, always seeking an edgeless world. The rivers they move on lie within them; their flights are those of the imagination. Like the womb that encloses the life within it, they create worlds within themselves. And these women are anchored, as the poet herself is, to houses and to Ballycastle Beach.

The value of such anchoring appears in McGuckian's own mother, the subject of "Woman with Blue-Ringed Bowl," (1988, 58), one of the final poems in the volume. Seeing her as the subject of a many-colored portrait, fit for a pen "that wrote in four colours," McGuckian presents her as an Irish woman who maintained a home despite difficulties:

Though six vigorous soldiers have occupied her house,
She has cried out only once, and laughed without a wrinkle.
As wine comes stepping from stones, adding death to death,
A quarter of her blood shows like a scar at moments
Of excitement through her belted dress of dusky grey.
You would think it grey, but I think her dress
Is worthy of her mind, the semi-darkness
Of a poem composed after illness.

That evening, when I printed "THE END" in my black,
Floral, author's hand, on the blended orangey page,
I gave my youth to my mother, whose heart is not
Supposed to beat, even on the stairs, and said to the
Moroccan April, stay the way you are.

A gust of wind and colour flies to the door
That cannot be kept so narrow, my notebook lies

> Useless as a womb on my knees. The blue ensnared
> Is a careful, sad, a Marie-Louise blue,
> And she has remained both woman and flaxen page:
> But, when I saw the picture again, the sun had gone.

Having learned from an earlier poem that "any colour lasts a second, three or four / Minutes at most—and can never be repeated," we understand the poet's response, and her own awareness that her mother's life, "ensnared" for a moment in color, is drawing to a close. In the face of death, womb and notebook, sources of creation, seem useless, as does the loving gesture of an enlightened child trying to give "youth" to her mother. Although she would like to keep her mother behind one of those doors her personae are always locking, the speaker here understands that when the sun is gone, "THE END" always comes, and nothing, even a Moroccan April, ever stays the way it is. Hence, the painter and the poet must try to catch the light: "Hold me in the light, she offers, turn me around, / Not the light controlled by a window, but the cool gold / Of turning leaves after their short career in the sky."

While there are many themes, motifs, and images in this volume, "Woman with Blue-Ringed Bowl" encapsulates the unifying idea that ultimately we are all victims of time. The opening poem, "What does 'Early' Mean?," focuses our attention on the passage of time; and whether McGuckian is writing about domestic, political, or artistic life, whether she is describing seconds or hundreds of years, time is always an issue. Art, and especially poetry, become for her speakers a momentary defense against time, and the worlds of sleep and dream represent their entry into a timeless world of the imagination. As often as not, these women are waiting, not traveling in the usual sense, but staying home, finding themselves in what lies around them.

The ultimate message of *On Ballycastle Beach* is that leave-taking inevitably involves loss, an idea reinforced in the final and title poem (1988, 59), in which a child wandering on a beach is carried home to be read to:

> I would read these words to you,
> Like a ship coming in to harbour,
> As meaningless and full of meaning
> As the homeless flow of life
> From room to homesick room.

Ship and house merge here, and the value of home, with its multiple meanings and many ramifications, comes through in the words and poems written by a "child of the North."

The relationship of one generation to another, of children to parents, always a central theme in McGuckian's work, is also the subject of many of the poems in *Marconi's Cottage* (1991), and the problem of time is again central. The volume draws its title from a two-room cottage Mc-Guckian purchased at the end of Ballycastle Beach. McGuckian says that she knew this house as a child and attaches a political significance to the fact that the cottage gives her a space in a landscape where the "Queen owns the other rocks." Describing the spot as fostering her father's roots, McGuckian also sees the cottage as a peaceful alternative to the "hell of Belfast," explaining that it became a retreat for her after a trip to the United States and a particularly trying time away from Ireland. Familial, political, and artistic themes surface in the volume as McGuckian ex-plores both the personal and public meanings embedded in the image of the cottage.

Ballycastle has been associated with Marconi since 1898, when the scientist was struggling with the problem of transmitting wireless mes-sages over water. Marconi's assistant, George Kemp, came to Ballycastle to see if it were possible to receive signals from a lighthouse on Rathlin Island. If so, ships at sea could signal to Rathlin and then to the main-land, where a telegraph office had been set up. Degna Marconi, in *My Father Marconi* (1962), describes the success of this venture: "At Bal-lycastle a 70-foot pole was erected and on August 25, George Kemp and an assistant named Glanville went to Rathlin. Near the lighthouse they put up a wire, first to 80, then 100 feet to clear the lighthouse. The assignment was accomplished and considered a marvel because there is a high cliff between Torr Head and Ballycastle" (63). The success of this venture showed that the wireless could cover great distances and make land-sea communication possible.

The metaphoric possibilities of such an image provide rich lore for McGuckian's poems. Marconi's cottage, as the backdrop for these poems, has significance on many levels. In evoking Marconi, McGuckian says she imagined the sea speaking to him and sees his work as an illustration of the way he responded to and understood nature.[18] Voices coming over telephones and answering machines appear in these poems, and nu-merous poems suggest an analogy between Marconi's wireless communi-cation and the work of the poet and artist. Allusions to Rilke, Rodin, Gwen John, Yeats, Balzac, Charlotte Brontë, and Sylvia Plath, among others, reinforce the need to see this volume as concerned with the art-ist's struggle to create and communicate.

18. McGuckian discussed *Marconi's Cottage* with me in Galway in July 1992. Some of the following comments and quotations draw on that conversation.

Marconi's Cottage, like McGuckian's other volumes, is full of multiple voices, highlighting the tension arising from a woman's double role as mother and poet: the desire, on the one hand, to have another child, and, on the other, to commit herself fully to her writing. As is typical of McGuckian, these two roles intersect; the yet unconceived child dreamed about in the first part of the volume becomes the child celebrated in the later poems. Parallels between this child and the unwritten and written poem are developed throughout the volume.

The last poem, "On Her Second Birthday" (1991, 107–108), dedicated to McGuckian's daughter, Emer Mary Charlotte Rose,[19] brings many of the preceding ideas and images into focus, reinforcing the imagery and tone of earlier poems. Sea, child, and poem merge as McGuckian's persona describes a characteristic process of change from mist to light. The speaker meditates:

> It seems as though
> To explain the shape of the world
> We must fall apart,
> Throw ourselves upon the world,
> Slip away from ourselves
> Through the world's inner road,
> Whose atoms make us weary.

The result of this fragmentation, this journey, is seen in the second half of the poem, where the image of a shadow materializes as the speaker "ripened" into light. Like a message over water, a part of the speaker moves towards the sea:

> But I flow outwards till I am something
> Belonging to it and flower again
> More perfectly everywhere present in it.
> It believes in me,
> It cannot do without me,
> I know its name:
> One day it will pass my mind into its body.

This image of conception and birth, of a part of self moving into something else, has numerous applications, not the least, given the dedication of the poem, to the daughter that this mother has produced. Lines in the beginning of the poem also allude to writing: "The wind like a soul / Seeking to be born / Carried off half / Of what I was able to say."

19. McGuckian already had three sons.

Like Marconi's message floating over water, however, the end of the poem suggests that the poet will "flower again" as her "mind" passes into the "body" of the poem.

Several other poems, including "Oval of a Girl" (addressed to "near-child, much-needed"), and "The Carrying Ring" (1991, 88–89), also highlight the birth of a daughter, emphasizing the parallel between different types of creation. Imagining the visible as "the carrying ring / For the invisible," McGuckian describes in the latter poem the process of waiting, for a poem and a child:

> Each languageless flake
> Of that night-filled mountain is a sleep
> And all that labour is to have
> An awareness of one's being
> Added to one's being, like a first daughter:
>
> The cloudy, the overcast, then
> Something shone upon.

Repeating the imagery of night to day, darkness to light, shadow to shape that recurs frequently in her work, McGuckian emphasizes the value of waiting, until the sun shines through the clouds and the "child" is born.

If "On Her Second Birthday" and others celebrating the birth of a daughter create one tone in *Marconi's Cottage,* another pervades the volume as well. Linking birth with death, and beginnings with endings, many of these poems reflect McGuckian's awareness of the approaching death of her father, who was ill while she was writing these poems. One of the most lyrical and elegiac, "Echo-Poem" (1991, 67–69), represents a new direction for McGuckian in the simplicity of its language; it is also one of the most moving poems in the volume.

Acknowledging her meeting with a female figure of death, the speaker describes the consequences:

> Now that I have kissed
> Her sound awake,
> She alliterates
> With my father,
> She unmoors him; though
> I modify
> His name by fond
> Diminutives, she ties
> Him to her stern.

If by conceiving a child, a woman sends off some part of herself into the world, in the death of her parent, she loses another part. Words associated with language and literature ("alliterates," "modify," "diminutives," "war-odes,") accentuate the link to writing, as does the identification of the figure of death with writing:

> She will choose
> Her body freely,
> As a word chooses its meaning
> Her shoulder-twist
> And cleavage feeds
> Some foam-born
> Germ in me.

In the image of unmooring, McGuckian suggests that the writer may have as little control over words ("a word chooses its meaning") as humans have over death.

In other poems, like "The Invalid's Echo," "The Watch Fire," and "The Rosary Dress" (where a father's death is compared to "a new kind of winter"), the awareness of a coming death appears in images of night, winter, invisibility. But death is also tied to new life in this volume; the last lines of "Charlotte's Delivery" (1991, 83) tell us: "In the wrecked hull of the fishing-boat / Someone has planted a cypress under the ribs."

McGuckian herself suggests the cyclical structure of *Marconi's Cottage* and points to two poems, "Swallows' Wood, Glenshesk," and "The Partner's Desk" as pivotal. In "The Partner's Desk" (1991, 70–71), a daughter and father both appear as the speaker mediates between them, McGuckian's familiar middle ground. Imagining a yet-to-be-born child, she describes a future where her own father is dead: "When I teach the continents / To my favourite daughter, my father is there / Though I do not see him." Although the father's "mood is towards evening," the bond between father, daughter, and granddaughter will survive. Reinforcing the generational links, the speaker's father, very much aware of his own mortality, tells his daughter of her own conception and birth: "'The finest summer I can ever remember / Produced you.'"

In the final lines of "The Partner's Desk," a persona speaks of the renewed rousing of her fingers, a metaphor for writing, as she describes the complicated feelings engendered by the overlapping birth of a daughter and death of a father:

> . . . He will leave me
> The school clock, the partner's desk, the hanging

Lamp, the head bearing the limbs, as I will leave her
The moonphase watch and the bud vase. I restart
My diary and reconstruct the days. I look upon
The life-bringing cloud as cardboard
And no reason for the life of another soul, yet still
Today is the true midsummer day.

Images of time, of clocks and watches, of seasons and months, of days
and diaries, of generational inheritances, reinforce the overwhelming
sense of time passing in this poem and throughout the volume. The "yet
still" of the penultimate line, the coming to terms with what time de-
livers—both good and bad—illustrates one of the many structures on
which *Marconi's Cottage* rests.

There are numerous images of writers and artists in *Marconi's Cot-
tage,* a good number of the allusions focused on the hardships individual
artists endured.[20] The struggle to create within a framework of other ob-
ligations, as well as the difficulty of persevering through the intense pro-
cess of creation, is highlighted in these allusions. In "East of Mozart"
(1991, 64–66), the musician's tempestuous isolation is compared to the
poet's:

> But some words like some notes
> That never pronounce themselves,

20. For example, the poem "Journal Intime" reminds us of the writer Henri-Frédéric
Amiel's *Journal Intime,* his account of long years of suffering. Amiel's continual search for
the relationship between the real and the ideal, his fascination with the invisible shadow
world McGuckian explores in many of the poems in this volume, is reflected in his journal.
Amiel's journal entry for October 4, 1873, parallels some of the feelings reflected in
McGuckian's poems:

> I have been dreaming a long time while in the moonlight, which floods my room
> with a radiance, full of vague mystery. The state of mind induced in us by this
> fantastic light is itself so dim and ghost-like that analysis loses its way in it, and
> arrives at nothing articulate. It is something indefinite and intangible, like the
> noise of waves, which is made up of a thousand fused and mingled sounds. It is
> the reverberation of all the unsatisfied desires of the soul, of all the stifled sor-
> rows of the heart, mingling in a vague sonorous whole, and dying away in
> cloudy murmurs. (268–69)

Many of Amiel's images appear likewise in McGuckian's poems; they share a world of
dreams, ghosts, mystery, moonlight, sea, waves, and clouds, a state where sorrow reverbe-
rates, and "analysis loses its way" and often "arrives at nothing articulate." It is not hard to
see *Marconi's Cottage* as McGuckian's own *Journal Intime.* Mrs. Humphry Ward's introduc-
tion to her translation of Amiel's *Journal Intime* provides a good nineteenth-century view of
Amiel's work.

Are meant for at most
Ten people in the world
Whose oxygen is storms.

Two female artists who appear in these poems, the painters Paula Modersohn-Becker and Gwen John, also struggled with some of the same problems McGuckian's personae express. Both are pictured in difficult relationships with male artists, John with Rodin, Modersohn-Becker with Rilke.

Paula Modersohn-Becker, who died after giving birth, was a close friend of Rilke's and the subject of his poem "Requiem für eine Freundin" (Rilke 1982, 72–87). In her study of Rilke, Patricia Pollock Brodsky explains that the more successful she became, the more the artist "feared being swallowed up, neutralized, by the traditional expectations of her family, husband and society" (1988, 17). Rilke's poem addresses these issues, lamenting the fact that her maternity led directly to her death. At the end of the poem, Rilke moves into more general questions about the relationship between life and art.[21]

In "To Call Paula Paul" (1991, 16–19), McGuckian calls attention to Modersohn-Becker's work. The speaker "embraces" the painter and suggests that they share "mother-to-be dreams," and an important image is the artist's wrist. The speaker describes her relationship with this other woman artist:

I did nothing, I didn't cry:
I held the permanent bangle on her wrist
For a long time. In the bright July
My window seemed too big, all day
Long to insult me, with its pale heaven,
Putting supple hands around my throat.

The image of a strangled voice suggested in the last line above is reinforced when Paula's face is seen in a "sordid light" and the mouth of the

21. Brodsky provides more details on this subject. Rilke often wrote about death, and many of his poems are requiems. Brodsky describes the influence of Jens Peter Jacobsen, saying that Rilke "came to believe that each person has a death of his own, as uniquely his as his life had been. He also frequently uses the image of death as the core or seed of a fruit: death is placed within us to ripen. For women, giving birth also implies bearing a death along with each life they create" (1988, 30). In a poem written in 1900 about Paula Modersohn-Becker and the sculptor Clara Westhoff, later his wife, Rilke warns both women about giving up their art (which he defines as a feeling in their wrist), for the more conventional life of a woman. These concerns are central to McGuckian's poems as well.

wind "outshouts" the speaker who identifies with Modersohn-Becker's conflict.

There can be no doubt here that the relationship between the artist and the mother, with Modersohn-Becker's tragic death after childbirth in the background, influences not only this poem but others in *Marconi's Cottage* as well. A woman's concern over bearing another child, and its effect on her writing career, is clearly expressed in this poem. Turning Paula into Paul, the masculine name suggesting the more traditionally "male" career of writer, McGuckian explores the conflict between the artist and "mother-to-be dreams," an intercourse the speaker and subject of this poem share.

In another poem, "Road 32, Roof 13–23, Grass 23" (1991, 42–43), McGuckian considers the tangled life of Gwen John. To identify tones, John had developed a color system based on combining the numbers 1, 2, and 3, recording in notebooks the colors in each of her paintings. The poem's title refers to this system, one we can connect with the recurring colors that take on numerous meanings in McGuckian's poems.

A number of characteristics would attract McGuckian to John: she shared the turmoil McGuckian describes in so many of these poems; many of John's paintings feature rooms and interiors, which figure so prominently in McGuckian's work as well; and, as Mary Taubman explains, John's "closely woven interaction of self and subject is a unifying theme running through her entire *oeuvre* from youth to maturity (1985, 11).[22]

McGuckian's poem begins as a portrait of John, highlighted by its color, which emphasizes the woman's suffering:

> The dark wound her chestnut hair
> Around her neck like the rows of satin trimming
> On a skirt with three flounces.
> She pressed firmly down the sides of her eyes
> The colour of the stem of the wild geranium
> And of the little ball holding the snowdrop petals.

In this poem, as in others in *Marconi's Cottage,* red is identified both with art and with suffering, the connection reinforcing the theme that the artist's life is often fraught with pain.

John met Rodin in 1904 while working for him as a model, and they soon became lovers. John's relationship with Rodin greatly influenced

22. McGuckian's attraction to late Victorian and turn-of-the-century life and art (like Gwen John's) is also illustrated throughout her work.

her melancholic life, though the significance of her work seems not to have been acknowledged between them.

McGuckian describes a conflict between different women embodied in John. Rodin knew one as the woman who wrote daily, loving letters to him; McGuckian imagines the other as totally different:

> She slept with his letter in her hand,
> And the longest letter she wrote
> Was on the back of his letter
> To a woman who never existed.

The darkness and mists so prevalent elsewhere in *Marconi's Cottage* appear in this poem as well, suggesting how John's gloomy, sunless life was overshadowed by Rodin:

> She did not light the lamp or the fire,
> Though he lit a station of candles
>
> In wine bottles for their first kiss;
> The candlelight left a film of woodsmoke
> Over everything. Her fear of light began
> While his coat still hung over a chair,
> The window seemed a picture eased out of her,
> She did not want her own face there.

On one level, the images in this poem allude to Rodin and John and the struggles she had combining two lives. But they also connect to recurring images in all of McGuckian's work: images of dark, light, smoke, mist, rain, letters, doors. The woman artist and writer, who in McGuckian's poems must close one door in order to open another, is epitomized in figures like Gwen John and Paula Modersohn-Becker.

The tone and imagery of *Marconi's Cottage* consistently demonstrate that the struggle to create and communicate involves pain. Drawing on the conventional association of winter with death and spring with rebirth, McGuckian sees art as the offspring of suffering, poetry as the fruit of winter, and the garden the reward for having come through. The seasons and months of the year, as well as the cycle of conception, birth, life, and death, unify the volume and express ultimately that for every loss there is a gain, for every death a birth. The final poems in the volume portray a woman who has survived, who has confronted both the power of death and the difficulty of writing. In "Teraphim" (1991, 104–5), the mystery is accepted, and the ordeal of waiting through the difficult times is described as the "mist in which we are swallowed" that "allows a garden to be planted, / To breathe with our breath." This breathing alludes to the image of the child which appears often in the volume and to the work of the artist, more specifically the poet.

In the title poem, "Marconi's Cottage" (1991, 103), the speaker addresses the cottage: "Maybe you are a god of sorts, / Or a human star, lasting in spite of us"; in "Red Armchair" (102), another speaker says: "If my father dies in the wasted arms of summer, / The sudden warm flood of his melted life / Will make new constellations." At its most universal level, *Marconi's Cottage* is about gods and stars, about the possibility of light when darkness seems overwhelming. This is an elemental volume, with earth, air, fire and water prominent images. In "The Watch Fire" (53–54), McGuckian tells us, "When spring hesitates / We must wait for it." For McGuckian's female personae the end result of this waiting is new life: both the child and the poem.

As we can see, consistent themes and images run throughout McGuckian's work, and, as I suggested in the beginning of this chapter, her subject is almost always the relationship between the different facets of a woman's life. Her poetry, especially the more recent work, is decidedly autobiographical, and details, if one is willing to accept her linguistic experiments, the most profound human experiences. McGuckian is much concerned with the role of the woman artist, but within the larger framework of women's multiple lives.

In one of her more subtle but extremely significant responses to the male tradition of Irish writing, McGuckian introduces a new image in the poem "Sky-Writing" (1991, 79), as she alludes to Yeats's famous poem, "Leda and the Swan." Talking from the sky to the town below her, Leda becomes a typical McGuckian heroine, describing her escape: "I forfeit the world outside / For the sake of my own inwardness." Like Yeats's Leda, McGuckian's speaker is swept away, but she is making her own choices: "I abandon myself to its incubative weight," she says, distinguishing herself from the helpless Leda over whom Zeus has total power. Again seeing writing as intercourse with her muse, Leda here poses the Yeatsian question: "Being seen like this by you, / A steeply perched, uplooking town, / Am I the same in a more strengthened way?" The final lines of this poem rewrite Yeats's drama, as a woman poet expresses how she feels after this union:

> I am on the point of falling
> Like the essence of rain or a letter
> Of ungiveable after-love into the next degree

Of spring, its penultimate tones:
Shall I ever again be caught up gently
As the rustle of a written address by the sky?

In this new version of intercourse with the gods, Leda is speaking, not spoken about. She has become the female poet, not the subject of the male poet, and is willing to abandon herself to the "incubative weight" of her *own* inwardness for some "Sky-Writing." The struggle described in this poem is a far cry from Yeats's image of a woman raped, and an important difference arises from the fact that in this poem Leda appears not as passive female but as willing participant in the development of her own "inwardness." In this poem, as in much of McGuckian's other work, the value of a very complex female consciousness, with all its multiple voices and variants, cannot be overestimated. "Sky-Writing" is about pregnancy and poetry.

Nuala Ní Dhomhnaill.
Courtesy of Wake Forest University Press.

6

Nuala Ní Dhomhnaill

For a contemporary Irish poet, the legacy of the Irish language presents both possibilities and problems. Schooled primarily in English, most of the well-known poets write in that language, a natural consequence of their upbringing and education and the broader audience they write for. But, attuned to the nuances of language, the links between language and culture, and the political implications of the disappearance of a native tongue, some modern poets try to keep Irish alive while writing in English. Seamus Heaney and Paul Muldoon, for example, make liberal use of Irish place names and fragments of the older language that survive in the English spoken in Ireland.[1] Other poets, including Eithne Strong, Rita Kelly, and Michael Hartnett, write in both Irish and English.

But in Ireland today an appreciable number of poets write only in Irish. Some of the best known of these are women poets, among them Máire Mhac an tSaoi and Biddy Jenkinson, who are recognized for their achievements in the Irish language.[2] Another poet, Nuala Ní Dhomhnaill, writes in Irish but has a wider audience because of translations that focused the attention of non-Irish speakers on her work, affording Ní Dhomhnaill not only a larger reading public but also recognition as a major force in contemporary poetry. The dual-language format of her *Selected Poems/Rogha Dánta*, issued in 1988 by Raven Arts Press, provides English translations by Hartnett and Ní Dhomhnaill her-

---

1. Ní Dhomhnaill describes Heaney's work in this regard as "clearing home fields" (1987, 42).
2. *Dánta Ban/Poems of Irish Women, Early and Modern,* an anthology of poems by and about women selected and translated by P. L. Henry, was published by Mercier Press in Dublin in 1990. Included are poems by Eibhlín Ní Mhurchú, Máire Mhac an tSaoi, and Nuala Ní Dhomhnaill.

In 1990 Máire Mhac an tSaoi reviewed five recent volumes of poetry in Irish, including four by women poets. She notes that the latest surveys suggest that there fewer than 9,000 people who still speak Irish in the home (1990, 96).

self. Her 1990 volume, *Pharaoh's Daughter,* a dual-language collection of forty-five poems, about half of which are new, contains translations by thirteen of Ireland's best-known poets. In another dual-language volume, *The Astrakhan Cloak* (1992), Paul Muldoon translates a selection from *Feis,* Ní Dhomhnaill's Irish collection.

Although a discussion of poems in translation creates inevitable problems and restrictions, I have chosen to do so because Ní Dhomhnaill's poems, in Irish and English, have had quite an impact over the last few years. Although Ní Dhomhnaill has translated some of her poems into English and has cooperated with others on translations, she defines herself as a poet of the Irish language. Anyone who reads the poems in Irish, or has ever heard Ní Dhomhnaill read her poems in Irish (for she is quite a good reader), appreciates that much is lost in translation. One can indeed argue that English cannot do justice to the Irish originals, that they are in fact very different poems. Interpretation and evaluation of a poem in one language will not necessarily work for the poem in another because the sound and style of the original have their own inherent values. But translations often pose such problems, and arguments about the value of translation are often raised.[3]

The larger issue, in a study of Irish women writers, concerns Ní Dhomhnaill's contribution to contemporary poetry, especially when these translations make her work available to non-Irish readers within and beyond the borders of Ireland. For those who read her work in English, an audience that, given the availability of the translations, is steadily increasing, Ní Dhomhnaill's unique voice and imagery open up a new perspective on the Irish woman, introducing a revolutionary image of the female to contemporary poetry. This image comes through quite clearly in the English translations, even though the subtle nuances of the Irish language are lost.

The last poem in *Pharaoh's Daughter,* "Ceist na Teangan"/"The Language Issue" (1990, 154–55), with its allusions to Moses' mother's choice between turning her infant over to the Egyptians or exposing him to the dangers of the Nile, touches on the politics of the Irish/English language question when Ní Dhomhnaill describes the unforeseen voyage a poem might take from writer to reader:

---

3. The issue of translation, and the relationship between Irish and English literature as this applies to the woman writer, is discussed by Máirín Nic Eoin (1992). In a review of Ní Dhomhnaill's *Pharaoh's Daughter,* Robert Welch notes that in these translations "Irish itself is being sustained by no less a presence than the English language itself" (1992, 129).

Cuirim mo dhóchas ar snámh
i mbáidín teangan
faoi mar a leagfá naíonán
i gcliabhán
a bheadh fite fuaite
de dhuilleoga feileastraim
is bitiúman agus pic
bheith cuimilte lena thóin

ansan é a leagadh síos
i measc na ngiolcach
is coigeal na mban sí
le taobh na habhann,
féachaint n'fheadaraís
cá dtabharfaidh an sruth é,
féachaint, dála Mhaoise,
an bhfóirfidh iníon Fharoinn?

Paul Muldoon translates:

I place my hope on the water
in this little boat
of the language, the way a body might put
an infant

in a basket of intertwined
iris leaves,
its underside proofed
with bitumen and pitch,

then set the whole thing down amidst
the sedge
and bulrushes by the edge
of a river

only to have it borne hither and thither,
not knowing where it might end up;
in the lap, perhaps,
of some Pharaoh's daughter.

The "hither and thither" Ní Dhomhnaill's poems have reached range from the Irish speakers in the *Gaeltacht,* areas where Irish is the primary language, to the English-speaking world and larger international poetry circles. Her Irish is both a literary and political statement: "I feel that what I represent," Ní Dhomhnaill has said, "is the aboriginal Irish somehow" (1987, 42).

Born in England but raised in the *Gaeltacht* in Kerry, Ní Dhomhnaill finds Irish a natural language in which to write. But the native language has another value: as a woman poet, she sees a way to recover the female voice in Irish poetry that the English male tradition gradually eclipsed. When Ní Dhomhnaill was asked about the connections she feels to ancient Irish women poets, she responded:

> A great one. There was Liadán, of the Corca Dhuibhne, my tribe of the Dingle Peninsula. She refused to marry her one great love, the poet Cuirithir, in case he stole her poetry, and she was dead right. Then there was Eibhlín Dubh Ní Chonaill and her great keen of love and lust and hate. And there in the *Táin* was Fedelm Banfhile. . . . Fedelm's poem is prophetic, it has a Cassandra quality, and I think that is what is emerging in our generation of women poets. As we aborigines are just now getting back to what we were going on about before the Norman invasions, likewise we female aborigines are beginning to get back to what we were going on about before we were interrupted by the male side of the psyche that caused Christianity and witch-burning. We are going back to where the sybil was interrupted in mid-sentence by the invasions. (Ní Dhomhnaill 1987, 43)

In Gaelic society before the sixteenth- and seventeenth-century colonization of Ireland, women enjoyed a higher status and greater independence than they have since. Although much work remains to be done in uncovering their role in pre-Christian and Early Christian Ireland, the historian Margaret Mac Curtain argues that literary evidence suggests that women shared equal status with men (Mac Curtain and O'Dowd 1991).

Much of the reconstruction of Gaelic society, however, comes from a study of mythology, and as Helen Lanigan Wood points out in "Women in Myths and Early Depictions," a study of Irish mythology leaves little doubt of the high status and powerful roles female deities enjoyed. Because "all the heroines of medieval Irish literature are adaptations in human terms of the archetypal female deity," Wood suggests, "all the authority and confidence of the goddess is extended in the literature to her human counterpart" (1985, 17).

In *The Serpent and the Goddess: Women, Religion and Power in Celtic Ireland,* Mary Condren traces the decline of matriarchal religion in Ireland under the influence of patriarchal Christianity. Condren describes the Celtic deities and their legacy in Irish culture:

> Goddesses permeated Ireland. Mountains, rivers, valleys, wells, all testified to her presence. Around the eleventh century, Ireland became known primarily as Éire, a name derived from the Goddess Éiru, one of the Triple Goddesses: Éiru, Banba, Fotla. In a famous story of one of the Celtic invasions, Éiru makes it clear that anyone wishing to enter Ireland would have to revere the goddesses if they wished to prosper and be fruitful. Ireland was also often called "the island of Banba of the women." (1989, 26)

Irish literature and legend, then, supply Ní Dhomhnaill with images of strong women, with goddesses and queens who wield authority equal to or greater than that of their male counterparts. The Irish female goddesses are particularly interesting because they combine the functions of fertility and land protection. In the latter role they have a great deal of prestige but also, as Miranda Green explains in *The Gods of the Celts,* "a propensity for death, chaos and destruction" (1986, 120). Green points out that though these goddesses did not themselves necessarily engage in battle, they "inspired terror and panic among contending warriors by magical means" (120). She cites examples from Irish mythology to illustrate:

> Badb confronted Cú Chulainn on the field of battle wearing a red cloak, with red eyebrows, driving a chariot, intent by her appearance, on unmanning the young hero. This goddess had the unpleasant habit, too, of metamorphosing into a carrion bird "Badb Catha" (battle Raven) gloating over bloodshed. That such goddesses could be spiteful and capricious is demonstrated by another Cú Chulainn incident: preoccupied with fighting, the hero spurned the attentions of a young girl who turned out to be the battle-Fury, the Mórrígan. In revenge she attacked Cú Chulainn in different zoomorphic forms. (120)[4]

In her study Condren maintains that emphasis on this warrior goddess evolved as the Irish goddesses underwent a change. Using the goddess Macha to illustrate, Condren suggests that the various stories of the curse and overthrow of this goddess are "*the* foundation myth of Irish patriarchal culture" (1989, 30). Over time Macha became one of the trio

4. For more on the female goddesses, see Clark 1991, which traces the decline of the power of the goddess and charts the appearance of this figure in Anglo-Irish literature. See also Bowen 1975 and Dalton 1974.

of war goddesses, and her "status declined from Mother Goddess to consort to daughter" (35). With what Condren defines as "male reproductive consciousness" and the "birth of the hero" (36–38), a new image of the goddess appeared:

> Men no longer need the Goddess in her life-giving form, yet the goddess of death is still active, seeking out their destruction. A major change has taken place: she has suffered a subtle transformation from the goddess of death into the goddess of war. In patriarchal culture, in fact, the only goddess who is tolerated is the goddess of war: she is the only one with any real part to play, whether her name be Mother Ireland, the motherland, or Britannia. She is the one against whom, or on whose behalf, men must constantly pit their wits and their strength, and if they fail in the attempt they can say, (as was said in Ireland of the leaders of the failed "Easter Rising" of 1916) that they died for her sake. (43)

In Christianity, the Triple Goddess was replaced by the Father, Son, and Holy Spirit of the Trinity. The pagan goddess Brigit gradually evolved into the saint venerated in Irish Christianity, who as a virgin, Condren maintains, could "prop up symbolically what had increasingly become a hierarchical, centralized power structure where women in general were left at the bottom of the ladder" (1989, 78).

Images of the Great Queen, Mór, and Badb appear in many of Ní Dhomhnaill's poems, showing up in both their life-giving and their death-giving forms, when Ní Dhomhnaill restores the goddesses to the independent and active roles they once had. The red hair, the red cloak, and the zoomorphic forms often associated with them appear as well.

Ní Dhomhnaill also translates the ancient goddesses' characteristics into attributes of the human psyche. Often speaking in her own voice, a goddess expresses multiple responses to the external world. Tones that range from assertive proclamation of their many powers to self-reflective examination of their motives create an image that restores the goddesses to the status they enjoyed in early Celtic Ireland. Ní Dhomhnaill also humanizes these figures—shows them laughing or angry, loving or vengeful—and suggests ways in which they may embody archetypal sensibilities.

Reading Ní Dhomhnaill's *Selected Poems/Rogha Dánta* we see how the poet establishes a relationship between mythological figures and contemporary women. In "Mór Cráite"/"Mór Anguished" (1988, 36–37), for example, the goddess tries to explain her own impulses and behavior:

Tá Mór go dlúth fé ghlas
ina meabhairín bheag fhéin; 3"/4"/2"
ábhar liath is bán—

dearg (a bhíonn na créachta
a bháthann leath na gcuileanna
faid is a dheineann an leath eile a mbiaiste
ar fheoil na n-imeall)

'Éistíg', in ainm Dé,' ar sise leis na préacháin
is cabairí an Daingin a thagann san iarnóin
ag suathadh a mbolg.

'Tá na héinne dúnta isteach
ina ifreann féiníín féin.'

Michael Hartnett translates:

Mór, firmly under lock and key
in her own tiny mind
(2" × 4" × 3")
of grey, pinkish stuff
(here be the wounds
that drown the flies
while other flies survive
to make their maggots
on the carrion fringe).

"Listen, in God's name," she begs
the magpies and the crows
that come at evening
to upset their guts,
"every one's enclosed
in their own tiny hells."

Trying simultaneously to explain and justify her actions, Mór invokes the Christian God and hell to try to make the birds understand the mysteries of survival and destruction. The poem pictures an anguished Mór, whose power isolates and confuses her, a humanized earth goddess living through her own inferno.

This humanizing of the goddess connects the mythological poems with others in *Selected Poems/Rogha Dánta* that identify instinctual and, at times, seemingly uncontrollable feelings. The "tiny hells" exist everywhere in Ní Dhomhnaill's poems. "Breith Anabai Thar Lear"/"Miscarriage Abroad" (1988, 50–51), for example, which describes the loss of the speaker's ten weeks' fetus, seems to have little to do with the Mór poems until we hear the speaker describe the jealousy she shares with the goddesses:

> Is ní raghad
> ag féachaint linbh
> nuabheirthe mo dhlúthcharad
> ar eagla mo shúil mhillteach
> do luí air le formad.

Harnett translates:

> And I will not go to see
> my best friend's new born child
> because of the jealousy
> that stares from my evil eye.

Ní Dhomhnaill's female deities, like their human counterparts, acknowledge their "evil" side. In "Mór Gorai"/"Mór Hatching" (1988, 32–33), the goddess is warned that she needs to turn poison into honey; the speaker addresses the ugly part of herself, the Mór, that keeps surfacing:

> Táimse á rá leat,
> a Mhóir mhíchuibhseach,
> go dtiocfaidh naithreacha uaithne
> amach as do bholg
> má fhanann tú ar gor
> ar nimh na haithne
> lá níos faide.

Hartnett translates:

> I'm telling you,
> unruly Mór,
> that green snakes
> will emanate from your womb
> if you stay hatching
> out this poisoned kernel
> one day more.

The evil eye, an image of the anger and frustration a woman who has miscarried shows toward her best friend's new child, becomes an emblem for very complex human emotions. When Ní Dhomhnaill describes the hag, she also probes the causes of her behavior. More often than not, the hag reacts to loss or rejection, and redeeming her involves understanding the causes of her behavior as well as challenging traditional beliefs about the sources of evil, particularly those that are applied to the female. First and foremost, such redemption requires an image of an active rather than a passive female, and a woman who speaks for herself about herself. Both of these are abundant in Ní Dhomhnaill's poetry.

Ní Dhomhnaill's emphasis on the great energy and authority of the female inevitably results in a devalued status for some traditional male heroes. In one poem, "Agallamh Na Mór-Riona Le Cú Chulainn"/"The Great Queen Speaks. Cú Chulainn Listens" (1988, 116–19), the Queen promises revenge for Cú Chulainn's rejection of her. Claiming that she came ready to grant him both power and glory, the Queen angrily chastises the hero:

> Ach nuair a shleamhnaíos
> 'on leabaidh chughat
> dúraís, 'Cuir uait!'
> Ní tráth imeartha í seo.
> Ní ar son tóin mná
> a tugadh ar talamh mé!
> Bhí an domhan mór uile
> le bodhradh fós
> le do ghníomhartha gaile,
> bhí barr maise
> le cur ar do ghaisce,
> is do thugais droim láimhe orm
> murar thugais dorn iata.
> *All right,* mar sin,
> bíodh ina mhargadh,
> beatha dhuine a thoil.

Hartnett translates:

> But when I slipped
> into bed with you
> you said "Get off!"
> This is no time for fun
> I'm not here on behalf
> of a woman's bum!
> The wide world was yet
> to be deafened

by your great deeds
your skills had yet
to be improved
and you gave me the back of your hand
if you didn't a closed fist.
All right, so—
it's a bargain—
please yourself.

Cú Chulainn's rejection of the Queen, and her subsequent reprisals against him, have parallels outside the mythological world; the back of the hand and the closed fist portray the abuse of women at the hands of dominating men. Suggesting that Cú Chulainn has been awarded a heroic status that he might not have earned were his treatment of the Great Queen taken into account, the poems present the Queen's rebuttal and describe her ability to avenge Cú Chulainn's treatment of her.

In another poem, "An Mhór-Rion ag Cáiseamh na Baidhbhe le Cú Chulainn"/"The Great Queen Berates the Badhbh to Cú Chulainn" (1988, 122–25), the goddess warns the hero that his fear of her "womanness," his spurning her when she came as a queen "like a tree begarlanded," has put him at the mercy of the merciless Badbh, the side of her that will show him no pity:

Is í an bhadbh í,
ar foluain os cionn an tslua.
Priocann sí na súile
as na leanaí sa chliabhán.
Is í an scréachán í,
éan búistéara;

Hartnett translates:

She is the hooded crow
hovering over the crowd.
She picks the eyes
from kids in cots.
She is the screecher,
the butcher-bird:

Certainly these images revise the portrait of Cú Chulainn, the great hero of the Ulster Cycle of Irish myth. Ní Dhomhnaill's Cú Chulainn appears in his weakest moments and under the worst circumstances. In "Cú Chulainn I" (1988, 112–13), translated by Michael Hartnett, the speaker addresses him as a "Small dark rigid man," one "who'd satisfy no woman," while reminding him that he spent his first nine months in his mother's womb. These poems put Cú Chulainn in his place, and restore the Great Queen to hers. The major charge against him involves his poor treatment of women.

This type of hero is not confined to mythology, however. As she links queens and goddesses with modern women, Ní Dhomhnaill continually draws parallels between contemporary men and their mythic counterparts. "Masculus Giganticus Hibernicus" (1988, 78–79) expresses such a comparison:

> Iarsma contúirteach ón Aois Iarainn,
> suíonn tú i bpubanna is beartaíonn
> plean gníomhaíochta an fhill
> ná filleann,
> ruathar díoltais ar an bhfearann baineann.

Hartnett translates:

> Dangerous relic from the Iron Age
> you sit in pubs and devise
> the treacherous plan
> that does not recoil on you—
> a vengeful incursion to female land.

Maintaining that this "giant male" is "always after the one thing," the speaker castigates him for continually turning the female garden (the Earth Mother) into a "trampled mess." In his mythic and animal guise ("antlered," with "two broad hooves"), this man is accused of always taking what he wants: "You'd live off the furze / of the heather that grows / on a young girl's sunny slopes." A poem like this has applications to both gender and politics, the "trampled mess" evoking both woman and land, and the associations made between the two in Irish history and culture.

In the battles between the sexes in Ní Dhomhnaill's world, however, women readily confront such men and sometimes become the aggressors, bent on their own "vengeful incursions." Hence, the appearance of Medb, the queen of Connaught, a much more powerful figure than her husband, Ailill, in the narrative of the *Táin*.[5] Taunted by Ailill, Medb sets out to find an animal superior to those in his herd, setting up the Cattle

---

5. The *Táin Bó Cuailnge* has been translated by the contemporary poet Thomas Kinsella.

Raid at Cooley and the struggles between the kingdoms of Connaught
and Ulster. Medb is determined to possess the notorious Brown Bull, the
greatest in all of Ireland. After an unsuccessful attempt to borrow the
animal, Medb leads the men of Connaught into battle with Cú Chulainn
and eventually captures the bull.

In Ní Dhomhnaill's poem "Labhrann Medb"/"Medb Speaks" (1988,
110–11), the queen announces her intentions, speaking as a woman who
moves into male territory. No Grecian princess, this woman demands
respect on her own terms. Again, the poem links gender and political
oppression:

> Fógraim cogadh feasta
> ar fhearaibh uile Éireann,
> ar na leaids ag na cúinni sráide
> is iad ina luí i lúib i gceas naíon,
> a bpilibíní gan liúdar
> is gan éileamh acu ar aon bhean
> ach le teann fearaíochta is laochais
> ag maíomh gur iníon rí Gréige
> a bhí mar chéile leapan aréir acu,
> is fógraím cogadh cruaidh feasta.
> . . . .
> Tabharfad fogha feasta
> tré thailte méithe Éireann
> mo chathláin réidh faoi threalamh,
> mo bhantracht le mo thaobh liom,
> is ní tarbh a bheidh á fhuadach,
> ní ar bheithígh a bheidh an chlismirt
> ach éiric atá míle uair
> níos luachmhaire, mo dhínit;
> is fógraím fogha fíochmhar feasta.

Hartnett translates:

> War I declare from now
> on all the men of Ireland
> on all the corner-boys
> lying curled in children's cradles
> their willies worthless
> wanting no woman
> all macho boasting
> last night they bedded

a Grecian princess—
a terrible war I will declare.

. . . .

I will make incursions
through the fertile land of Ireland
my battalions all in arms
my amazons beside me
(not just to steal a bull
not over beasts this battle—
but for an honour-price
a thousand times more precious—
my dignity).
I will make fierce incursions.

Contrasted to this world of "corner boys . . . curled in children's cradles" is one in which women and children are heroes. In "Ag Cothú Linbh"/"Feeding a Child" (1988, 86–89), for example, a mother describes a different type of exploring hands as she addresses her nursing infant:

is do dhoirne beaga
ag gabháilt ar mo chíoch.
Tánn tú ag gnúsacht le taitneamh,
ag meangadh le míchiall.
Féachaim san aghaidh ort, a linbh,
is n'fheadar an bhfeadaraís
go bhfuil do bhólacht
ag iníor i dtalamh na bhfathach,
ag slad is ag bradaíocht,
is nach fada go gcloisfir
an "fí-faidh-fó-fum"
ag teacht thar do ghuaille aniar.

Tusa mo mhuicín a chuaigh
ar an margadh,
a d'fhan age baile,
a fuair arán agus im
is ná fuair dada.
Is mór liom de ghreim tú
agus is beag liom de dhá ghreim,
is maith liom do chuid feola
ach ní maith liom do chuid anraith.

> Is cé hiad pátrúin bhunaidh
> na laoch is na bhfathach
> munar thusa is mise?

Hartnett translates:

> As my breast is explored
> by your small hand
> you grunt with pleasure
> smiling and senseless.
> I look into your face child
> not knowing if you know
> your herd of cattle
> graze in the land of giants
> trespassing and thieving
> and that soon you will hear
> the fee-fie-fo-fum
> sounding in your ear.
>
> You are my piggy
> who went to market
> who stayed at home
> who got bread and butter
> who got none
> There's one good bite in you
> but hardly two—
> I like your flesh
> but not the broth thereof
> And who are the original patterns
> of the heroes and the giants
> if not you and I?

Exploring the world of fairy tales and myths for expressions of values, the mother speaking here claims her and her child's status as heroes; like her alter ego, Medb, she demands something a thousand times more precious than a bull—her dignity.

The poem has historical connotations as well, with the English-Irish conflict echoing throughout. Allusions to "fee-fie-fo-fum" and smelling the blood of Englishmen, to Swift's sardonic image of Ireland as a sow who eats her children, or to "trespassing and thieving" giants of which the child "will hear" are contrasted here to the more important "original patterns" of the love between mother and child.

Another side of these mythological women involves their fertility. Their value is not restricted, as it often is in Irish Catholic female saints, to virginity or maternity. As Ní Dhomhnaill presents them, the ancient females and their modern counterparts delight in their sexuality, continually welcoming lovers to their beds and initiating sexual activities. In "Dúil" (1988, 30–31), when Mór's anguish gives way to pleasure, the tone of the poem changes, as the goddess relishes the "cornucopia" set before her:

> An fear
> lena mhealbhóg
> ag cur oscrais orm;
> na torthaí úra
> fém' shúile
> ag tarrac súlach
> óm' cheathrúna
> is an smuasach
> as croí mo chnámha;
> ag lagú
> mo ghlúine
>   go dtitim.
>   oop-la!
>   barrathuisle,
>   Mór ar lár.

Hartnett translates:

> "This man
> with his hamper
> makes me hungry,
> his fresh fruits
> before my eyes
> drawing juice
> from my thighs
> and marrow
> from my joints
> weakening my knees
> to falling point."
>   Oop-la!
>   She stumbles.
>   Mór is down.

In poem after poem, Ní Dhomhnaill's speakers celebrate the sensual pleasures of dancing, singing, eating, and sex. "Leaba Shioda" / "Labysheedy (The Silken Bed)" (1988, 154–57), translated by Ní Dhomhnaill herself, describes a speaker who makes a bed in the grass and anticipates her lover: "and what a pleasure it would be," she says, "to have our limbs entwine / wrestling / while the moths are coming down." For Ní Dhomhnaill's personae, sex involves choice, not obligation, as they actively pursue their roles as daughters of Earth. Blatantly sexual, they can be simultaneously lovers and mothers, symbolized by the Shannon Estuary (1988, 158–59), who welcomes a graphically phallic, leaping salmon:

> Is seinim seoithín
> Do mo leannán
> Tonn ar thonn
> Leathrann ar leathrann,
> Mo thine ghealáin mar bhairlín thíos faoi
> Mo rogha a thoghas féin ón iasacht.

Ní Dhomhnaill translates:

> And I will sing a lullaby
> to my lover
> wave on wave,
> stave upon half-stave,
> my phosphorescence as bed-linen under him,
> my favourite, whom I, from afar have chosen.

In their forays back into the old religion, Ní Dhomhnaill's speakers sometimes find themselves in conflict with the newer creeds, in which the image of woman changed when the earthy, sexual, and powerful goddesses gave way to asexual saints. In "Scéala"/"Annunciations" (1988, 44–45), Ní Dhomhnaill pictures Mary remembering the angelic vision, while Christ "went away / and perhaps forgot / what grew from his loins—": the two thousand years of "smoke," "fire," and "rows" that Christianity generated. The speaker addresses Mary, the Christian saint, in the words of the Catholic prayer, "Memorare," remarking, woman to woman, on her lack of sexuality:

> Ó, a mhaighdean rócheansa,
> nár chuala trácht ar éinne riamh
> ag teacht chughat sa doircheacht
> cosnocht, déadgheal
> is a shúile lán de rógaireacht.

Hartnett translates:

> Remember
> O most tender virgin Mary
> that never was it known
> that a man came to you
> in the darkness alone,
> his feet bare, his teeth white
> and roguery swelling in his eyes.

The obvious contrast with older goddesses, who were neither "tender" nor "virgin," points to the problems with the images of women that the Christian fathers created and promoted.

Such a woman, identified as the source of original sin and the seducer of Adam, comes to explain herself in the poem "Manach"/"Monk" (1988, 56–57):

> Mise Temptation,
> aithníonn tú mé.
> Uaireanta is Éabha,
> uaireanta is nathair nimhe mé.
> Éirím chun t'aigne
> i lár an lae ghléighil ghlé.
> Soilsím mar ghrian in úllghort.

Hartnett translates:

> I am Temptation.
> You know me.
> Sometimes I'm Eve,
> sometimes the snake:
> I slide into your reverie
> in the middle of brightest day.
> I shine like the sun in an orchard.

The monk, like his ancestor Cú Chulainn, fears "womanness"; the threat she presents to his highly valued chastity forces him to turn woman into an image of evil, to deny her sexual worth and make sinful the pleasure that she brings. In the final lines of this poem, however, the speaker describes another kind of annunciation, restoring the value of female sexuality as she explains to the monk what he should see:

> Is ní chun do chráite
> a éirím gach lá,
> ach chun do bháite

faoi leáspairtí grá.
Léim gaiscígh i bhFlaitheas
de dhroim dhroichead Scáthaigh
faoi deara dhom triall riamh ort
a apstail, a mhanaigh.

Hartnett translates:

But it's not to torment you
every day I rise—
but to drown you
in love's delights.
I'm a dead hero leaping
from the edge of the bridge of fear—
That's the only reason I haunt you:
my monk, my apostle, my priest.

This welcoming woman, with her corrective revision, appears often in Ní Dhomhnaill's poems, even when her visitor arrives unexpectedly. Her message is always the same, whether she greets a human lover or a god come down to earth. In "An Cuairteoir"/"The Visitor" (1988, 48–49), we hear her offer hospitality to Christ:

'A Dhé dhílis, dé do bheatha,
fág uait do Choróin Spíne is do Chrois,
druid suas i dtreo na tine is bí id' shuí,
dein do chuid féin den tigh is lig do scíth,
fearaim na céadta fáilte romhat, a Rí.'

Hartnett translates:

"You're welcome here, my Lord,
uncross, uncrown yourself of thorns:
shove up to the fire and sit yourself,
make yourself at home and rest,
My King, I garland you with welcoming."

The image of the garland links this speaker with the Great Queen, who appeared "be-garlanded" before Cú Chulainn only to be rejected. The ancient goddess speaks here in the voice of a contemporary woman who offers comfort to the new religion's God in his human incarnation.

The rest of the poem suggests, however, that he cannot accept her gifts, as Cú Chulainn could not accept Medb's. Ní Dhomhnaill's speaker assumes an importance equal to that of her visitor but complains that the

"Lord" takes no notice of her. When he clasps her hand and squeezes the air out of her lungs, her belly swells and her breasts go slack as she becomes a nonsexual, silent mother. The final lines of the poem delineate the tragic fate the Great Mother suffered as she turned into the Blessed Virgin. Ní Dhomhnaill's speaker usurps the words of the victimized Christ to plead her own case. The words, "Lord, I am not worthy," spoken in the Catholic Mass as a communicant accepts the body of Christ, echo ironically as a woman suggests how her gifts, including her body, have been made unworthy by the followers of Christ. This is the burden, the "chalice," that the Great Mother and all women have to bear in the history of Christianity.

Mary Condren, in her study of Celtic goddesses, which Ní Dhomhnaill has called "exciting and pioneering," explains the effects of these biblical images of women:

> Women have been identified with Eve, the symbol of evil, and can only attain sanctity by identifying with the Virgin Mary, the opposite of Eve. But this is an impossible task since we are told that Mary herself "was conceived without sin" and when she gave birth to Jesus remained a virgin. To reach full sanctity then, women have to renounce their sexuality, symbol of their role as Temptresses and the means by which they drag men down from their lofty heights. For this reason most of the women saints of the Catholic Church have been either virgins, martyrs, widows, or married women who have taken a perpetual vow of continence. Sex and spirituality have become polar opposites in Christian teaching (1989, 5).

Ní Dhomhnaill's poem "Cnámh"/"Bone" (1988, 96–97), translated by Michael Hartnett, works from the same premise when it suggests that traditionally Eve is seen as either evil temptress or sacrificing mother. The first mother complains that her sexuality has made her an archetypal sinner, for, when pleasure became sinful, Eve and her descendants became sinners. Such revising of Eve links Ní Dhomhnaill not only to other contemporary Irish poets like Eavan Boland and Eithne Strong but also to women poets in other nations who offer alternatives to traditional mythic and religious female figures.

In "Táimid Damanta, a Dheirféaracha"/"We Are Damned, My Sisters" (1988, 14–17), Ní Dhomhnaill comments on the legacy of Eve when she describes a group of women who defy it:

> Chaitheamair oícheanta ar bhántaibh Párthais
> ag ithe úll is spíonán is róiseanna
> laistiar dár gcluasa ag rá amhrán

> timpeall tinte cnámh na ngadaithe,
> ag ól is ag rangás le mairnéalaigh agus robálaithe
> is táimid damanta, a dheirféaracha.

Hartnett translates:

> We spent nights in Eden's fields
> eating apples, gooseberries; roses
> behind our ears, singing songs
> around the gipsy bon-fires
> drinking and romping with sailors and robbers:
> and so we're damned, my sisters.

Refusing to play roles assigned to them, these women explain how they choose not to be handmaidens or helpmates, neither darning stockings nor making tea, but dancing on the shore. A mixture of celebration, defiance, and loss creates the tone of this poem; the shift from the present tense, "We are damned, my sisters," at the end of the first stanza, to the future, "when we are damned," in the final line, suggests that while the condemnation has already had its effect, the voice of the sisters has not totally been silenced. The poem seems as much a rallying call as a memorial, more challenge to the damnation than acquiescence.

Despite her questioning of Christianity's vision of women, especially of Mary, Ní Dhomhnaill is still attracted to its symbols and its stories, some of which, like the Annunciation and the Virgin Birth, can be traced back to pre-Christian narratives. "Parthenogenesis" (1988, 132–35) tells the story of a lady of the Ó Moores, married and childless, who, while swimming one day, sees a shadow come close enough to touch her. Frightened and numbed, the woman metamorphoses into a mermaid and, escaping under water, changes into coral. After a long sleep she swims to shore, lingering near death for nine months until giving birth to a boy, much to her own and her husband's satisfaction. Noting that this story is told in many different versions in the coastal areas of Ireland, the speaker comments on the miracle birth, stressing how the woman feels:

> Ach is cuma cér dhíobh í, is chuige seo atáim
> gurb ionann an t-uamhan a bhraith sí is an scáth
> á leanúint síos is an buaireamh a líon
> croí óg na Maighdine nuair a chuala sí
> clog binn na n-aingeal is gur inchollaíodh
> ina broinn istigh, de réir dealramh, Mac Dé Bhí.

Hartnett translates:

> But whoever she was I want to say
> that the fear she felt
> when the sea-shadow followed her
> is the same fear that vexed
> the young heart of the Virgin
> when she heard the angel's sweet bell
> and in her womb was made flesh
> by all accounts
> the Son of the Living God.

The poem suggests that the conception of Christ, when the shadow of the Holy Spirit passed over the Blessed Virgin, has analogues in other tales, part of a female "heroic heritage" not unique to Christianity. The title "Parthenogenesis" highlights the major role of the female in this creation, and with her seemingly offhand and certainly understated remark, "Whoever she was," the speaker moves the spotlight from the male child to the archetypal mother-creator who bears the Son of God.

With this change in emphasis, Ní Dhomhnaill places the Christian story within a larger mythological framework, where the mother and her husband, "so full of love for this new son / forgot the shadow in the sea." Indeed, this shadow, described as "like a man's," might be seen as the woman's own: "And every twist and turn she made / the shadow did the same / and came close enough to touch." A poem like this reminds us that there are many stories that attempt to explain the sources and mysteries of human life; ultimately, it insists that a creator need not be, nor has always been imagined as, a male. The female role of creator is highlighted, and an Irish tale, older than the New Testament story of the birth of Christ, is given equal status.

In her introduction to Ní Dhomhnaill's *Selected Poems/Rogha Dánta*, Máire Mhac an tSaoi, whose poetry has been cited as some of the best in the Irish language, claims that Ní Dhomhnaill's Irish is "like that of children brought up by their grandmothers, a hundred years old, a kind of miracle of survival" (Ní Dhomhnaill 1988, 9). She also explains that Ní Dhomhnaill's poetry is relevant to our age because of what it brings from the west of Ireland:

> The idyll of Irish rural life was not simpleminded; it had an overt and articulated darker side, which can come effortlessly to terms even with

the sadism and Satanism of our present rootless and drifting mass culture, teach us the control techniques we need to survive in such a world—nothing new under the sun! It is strange and deeply heartening that the forces of darkness, once confronted and reduced to numbers, are less scary. (9)

In some poems, Ní Dhomhnaill dramatizes those forces in a modern setting, where the Great Mother becomes the perpetrator of contemporary disasters, rebuking us for our abuse of the earth. In "An Ollmháthair Mhór"/"Great Mother" (1988, 58–59), translated by Michael Hartnett, Ní Dhomhnaill suggests that the effects of bombs and acid rain are the Earth Goddess's reprimand for our failure of respect: "Tá sciorta det fhallaing le feiscint ag íor na spéire." / "The fringe of your cloak is on the horizon." Like Cú Chulainn, who rejects the love of the Great Goddess, those who desecrate the earth suffer as she appears on the horizon, Badb come again. Union with her becomes a perverse form of love where the Earth Goddess answers our arrogance with a terrible embrace in which the very clay of the earth, her great-coat, will cover us. Set next to the poem, "Agallamh Na Mór-Riona Le Cú Chulainn"/"The Great Queen Speaks. Cú Chulainn Listens," this image of a world destroyed by technological abuse shows how much the old stories can still teach us.

Ní Dhomhnaill's poetry insists that we respect and value nature in its numerous aspects, that we accept and try to understand both pleasure and pain. Repressing natural instincts, Ní Dhomhnaill suggests, denies us the comfort we need to counteract the tragedy and disaster we must also cope with. In poem after poem, Ní Dhomhnaill exhorts us to enjoy the fullness of the natural world, accepting the gifts of the senses. In "Dán Do Mhelissa"/"Poem for Melissa" (1988, 136–37),[6] the goddess becomes a contemporary woman who grants her young daughter the gifts of the earth:

Bheadh geataí an ghairdín ar leathadh go moch is go déanach,
ní bheadh claimhte lasrach á fhearadh ag Ceiribín,
níor ghá dhuit duilliúr fige mar naprún íochtair
sa domhain úrnua a bhronnfainn ort mín mín.

A iníon bhán, seo dearbhú ó do mháithrín
go mbeirim ar láimh duit an ghealach is an ghrian
is go seasfainn le mo chorp féin idir dhá bhró an mhuilinn
i muilte Dé chun nach meilfí tú mín mín.

6. Ní Dhomhnaill has a daughter named Melissa.

Hartnett translates:

> The garden gates forever wide open
> no flaming swords in hands of Cherubim
> no need for a fig-leaf apron here
> in the pristine world I would delicately give.

> Oh white daughter here's your mother's word:
> I will put in your hand the sun and the moon
> I will stand my body between the millstones
> in God's mills so you are not totally ground.

This mother's gift, a "pristine world" before the Fall, is essentially the world of the "sisters" who are damned, a world Ní Dhomhnaill redeems. In the voice of her persona, we hear the strength of the Great Mother, the power of Queen Medb, and the courage of all women who demand "dignity" and insist that they not be damned for accepting the pleasures of the natural world. This theme appears again and again in Ní Dhomhnaill's *Selected Poems/Rogha Dánta*.

In *Pharaoh's Daughter* (1990), Ní Dhomhnaill's imagery stresses the connections between cultures, as she continues to focus on women. Half of the poems in this collection are new, and the list of thirteen translators, among them John Montague, Medbh McGuckian, Ciaran Carson, and Eiléan Ní Chuilleanáin, includes some of the most important voices in contemporary Irish poetry. The image of Pharaoh's daughter, explicit in the final poem, "Ceist na Teangan"/"The Language Issue" (1990, 155), translated by Paul Muldoon, is part of a pattern of imagery in which biblical stories are set beside the tales of Irish folklore.

Merging mythic and biblical Creation stories, the speaker in "Mac Airt" (1990, 76–79) describes a dream in which a bear takes her in "his hairy grip." Alluding to legends in which "the fish jumps / into your hand" or "the Christ seed / sprouts within," the pregnant speaker says that she will not name her child Emmanuel, David, or Jesus; she will call him after Cormac Mac Airt, a fourth-century king of Ireland. Seeing herself as Mary (the "brute groan" her Angelus), the speaker imagines herself as kingbearer, creatrix of the Savior. The second part of the poem, the ironic "Fonóta feimineach bliain ina dhiaidh sin:"/"Feminist footnote a year later," carries the revising one step farther as the seed blossoms into a baby girl, the latest version of Ní Dhomhnaill's female deity:

> Mar a tharlaíonn,
> séard a bhí agam sa deireadh
> ná iníon.
> Tá clúmh mín ar ghach orlach

dona corp
is ní baol di—
tá sí ciotarúnta gramhsach.

Tom Mac Intyre translates:

Unto me
as it happened
a daughter was given,

on every inch
of her body
this fine down—

no harm to her—
berserk the light
of her impudent eye.

A fascination with miracles, whether in the fantastic stories of Irish folklore and biblical history or in the seemingly more ordinary birth of a daughter, blends the world of everyday experience with the transcendental world of religion, legend, and myth. While many of these poems, like "Féar Suaithinseach"/"Miraculous Grass" (1990, 32–35), translated by Seamus Heaney, merge these two worlds, in the final lines of "Chomh Leochaileach le Sliogán"/"As Fragile as a Shell" (84–89), translated by Derek Mahon, a dejected speaker simplifies the definition of miracles to its most basic:

Mar is istigh sa sícé amháin
a tharlíonn míorúiltí
an cheana, an mhaithiúnachais
is an ghrá
mar is i dtaibhrithe amháin
a bhíonn an ghrian is an ré ag soilsiú
le chéile is spéir na maidne
orthu araon ag láú.

It is only in the soul
that the miracles take place
of love, forgiveness and grace;
it is only in dreams
that the sun and moon shine together
in a bright sky
while day dawns on them both.

The fantastic and its place in the lives of the Irish is given high status in Ní Dhomhnaill's poems. So in "An Ceann"/"The Head" (1990, 14–19), translated by Ciaran Carson, we hear the story of Tom the Head, who, among other achievements, used his giant skull to put "a cracker of a head butt / Clean through" a coffin. But, the poem tells us, Tom's miracles were minor compared to those of the Child of the Glen, who, according to local legend, lived in the 1780s. This child picked up a grown man, Tommy Connor, and was ready to toss him over a cliff when his mother intervened. When the child died at thirteen, the story goes, it took six strong men to lift his coffin. The speaker explains the value of such tales:

> Ach cén bhaint atá aige seo go léir liomsa
> nó caith uait na céapars, a deireann tú.
> Tá, go siúlann na daoine seo go léir, go reigleálta
> isteach i mo thaibhrithe. Inné roimh lá
> bhí fathach mór d'fhear óg, an Leanbh, ní foláir,
> trasna an chuain uainn is bhíos-sa agus na leanaí
> ag iarraidh é a mhealladh chughainn anall
> tré sholas a lasadh, faoi mar a bheadh tóirse gluaisteáin
> ann/as, ann/as, ann/as—trí lasadh fada
> is trí cinn ghearra arís, ar chuma S.O.S.
> Féachaint an dtuigfeadh sé an scéala
> is go dtiocfadh sé i leith;
> féachaint an bhféadfaimis teangmháil a dhéanamh leis ar
>   deireadh.

Carson translates:

> But what has this to do with anything, you might say, all this
>   bullshit?
> Just this: these people swim into my ken with marvellous
> Regularity. Just yesterday, before first light, an enormous
>   giant of a youngster—
> It could only be the Child—was signalling across the bay to us
> And the children and myself were trying to guide him over to
>   our side,
> Flashing a light—a car flashlight, maybe—on/off, on/
> Off, on/off . . . three long bursts and three
> Short bursts, three long ones again, for all the world like
>   S.O.S.—
> Hoping he would get the message, trying to see if he would talk
>   to us,
> Or, finally, if we could talk to him.

In poems like this in *Pharaoh's Daughter,* Ní Dhomhnaill continually links the sacred and the sensual, the religious and the secular. In "Caoineadh Mhoss Martin"/"Lament for Moss Martin" (1990, 44–47), an elegy for the musician Moss Martin (translated by George O'Brien), Ní Dhomhnaill imagines him as another Moses, the piper who will "play up now, lure us / to the Promised Land." The Ark of the Covenant has counterparts in nature: the pike in the "flat stomach of the lake"; the seed that "lies dormant in the damp, sunless clay / Despite the world's having difficulty breathing." And the female speaker in "Iarúsailéim" / "Jerusalem" (1990, 138–39), translated by Tom Mac Intyre, imagines herself as the sacred city, using Old Testament imagery. Rewriting the major western narratives from an Irish and a female point of view, Ní Dhomhnaill undercuts the expectations of her readers while she reimagines conventional literary images.

One image that undergoes revision is the muse. Several of these poems have as their subject what Ní Dhomhnaill calls the "male muse." She describes herself as a woman writer "returning the compliment" to males who, inspired by a female muse, have written in praise of the female body (Somerville-Arjat and Wilson 1990, 150–51).

The traditional image of Ireland as female is evoked in the poem "Oileán"/"Island" (1990, 40–43), which describes a man's body:

> Oileán is ea do chorp
> i lár na mara móire.
> Tá do ghéaga spréite bhraillín
> gléigeal os farraige faoileán.

John Montague translates:

> Your nude body is an island
> asprawl on the ocean bed. How
> beautiful your limbs, spread-
> eagled under seagulls' wings!

"Gan do Chuid Éadaigh"/"Nude" (1990, 90–93), translated by Paul Muldoon, is more direct: "The long and short / of it is I'd far rather see you nude—." "Fear"/"Looking at a Man" (1990, 140–43), translated by Eiléan Ní Chuilleanáin, blends the ideal with the real in a woman's description of her physical attraction to a man.

Images of women appear frequently in *Pharaoh's Daughter* in poems that range from a modern view of the Shan Van Vocht to an elegy for one of Ní Dhomhnaill's female relatives. While there are few poems in this volume about goddesses, there are many that explore diverse images of the female.

The Shan Van Vocht, the old woman celebrated in a 1798 ballad, is an enduring figure who appears in many guises in Irish legend and culture but is best known in the modern age in the literature of the Revival. David Cairns and Shaun Richards describe her modern reincarnation and the gender implications of this image:

> In plays of the Revival the presentation of "Ireland" as the "Poor Old Woman" or "Shan Van Vocht" had obvious advantages for dramatists, stemming from the popularity of the trope in ballads and Irish language poems, and its familiarity to audiences whose reading of it was unambiguously nationalist. . . . Thus endorsed, the notion of an Ireland, symbolically represented as "woman," whose destiny was to be independent and united, passed into the educational and cultural formation of two generations of Irish men and women. (1991, 129–130)

In another form, as Cathleen Ní Houlihan, the old woman became identified with self-sacrifice for the nation. In Yeats's play, for example, Cathleen faces a choice between her personal needs and those of the nation; she sacrifices and gets what Cairns and Richards call "consequent immortality for those who heed the call, and rejuvenation for the Mother/Nation." This rejuvenation is reflected in the transformation of the old woman into a young girl, who had, in Yeats's play, "the walk of a Queen."

In Ní Dhomhnaill's poem, "An tSeanbhean Bhocht"/"The Shan Van Vocht" (1990, 128–131), translated by Ciaran Carson, the Shan Van Vocht comes under the scrutiny of a cynical speaker who sees her as an old crank. Alluding to the effect of the traditional transformed Cathleen, Ní Dhomhnaill writes of those betrayed by this image:

> Féachann sí orm anois leis an dtruamhéil fhuar
> a chífeá go minic i súile a bhí tráth óg is breá,
> ag meabhrú di féin im fhianaise, leath os íseal
> is leath os ard, gur mhéanar don té a fuair amharc
> ar an gcéad lá a shiúil sí go mómharach síos an phromanáid
> mar ríon faoina parasól; ar na céadta céadta gaiscíoch
> is fear breá a chuaigh le saighdiúireacht in arm na Breataine
> nó a theith leo ar bord loinge go dtí na tíortha teo,
> aon ní ach éaló ós na saigheada éagóra
> a theilgeadh sí orthu de shíor faoina fabhraí tiubha.

Carson translates:

> That icy-blue pity stares through me, she
> Whose eyes were radiant once with youth and blue fire—
> How privileged they were, the poor unfortunates
> Who caught a glimpse of her in all her majesty, gliding
> On the promenade beneath a queenly parasol; the regiments
> Of stricken youths who took to soldiering, who
> Laboured in the White Man's Grave, anything
> To flee the blue illicit lightning
> She squandered from those eyes.

Describing the Shan Van Vocht now as "cantankerous / And cancered," the poem presents her as a self-pitying old woman in a wheelchair, remembering halcyon days, nightingales ("no common birds"), and diamonds dripping from her ears. The source of neither wisdom nor terror, she has become a babbling old woman, out of touch with the world around her. Venting her frustration, the persona comments:

> is gur ag dul i mínithe is i mbréagaí atá gach dream
> dá dtagann: gach seanrá thagann isteach i mo chloigeann,
> aon rud ach an tseanbhean bhaoth seo a choiméad socair

Carson translates:

> Folly, I'm saying, gets worse with every generation:
> Anything, every old cliché in the book, anything at all
> To get this old bitch to shut the fuck up.

No longer transformed, Ní Dhomhnaill's Shan Van Vocht becomes an emblem whose jaded past embodies the destruction of those enamored of her. Cutting through the romanticism of the traditional figure, Ní Dhomhnaill reconstructs her as a privileged, aristocratic "lady" who had no sense of the real lives of others around her, a "cliché" talking for too long.

In contrast to the figure of the Shan Van Vocht is a portrait of a real woman at the turn of the century, one of Ní Dhomhnaill's aunts, the subject of "In Memoriam Elly Ní Dhomhnaill (1884–1963)" (1990, 24–27), translated by George O'Brien. An honors graduate in biology, this woman returned from the university to her home, but she never married because "No one around was good enough for her." Spiteful, she fought with her brother, with her father, even with the parish priest over his reading the pledges aloud in the middle of Mass. Her righteous challenge to male authority becomes her hallmark and the poem ends with a description of her behavior:

Thuig sí an t-uaibhreas
a chuirfeadh ar dhaoine bochta
íoc thar a gcumas don Eaglais
ag fágáil a leanaí ocrach.
Dá réir sin,
shuíodh sí ina piú féin go sásta
a lámh ar a bata draighneáin
is ar a ceann hata,
fad a nglaoití amach ón altóir
'Elly Ní Dhomhnaill—dada'.

O'Brien translates:

She saw right well the cheek—
imposing on the poor
to pay the Church beyond their means
and leave their children hungry.
On that account, she'd sit
satisfied in her own pew,
hand on her blackthorn,
hat on her head,
awaiting the call from the altar,
'Elly Ní Dhomhnaill—nothing.'

As Maureen Murphy says, Ní Dhomhnaill "would count her aunt Elly Ní Dhomhnaill one of her 'sisters' not for the public virtues of lineage, physical courage, and generosity, but for the private ones: integrity, autonomy, moral courage" (1989, 146).

These images of women continue in *Feis,* Ní Dhomhnaill's 1991 collection. A selection of thirty-one poems from this volume, including the sequence, "Immram"/"The Voyage," were selected, translated, and retitled *The Astrakhan Cloak* by Paul Muldoon. This collection might best be described as a collaboration because Muldoon, freely translating, creates a poem as much his as Ní Dhomhnaill's. He ignores the original order of the poems in *Feis* and thus the volume's structure.

Briona Nic Dhiarmada, in a review in the *Irish Literary Supplement,* comments that Muldoon as translator is "particularly promising" because of similar themes and styles in his and Ní Dhomhnaill's work; both poets draw from numerous cross-cultural sources and challenge poetic conventions and clichés. But Nic Dhiarmada notes that we need to understand Muldoon's contribution as translator:

In his previous encounters with Ní Dhomhnaill's work, Muldoon didn't so much translate the poems as re-imagine them. That same tendency is also much in evidence in this collection. Indeed the title of the present volume could serve as a benchmark for Muldoon's style of translation in general. The reader will search in vain for a poem of that name, or its Irish equivalent, in the work of Ní Dhomhnaill. It comes in fact from Muldoon's version of a line from the poem "Deora Duibhshléibhe"/ "Dora Dooley." Ní Dhomhnaill's "faoi chlóca uaithne" which translates literally as "under a green cloak," becomes in Muldoon's poem, "with the cloak of green astrakhan" from which he takes the book's title which also serves as a pun on the Irish word "aistriúchán," which of course means "translation"!(1993, 3)

Muldoon also adds his own images and supplements Ní Dhomhnaill's text with allusions to non-Irish literatures and cultures. The tension between Irish and English is heightened by the collaboration of the two poets, highlighting both the cross-cultural nature of Ní Dhomhnaill's work and the international community in which she is read. Readers need to be aware, however, that the poems in their English translation vary considerably from the Irish originals. In the *Irish Studies Review,* Aubrey Malone argues that there are "occasions where the overblown passages fail to do justice to the original," and that Muldoon sometimes "alters the whole dynamic of the poem" (1993, 38).

Although not translated literally, the poem "Deora Duibhshléibhe"/ "Dora Dooley" (1992b, 46–47) still remains faithful to the images we have come to expect in Ní Dhomhnaill's work. Dora is a contemporary banshee, a modern version of the female messenger of death.[7] Ní Dhomhnaill's traveling speaker imagines meeting this banshee on the road, and we see a characteristic Ní Dhomhnaill deflation:

> seanbheainín liath faoi chlóca uaithne
> is madra beadaí faoina hascaill
> (*chihuahua,* ní foláir)

Muldoon translates:

> with her cloak of green astrakhan
> and a lap-dog under her oxtereen
> (a chihuahua undoubtedly)

We sense the speaker's apprehension about the arrival of the banshee when she wonders whether she could have the "wit" and "presence of

7. For more information on the banshee, see Lysaght 1986.

mind" to confront her. What she describes as her more likely response is one that illustrates how we often deal with the possibility of death:

> Nó ab ann ab amhlaidh
> a bheannóinn di go simplí
> is í ag dul thar bráid
> faoi mar a dheineas anois
> ó chianaibhín
> le bean ó áit.

Muldoon translates:

> It's more likely, though,
> that I'd merely give her a wave
> as she went by
> just as I did
> only a short time ago
> to a little, old, local lady.

As is typical in Ní Dhomhnaill's poetry, the little old lady merges with the banshee, the folkloric figure metamorphosed into a contemporary woman. In a poem about the difficulty of facing the inevitable, of looking for a rainbow and finding one "that's only partially bent," both evoke a coming death.

Ní Dhomhnaill herself calls attention to the relationship between folklore and contemporary life in such poems as "An Bhatráil"/"The Battering" (1992b, 24–27).[8] Suggesting that folk tales sometimes reflect anxiety, Ní Dhomhnaill notes that women and children are often subjects of these cautionary tales, some of which focus on children abducted by fairies. In the poem a persona tells of rescuing her baby from the fairies who had stolen him, of the rituals she had to perform (drawing the child through a hank of undyed wool, cutting a briar with a black-handled knife), and of confronting a stranger who tried to bar her exit from the fairy fort. At the end of the poem, where both her fear and her hostility are evident, the speaker reveals her psychological state:

> Is má chuireann siad aon rud eile nach liom
> isteach ann
> an diabhal ná gurb é an chaor dhearg
> a gheobhaidh sé!

8. Ní Dhomhnaill discussed "An Bhatráil/The Battering" in this context at a reading at Villanova University in Pennsylvania in March 1993.

Chaithfinn é a chur i ngort ansan.
Níl aon seans riamh go bhféadfainn dul in aon ghaobhar
d'aon ospidéal leis.
Mar atá
beidh mo leordhóthain dalladh agam
ag iarraidh a chur in iúl dóibh
nach mise a thug an bhatráil dheireanach seo dó.

Muldoon translates:

If they try to sneak anything past
that's not my own, if they try to pull another fast
one on me; it won't stand a snowball's
chance in hell:
I'd have to bury it out the field.
There's no way I could take it anywhere next
or near the hospital.
As things stand,
I'll have more than enough trouble
trying to convince them that it wasn't me
who gave my little laddie this last battering.

In these final lines, "An Bhatráil"/"The Battering" takes us into the area of child abuse and how a woman might rationalize having beaten her child as violence done at the hands of the fairies.[9] Using what she calls "undifferentiated other world stuff," Ní Dhomhnaill connects folk tales with modern psychology in an attempt to describe the disturbed mental state of the speaker, making the tale a paradigm for the woman's troubles. Citing the work of Mircea Eliade,[10] Ní Dhomhnaill sees such tales as beyond history, where all time is an eternal now, and where the story always has contemporary applications.

Angela Bourke points out that in the Irish legends, women do not usually speak in the first person, and Ní Dhomhnaill's poems, where a woman speaks in her own voice, breaking this silence, are revolutionary.[11] Suggesting that such legends give women, and the woman poet, a way of

9. Ní Dhomhnaill mentioned the Kerry Babies case as an example of an incident which brings up related questions. For more information on this case, see McCafferty 1985.

10. See, for example, Eliade 1957.

11. Bourke, a writer and critic on the faculty at University College Dublin, appeared with Ní Dhomhnaill at Villanova University in March 1993 in a program on Irish folklore. Bourke's own work in folklore has examined such topics as the literary techniques of keening.

anchoring material and establishing a relationship with the community, both Ní Dhomhnaill and Bourke stress the importance of the oral tradition as distinct from the Fenian stories, which constitute a different kind of Irish mythology. This oral tradition, very much alive in Ní Dhomhnaill's poetry, works against the notion of an ideal, romanticized past articulated in a language monopolized by men.

Ní Dhomhnaill also gives us another way to read "An Bhatráil"/"The Battering" when she suggests the relationship between these legends and the work of the poet. In a conversation with Rebecca E. Wilson, Ní Dhomhnaill explains:

> For poetry to occur it has to come from a deeper level of the psyche. I call it the *lios* or "faery fort." There's supposedly sixteen hundred of them in the Irish countryside. . . .
> My attitude is that the *lios* is not there at all. It's within, the subconscious, which generally you can't get into, and poetry is bringing stuff from that other world into this world. Anything that comes from there will be imbued with an extraordinary charge, a luminous quality that will make it jump off the page. (Somerville-Arjat and Wilson 1990, 149–50)

Explaining that "An Bhatráil"/"The Battering" was written in a bout with postpartum depression after the birth of one of her children, Ní Dhomhnaill talks about some "level of the self" that is lost in such "passages" as birth and marriage and about the significance of an image like the fairy fort to articulate the anxiety a woman might feel as she negotiates with the subconscious. Ní Dhomhnaill maintains that folklore allows us to realize we are not alone in our anxiety, and she describes the abduction by the fairies as a paradigm for a troubled woman trying to deal with loss. This legend also suggests the poet's wrestling with the subconscious (the tall, dark stranger) to reach those deeper levels of the self from which poetry springs.

In *The Astrakhan Cloak*, Ní Dhomhnaill alludes often to traditional Irish female figures; in "Caitlín"/"Cathleen" (1992b, 38–41), she portrays Cathleen Ní Houlihan as a woman of the Roaring Twenties. The noise we hear in the background recalls the 1916 Rising and the Irish civil wars; this Cathleen, we are told, has a "Black and Tan Bottom." Depicting Cathleen/Ireland as a woman created to serve many causes, where "every slubberdegullion once had a dream-vision / in which she appeared as his own true lover," the poem tells us that Cathleen is still talking, "bending your ear / about the good old days of yore." Imagining the young maiden turned into an old widow, the speaker warns that her days are "truly over."

Nevertheless, this image of Cathleen endures, Ní Dhomhnaill writes:

> Cuirfidh mé geall síos leat nár chuala sí leis
> mar tá sé de mhórbhua aici agus de dheis
> gan aon ní a chloisint ach an rud a 'riúnaíonn í féin.
> Tá mil ar an ógbhean aici, dar léi, agus rós breá
> ina héadan. Is í an sampla í is fearr ar m'aithne
> de bhodhaire Uí Laoghaire.

Muldoon translates:

> And I bet Old Gummy Granny
> has taken none of this on board because of her uncanny
> knack of hearing only what confirms
> her own sense of herself, her honey-nubile form
> and the red rose, proud rose or canker
> tucked behind her ear, in the head-band of her blinkers.

The female image that serves as emblem, Cathleen the maiden "of beauties most beautied," or "poor, without blemish or blight," continues to exist for those who manipulate images of women for their own ends. In poems like this, Briona Nic Dhiarmada maintains, Ní Dhomhnaill turns poetic clichés on their heads, "deconstructing the idealized personification of Ireland sanctified in song and story since the 18th century" (1993, 3).[12]

This deconstructing appears in other poems in *The Astrakhan Cloak*. Ní Dhomhnaill's "Immram," a fourteen-poem sequence drawing on the medieval journey poem,[13] begins with "Cathair Dé Bhí"/"The City of God" (1992b, 72–73), in which the speaker alludes to the heavenly cities of the Bible. In this sequence, however, the holy city is identified with the mysterious island that appears in Irish folklore. In "Immram" the island becomes, among other things, a symbol for the deeper levels of the psyche from which poetry originates. For Ní Dhomhnaill, this search for, and sighting of, the island has specific value for the woman poet:

12. In another poem, "Mo Theaghlach"/"Household" (1990, 150–53), the speaker describes a secret room at the top of the stairs and an Irish version of the madwoman in the attic. Eiléan Ní Chuilleanáin translates: "Nobody pays any notice, especially not / When she screams that she is Caitlín Ní hUallacháin. / I met her one time on one of her good days / And she told me her real name was Grace Poole."

13. Muldoon's own poem, "Immram," appears in *Why Brownlee Left* (1981, 38–47).

What women find when they go in there is very different from what men have written about. That's the really exciting thing. Lots of women's poetry has so much to reclaim; there's so much psychic land, a whole continent, a whole Atlantis under the water to reclaim. It's like this island, again in Irish folklore, which surfaces from under the water every seven years, and if somebody can go out to it and light a fire, or do something, it will stay up forever. (Somerville-Arjat and Wilson 1990, 152)

The "psychic land" Ní Dhomhnaill describes here is the foundation for many of the themes and images in her poetry. Like Medbh McGuckian, Ní Dhomhnaill travels through a female psyche, imagining a whole continent, a new Atlantis, to be reclaimed. Whether we read her in Irish or English, in the original or mediated by a translator, the energy of that psychic landscape comes through vigorously, to express an Ireland tied to the past, set in the present, and heading for the future.

7

New Directions in
Irish Women's Poetry

In much of the poetry by Irish women published since 1980, a growing consciousness of the importance of self has led not only to the proliferation of female personae but also to a more confident female voice expressing the value of women's experience and perception. In one of the most notable developments in recent Irish poetry, speakers clearly identify themselves as women, and often as poets, accepting without qualification their right to speak as both.

Several factors account for the increasing visibility of the woman poet in Ireland. As the influence of women's rights movements has gradually spread over the last twenty years, interest in the lives of Irish women has taken on a life of its own. In universities, women scholars and Women's Studies programs have begun to focus on the neglected lives of women in Ireland, and the students in these universities are exposed to the contributions of women to Irish history and culture.[1] From an emphasis on the condition of contemporary women, scholars have broadened their scope to look at women in historical, cultural, and literary contexts. Books like *Women Surviving: Studies in Irish Women's History in the 19th and 20th Centuries,* which grew out of meetings of the Irish Feminist History Forum and is, in the editors' words, an attempt to debunk the myth of "woman as passive victim" (Luddy and Murphy 1989, 1), attest to a growing commitment to uncover a more complex and realistic image of Irish women.

Work in Women's Studies has also led to increased interest in writing by women, and to expanded publishing opportunities for contemporary writers, as well as to publication of works by their female literary predecessors. Anthologies like *Wildish Things, Pillars of the House, The Female Line,* and an increasing representation of work by and about

1. By the beginning of the 1990s, Women's Studies programs were established at universities in both Northern Ireland and the Republic.

women writers in periodicals like *Cyphers, Poetry Ireland Review,* and *Krino* bring this work to readers who in the past had little or no access to it.

Writing workshops have also sprung up all over Ireland, offering women the opportunity to read and discuss their writing. Some of these, like those under the auspices of the Dublin-based Women's Education Bureau (WEB), were initiated in the early 1980s specifically to create forums for women writers. In June 1987, in an editorial in *The WEB,* which published material generated in these workshops, Eavan Boland described them as outlets for what she calls "a great deal of underground energy seeking expression."

Noting gender-related difficulties, in her editorial Boland stresses the value of such workshops for women as she contrasts male and female writers:

> The young male writer tends to emerge in his twenties in Ireland. He is often unmarried, economically free of family restriction, able to move with some ease to the centres of population where he will find stimulus and sustenance. The woman writer is Ireland is different. She more often starts writing—or starts again—in her thirties. She tends to have children, be economically dependent, be restricted in movement. Both types of writers will have a long journey ahead of them. But the sustenance, support, funding and structural nature they require at crucial times are quite different. (1987c, 1)

The growth of writing workshops and writing groups across Northern Ireland and the Republic has allowed women, especially those outside of Dublin, to participate in a community of writers where the "underground energy" Boland writes about surfaces. Such structures often serve as an impetus to continue to write. As Boland says, "People do give up. They get discouraged," but, despite the fact that workshops are "unwieldy, transient, ephemeral" (1987c, 1), they create the opportunity, for women especially, to read and be listened to. While young poets like Sara Berkeley and Rosita Boland, both published before they left Trinity, may signal a new generation of women publishing much earlier than their predecessors, many of the women poets published in Ireland today were late starters, more tied to a particular locale than their male colleagues. For many of them, workshops have provided the needed encouragement to keep writing.

All of these changes and opportunities have given rise to new voices, imagery, and language in the poetry of Irish women. New points of view transform old heroines; we see Eve and Mary, Ariadne and Penelope, the hag, the banshee, the Shan Van Vocht, and the Irish goddesses in re-defined roles. The range of women we meet broadens as a much more expansive cast of characters challenges many traditional female figures. To complement an older and quieter lyric voice, recent poems express a range of emotions: anger, humor, ambivalence, cynicism, and satire sur-face as women explore the complexities of their lives and their feelings. The pleasures of love and sex balance the conflicts these engender, and the difficulty of women's choices echoes through much of this work.

Anne Le Marquand Hartigan's volume *Long Tongue* (1982), typical of this new poetry, opens with an explanatory note about its title: "Long ago in Ireland the poet was thought to have fearful powers. It was a misfortune to have a poet in the family: doubly so if the poet were a woman, as her powers were twice as strong as a man's. A poet was recog-nized by the possession of an extra long tongue." Harking back, like Nuala Ní Dhomhnaill, to an earlier culture that recognized (and feared) women for their poetic talent, Hartigan writes poems that blend conven-tional and experimental forms.

In "The Milkman's Wife" (1982, 34–35), Hartigan connects old and new as the speaker addresses the "Old hag death" who "took the milk-man's / Wife away":

> Why old bitch
> Did you take her hand,
>
> O tell us what's your meaning,
>
> She'd done no harm
> And she hadn't lived long,
>
> O sing a song with feeling.

The hag answers:

> There is no reason,
> There is no rhyme
>
> And I'm bloody well coming
> In my own good time,
>
> That's what I do be singing.

Evoking both the banshee and the Irish keening woman, Hartigan con-fronts the power of death, acknowledging, in the ironically assertive voice of the speaker, her helplessness in the face of this force. In a poem filled with rhyme and, in its own way, with reason, we are asked to accept that "There is no reason, / There is no rhyme." While Hartigan personifies death as a hag and a bitch, the poem undercuts stereotypical images of the terrifying female monster.[2] Though "We love her not," this hag "does no wrong" and thus should not be blamed for her power. Equally important is that the speaker focuses on a real female in the inexplicable tragedy of the milkman's young wife, as an elegy for a specific woman becomes also a meaningful poem on our powerlessness in the face of death. Rather than hate the old hag, we are warned to respect her, and loaded words like "bitch" and "old bag" suggest more about fate than gender.

The female speakers in *Long Tongue* have many different voices, and the tone changes as often as the form. In the final lines of the ballad "Song" (Hartigan 1982, 36), a woman deserts her kitchen for the singing and spinning she hears in her head:

> I have undone my apron strings
> It's fallen to the floor,
> The moon has winked her eye at me,
> My hand is on the door.

Images of a lamp in the mind and the moon in the sky, both traditionally associated with imagination, lead us to read this poem as a song about loosening apron strings to respond to the lure of the imagination—literally, as the need to get out of the kitchen to write a poem.

When Hartigan's speakers move beyond the kitchen door, they view nature through a woman's eyes, as we can see in the imagist poem "April" (1982, 62–63), built upon metaphors from a woman's world. The poem describes birds in the trees overhead:

> Craw and crack,
> The bedmakers overhead
>   Black
> Mammies bicker,
> And twicker, twicker
> The thick clouds, you
> Rook-a-bye-babies;
> Swing sideways
> Beech bedded

2. Images of female monsters are discussed in Keane 1988 and in Caldecott 1988.

High headed,
> Shitters.

White, ice,
Blackthorn winter
> Slice
Bright patterns
In the hedgerows
Lace curtains
Twitch, twitch,
The green fingers
Itch the buds out
> Overnight.

. . . .
Bedspreaders,
Husk shedders and coverers
Quilting the skyscape
> Green.
Nest knitters, twig sitters,
Needle the patchwork
> Space.

Images of lace curtains, bedspreads, patterns, and rocking cradles create a landscape out of scenes culled from a woman's life. The birds overhead mirror the maternal world below them; and the landscape, with images of bedmaking, nestmaking, quilting, and needlework, delineates a spring world of women. The speaker's voice, which draws on poetic conventions but reverberates with rhythmic originality and intensity, depends on her own acceptance of the gift of the long tongue. Hartigan depicts her persona in another poem, "Invisible Candles," (1982, 28–29), as "this scribbler" who "Made signs / Charms and rubrics."

An awareness of the role of gender differences in poetry also surfaces in Paula Meehan's poetry, as "The Apprentice" from *Return and No Blame* (1984, 27–29) demonstrates. Addressed to the "masters," male poets, but specifically Yeats, the poem rejects the images of women these men have created:

Your swanlike women are dead,
Stone dead. My women must be
Hollow of cheek with poverty
And the whippings of history!

Declaring that "You are no master of mine, / Who gilds the heart / And blinds the eye," the speaker-poet says that her rhyme and chant, the story she must tell, will detail a real city and real people. Arguing that Yeats missed much while spying from high Georgian windows, Meehan explains, with ironic suggestions of his Crazy Jane poems (Yeats 1990, 264–68), why she cannot follow him:

> Strange the things that reach my ears—
> A voice that whispered in the ditch
> A secret to sneak up through chance and time
> To make a rhyme, a chant for me.
>
> The times I've had to listen,
> Watch and listen. Now I learn
> The story in the telling. . . .

Echoing sentiments in Eavan Boland's work, Meehan sets out to depict women as she herself sees them, rather than as Yeats—the prototypic "master"—depicts them. For many contemporary women poets, the story is "in the telling": they reject inherited images in favor of those they themselves create.

For these poets an attempt to draw more truthful portraits of women yields a complicated array of characters and a much more complex range of female experiences and emotions than Irish literature has previously offered. Many of these portraits are of ordinary women, or women who live on the fringe of society, lost in worlds of their own. The young poet Sara Berkeley in *Penn* draws a picture of "Agatha" (1989b, 18), who "likes it near the edge":

> So sure she can see straight.
> Walks to the end of walking,
> She strings words and shakes the raindust
> From her curls—Agatha
> Can't remember what she's fighting for,
> Notes shed their octaves in her inner ear.
>
> All her time is swirling down the drain
> With leaves and bits of eddying soul
> While Winter folds into the ruffles on the lake
> She thinks maybe she runs in last year's race
> And finishes late, with three days of darkness
> Warping the moon; Agatha hums a piano tune

She's not so
Very plain, she'll get washed away.

Berkeley's tragic portrait shows us a woman whose shell of "ordinary dust" breaks before an indifferent winter. Sound complements imagery, especially of water, in the alliterative and ironic "So sure she can see straight," and the rhyming "lake" and "late," "moon" and "tune," and "shakes" and "shed."

Class boundaries also collapse as writers like Juanita Casey, Rita Ann Higgins, and Leland Bardwell detail life on the edge. Casey, the daughter of gypsy parents who was adopted by an English family, eventually returned to the life of Ireland's traveling people that her poems celebrate (Henderson 1972). In *Eternity Smith and Other Poems* (1985), "We Grow Older," "Sailing to Byzantium," and "What Rough Beast" counterbalance the imagery of Yeats and T. S. Eliot with the more primitive landscape and life that traveler's know. The title poem, "Eternity Smith" (Casey 1985, 23–27), mimics Eliot's "Journey of the Magi," substituting traveling people for Eliot's wise men, and parodying Eliot's more formal diction with colloquial phrases like "That was a cold night alright." Retelling the birth of Christ from a traveler's point of view, Casey draws on a legend of gypsies forever cursed to wander because they forged the nails for Christ's Crucifixion. The implicit contrast between the world views and assumptions of Casey and those of Eliot opens our eyes to the narrowness of Eliot's vision and the need to supplement his male, high-brow Christian voice with that of an Irish traveling woman.

In another poem, "Venus" (1985, 12–14), Casey retells the goddess's story as a clash between a life of freedom, symbolized by the liberty to roam the hills, and a housewife's chores of cooking and dusting. The conflict in the poem arises when women are promised the former but expected to perform the latter. At the end of this poem we see two visions of Venus, one a contemporary housewife, the other a statue in the Louvre:

> Now swept and polished even
> Cobblestones,
> And removed from behind the sofa spaghetti,
> Fag-ends, knittings, one stiff left sock,
> Cheese rinds, dead goldfish, paint-lids,
> Half a marrow, a mummified hamster, two
> Chinese pennies, a hibernating bat and
> Bones,
> And applying Brighto to every floor

And wall,
The Goddess cobwebbed, flailed and besomed
Kitchen, lounge and hall,
And taking orphaned kittens from the oven
Tried her hand
At steak Rossini, cuisses de grenouilles,
And chicken Maryland.
Back on her pedestal, you'll see her in
The Louvre.
With the strained expression of one who
Cannot prove
To be all things to all men's love . . .
For, slamming shut the oven door—
Bent low—
Look dear, no hands!—they're in the
Escallopes de veau . . .
Time proves she never lost her charms,
Her smile, her poise, but merely both
Her arms.

To say the least, this is not the Venus we have been told and read about. When Casey suggests that the missing arms of the Louvre statue might have been lost in Vulcan's oven ("Look dear, no hands"), her flippant, comic tone reinforces the serious message that the multiple roles defined for women (among them, "Housewife, Tart, Witch, / Goddess or Gilded Lily") will ultimately lead to trouble. Her revision of Venus, in a frenzy over housework, charts a new direction in imagemaking, and the frenetic pace of the poem, with line tumbling into line, one image into another, imitates the harried life of women who try to "be all things to all men's love."

A distinctive new tone and imagery also marks the work of the Galway poet Rita Ann Higgins; all pretense to establishment decorum fades as Higgins directly confronts and details the world she sees. Her poems take us into the streets: into community welfare offices, prisons, dole queues, and shirt factory toilets, where we see the fantasies, failed dreams, anger, and violence in working-class lives. In the introduction to *Goddess and Witch* (1990), which combines Higgins's 1986 and 1988 collections into one volume, Eva Bourke comments that "Rita Ann Higgins' goddess and witch live around the corner from each other. The goddess's beauty might be awe-inspiring but she travels by bus to her council house; the witch might be watchful and mercurial, but she is trying to solve her financial and marital problems."

In Higgins's "Goddess on the Mervue Bus" (1990, 23–24), we find an "Aphrodite / of the homely bungalow." This antithesis of the classical goddess still must listen to her father's warnings:

> Your father
> (who is no Zeus)
> turns old scrap
> into rolled gold
> nightly from memory,
>
> looks down on you
> from his scrap mountain,
> hurling forks of caution
> about the tin-can man
>
> who fumbles in the aisle
> of the Mervue bus,
> longing for the chance
> of a throwaway smile,
> a discarded bus ticket.

In Higgins's poetry, we also meet the "Lotus Eater from Bohermore" (1990, 33), "no hopers" like Tommy, who "likes Guinness, sex and unemployment" (1990, 8–9). Fortune appears in the bingo games where Lizzie Kavanagh's "maroon imitation fur" (1990, 25–26) coat is treasured as a good luck charm. The real power in this world belongs to the "God-of-the-Hatch Man" (1990, 45–46), the community welfare officer to whose "hole in the wall" people make pilgrimages every Thursday:

> like visiting the holy well,
> only this well purports to give you things
> instead of taking them away.
>
> Things like scarlatina, schizophrenia,
> migraine, hisgraine but never your grain,
> lockjaw and wind, silicosis,
> water on the knee, hunger in the walletness.

Higgins introduces us to a harsh environment, her women and men burdened with the economic pressures and strains of their world. The "Witch in the Bushes" (1990, 76–79), "wearing a black patch / and a questionnaire," interviews Old Rockie Jaw, a typical Higgins deflation of Prometheus. Rockie Jaw chews on a big grey rock, symbolizing his attempts to overcome "the savage seas" that rise above dreams. The voices he hears tell him that a "real man / must spit feathers," while the witch continues to ask him "if all that anger / for all those years / was worth it." The Cyclops-like prison warders in "They Believe in Clint Eastwood" (1992, 1), who uphold the letter of the law, or the speaker in "Misogynist" (1992, 17), who needs a tow because "the engine's after / collapsin' on me again, / she is, the bitch," illustrate similar characteristics of destructive machismo.

Women often respond to these men by imitating the battle stance. In "The Deserter" (1992, 18–20), a wife complains of her husband's death as she irons his shirt: "that's the type / of person he was, / would rather die / than please you," and the poem ends with her useless threat: "The next time / I spend two hours / ironing shirts for him / he'll wear them." In another poem, "Crooked Smiles" (1992, 26), a woman brags: "The force of his fist / made my smile crooked a few times / but I got over it."

The social consequences of the pressures of the life Higgins portrays are evident in scenes describing the relationships between men and women. In "She Is Not Afraid of Burglars" (1990, 59–60), a wife explains why she has no fear when her husband is in the house: "the dog disobeyed my husband / and my husband beat him across the head / with a whip made from horse hair." When this husband orders her, like the dog, to "Stay there / His wife obeys him." Other men, like those described in "The Barmen of Sexford," "No Bliss in Newbliss," or "The Did-You-Come-Yets Of the Western World," view women only as sexual targets, objects of conquest. The sexually uninhibited woman in the third (1990, 67–68) gives advice to other women about these playboys, advice Pegeen in Synge's play might have found helpful: "Don't necessarily hold out / for the biggest one; / oftentimes the biggest ones / are the smallest in the end." Warning women about lovers "fishing up your independence," the speaker rejects men who fantasize about their power to make women "come," and advises her listeners to look for those who grant women their own sexual power:

> In time one will crawl
> out from under thigh-land.
> Although drowning he will say,
>
> "Woman I am terrified, why is the house
> shaking?"
>
> And you'll know he's the one.

Higgins's sardonic tone reveals a serious purpose; she explores both the humor and the suffering in the lives of people she never demeans. In a review in the *Honest Ulsterman,* Medbh McGuckian has accurately described Higgins's as a "mock-heroic style" that is "plainly controlled by a very far from naïve intelligence" (1988a, 60–62). The richness of Higgins's poetry depends very much on her graphic portrayal of the intimate details of her Galway people, and her talent for making poetry from their words and voices bears witness to the opening of new territories in contemporary poetry.

Higgins's poetry shares some of the characteristics of the work of Leland Bardwell, novelist, poet, and one of the editors of *Cyphers,* who since the 1960s has drawn the reader's eye away from mainstream subjects in Irish literature, especially in her female subjects and speakers. Bardwell's 1984 volume *The Fly and the Bedbug* is full of portraits of women: Sheila, in the poem of that title (7), "ninety years a spinster"; the title character in "Mrs. Katherine Dunne" (8), whose quiet dignity and generosity become her legacy; the woman in "Blackbushe" (14) who "sleeps on the shoulder of the aerodrome."

A remarkable courage comes through in the down and out women Bardwell often describes.[3] Lily, the heroine of "The Lady That Went On Strike Against the Early Closing Hours of the Iveagh Hostel" (1984, 11–12), frustrates the Garda when she camps on the street, but she gets through the night:

> They had to thumb through old books,
> Read old laws, invent new cruelties,
> (One fresh-faced young guard suggested
> Holding her head down the lavatory.)
>
> They got nowhere, seemingly, because
> When morning came, Lily was still there—
> Neatly tucked, umbrella for a roof—
> She could sleep in, fine, till Larry opened up.

While Bardwell shows us the lives of the homeless and the mad, lives symbolized by the fly and the bedbug in the title poems, she still manages to find innate dignity even in death. "Sheila" (1984, 7) eloquently describes the ironic beauty of a dying woman:

3. In a conversation with me in 1989, Bardwell said that the ten years she spent "on the bread line" gave her a greater understanding of some of these women's lives.

Silence spreads like the snowberries on her island.
She lifts three fingers like a queen,
Lets time press on the brows of strangers.
She has returned inland to where
The ponies graze. Sheila! The raspberries drip red
A wisp of wind makes the pippins fall.
She runs to her mother's parsley smelling garden
To hear the gladiolae stiffen.

This natural scene might be set beside one in the fifth of the "Prison Poems,"[4] a sequence in *The Fly and the Bedbug* (1984, 44–48), to give us a sense of Bardwell's range and her success at capturing in her images the sights, sounds, and movements of a particular place. In "Prison Poem V" (48) a woman is lead to a cell and another kind of death:

Her own identity is something left behind
With generous other days on dirty Dublin streets
Like watching the sad expression on her landlord's face
Or fixing the metre quickly before it's read
Or even a morning queuing for the dole.

But the crash of the heavy lock resounds;
The childhood mortice of an unknown room
And she is again a child on whom fleshless silence
Clamps its morbid teeth.

She lies under the weight of it
In the air as cold as salt and with her stare
Breaks up the surface of the cobbled wall
Beneath whose cloak of dust, graffiti, blood,
A million creatures whisper; with or without her
Their parliament is never still.

In "Sheila," and in this prison poem, women become as powerless as children; unable to escape the walls closing in on them, they retreat into childhood. The haunting silence in both scenes links them, yet the tone is different: Sheila presides over a landscape of raspberries, pippins, and parsley, with the stiffening gladiolae and dropping apples the only hint of coming death. The woman prisoner, on the other hand, enters a world where an insect "parliament" under the wall's surface seems to be more significant than she is, can live "with or without her," and childhood is imagined as a silence that "clamps its morbid teeth" on her. The dust,

4. Bardwell said she had in mind the Maze Prison when she wrote these poems.

graffiti, and blood that decorate the prison walls contrast with the snow-berries and ponies on Sheila's island. Significantly, both poems describe a silent world Bardwell ironically allows us to hear, even though noise—the strangers around Sheila, the war in which the woman is taken prisoner—echoes in the backgrounds. Like Higgins, Bardwell has moved beyond conventional settings to give us images of women that we have rarely seen in Irish poetry before.

New images in the poetry of contemporary women have also led, as we have seen in the poetry discussed in earlier chapters, to a revising of mythic and religious figures. This trend has increased since the 1980s. Ruth Hooley's "Woman Alone" (1986, 50) stands in a doorway, "Cast in her own role" but attached by an invisible string to shadows of herself within the house. "This is the person she is," Hooley's poem tells us, as she comes out from shadows into an identity of her own: "Leaning out of doors against the wall, / Sun after rain, seeding her own grain—/ Lifting the mist over Eden." Self-propagating, the woman emerges from the mist, a new Eve pictured in her own light.

The symbolic lifting of the mist sometimes means rewriting the story of Eve or challenging the image of women handed down in religious tradition. In Maeve Kelly's "Spring in Meelick," from her volume *Resolution* (1986, 13), the speaker presents a woman's view of a prelapsarian world, with emphasis on the natural beauty of the scene:

> Just budding is the willow;
> Baby finger leaves
> Open to the warmth of sun.
> This noon
> Is a golden glow;
> Daffodils in streams
> Spill across the lawn,
> Such green
> Shimmering with yellow,
> Innocent as Eve's
> First loving look.
> No harsh god here.

Kelly associates the spring landscape with Eve, so that we see her not as the traditional seductress, banished from paradise, but as the mother of the human race with her "first loving look." Images like "baby finger leaves" highlight this revising of Eve as First Mother, but we must imagine her before the Fall, in a green and golden landscape we can know every spring. To do this, we must ignore Eve the temptress, responsible for sin and the world's suffering.

Irish women poets, like women poets elsewhere, have begun to challenge the subordinate role created for women within religious tradition. In "Lot's Wife," in *The Goose Herd* (1989, 36), Roz Cowman looks at the fate of the housewife forced to follow her husband's lead:

> What else could she do, when that old fool,
> pickled in prudence, holier than she,
> God's loudspeaker, forced her to climb
> up out of the plain, start again with him,
> housewife to a tribe, getting back
> to Nature as he called it, milking
> his camels, hoarding their dung
> for fuel, hearing him talk to his dreadful god
> while the stars hummed like bees
> in the white nights of the desert.

A newly discovered freedom, especially sexual freedom, accounts for the more graphic portrayals of female sexuality found in recent women's poetry. Seeing their women as sexual beings, many of these poets ignore taboos earlier poets respected. Lynda Moran's "The Man-Eater" in *The Truth About Lucy* (1985, 42), cleverly develops a curtain image to portray the attraction of female sexuality:

> He who found comfort
> In her heavy curtains
> Could call out for warmth
> From her arms.
>
> Yet he in boots of bones
> Would dance her nunsome
> Weed-seed dance. Between
> their flesh-sheen powdered sheets
> His embers might explode.
>
> Who would suspect
> When her curtains were closed
> What her appetites hungered for?
>
> Or who would connect
> Such a "nice" girl
> With the primitive
> Or the taste for trophies?

Moran reverses stereotypical roles with the man (in "boots of bones") dancing to the woman's sexual tune, the curtains here suggesting openings other than windows. The pun on "nunsome" distances this woman from the chaste nun's life, and her "taste for trophies" becomes an ironic comment on women as men's sexual conquests.

Roz Cowman's "Taking the Veil," from *The Goose Herd* (1989, 44), carries this challenging one step further by questioning the emphasis on the vocation that Irish Catholic women have often been taught to see as ideal. Cowman's tone and language express another point of view about the value of the celibacy nuns accept:

> Zip into the honeycomb,
> sister; lie jelly coddled
> in your hexagon; listen to bees
> drilling bee-paths in oxygen, outside,
> and the hush of hatchery.
>
> See sun filtered
> in mica flakes through wax;
> mote-pollened stamens
> of light piercing
> cracks of the wall.
>
> Lie fallow; few
> are chosen for the flight
> into the sun's eye,
> the disemboweling,
> the fall.

Suggesting that a cloistered and celibate life might not be ideal, the speaker here endorses the value of sexuality and childbearing. While the nun lies "fallow," other women fly "into the sun's eye." The "disemboweling" and the "fall" at the end of the poem can be read both as a metaphor for the sexuality nuns surrender and as an image of childbearing. The nun who removes herself and lies "jelly coddled" while the world around her reproduces ("bees," "hatchery," "stamens") must not, this poem suggests, be given as the perfect model for women. The irreverent tone of the opening lines leaves no doubt that Cowman invites us to consider why celibacy is given such exalted status in Irish Catholic culture. With the image of the sun filtering through the cloister walls, Cowman also links the Christian nun with the mythic Danae, imprisoned in a chamber by her father but impregnated by Zeus in a shower of gold. In this poem "sister" has multiple meanings.

The image of the *sheela-na-gig*, her open vagina exposed on stone monuments throughout Ireland, has received numerous interpretations over the years.[5] It also becomes the focus of new poems. Susan Connolly's "Sheela-na-gig," from *For the Stranger* (1993), presents the figure as the object of numerous reactions ("wide-open . . . / to mirth / and wonder, / trust disgust") but gives her a broader meaning:

> Sheela-na-gig
> compels . . .
> not ugly
> but sad—
> everything
> about her
> so exposed.

Like Eiléan Ní Chuilleanáin's "Permafrost Woman" (1991, 15), another image alluding to the sheela-na-gig, Connolly's figure becomes an emblem for an Irish response to female sexuality.

Questioning religious values handed down to women, and challenging the rewards promised for certain kinds of behavior, some recent poems offer a new definition of female sexuality that emphasizes its pleasure and its value. Often this involves converting inherited images to new use. Adopting the voice of a sexy vampire or an evil witch, the speakers in some recent poems take comic advantage of the roles they can play. In Rita Ann Higgins's "Sunny Side Plucked" from *Goddess & Witch* (1990, 49–50), a woman tells us that the witch in her "wanted to scramble / his eggs," while the "devil in him / wanted to pluck / my chicken." Maeve Kelly in "Cognomens," from *Resolution* (1986, 47), describes how some contemporary women discuss their sexual organs:

> I have a friend who calls her uterus her gearbox,
> and this unlikely terminology,
> clanking aeons away from the Greek,
> somehow gives her comfort. She can then laugh
> at the shifts and changes which transport her,
> protesting, but inexorably, on her journey
> away from wooden horses and towards—
> one must assume—rockets and new moons.

5. For more information on the *sheela-na-gig*, see Dunn 1977.

Having none of this new technological terminology, the speaker in this poem explains her choice of terms, demythologizing and degenderizing, as her friend does, her own sexuality:

> My obsession is named Tiger.
> Grr, grr, she growls intermittently in her cage,
> sometimes stretches and yawns,
> velvety smooth, pulsating with power,
> langorous and warm.
> Prr, prr, prr. Stroke me and I will neck-nuzzle,
> gnaw you into passion, devour with kisses
> and lick and lollop, slavering for love.

In this challenging of taboos, poems about love and sex are also no longer restricted to heterosexual relationships. Mary Dorcey's *Kindling* (1982) and *Moving into the Space Cleared by Our Mothers* (1991), which includes some of the poems from *Kindling,* depict the pleasures of lesbian love and, in a poem like "Night" (1991, 90), the feelings of loss these sometimes engender:

> I remember your neck, its strength
> and the sweetness of the skin at your throat.
> I remember your hair, long, in our way
> drawing it back from my mouth.
> How my hands slid the low plain of your back
> thrown by the sudden flaunt of your loins.
> I remember your voice, the first low break
> and at last the long flight
> loosing us to darkness.
> And your lips along my shoulder,
> more sure, even than I had imagined—
> how I guarded their track.
>
> I ask you then what am I to do with all these
> memories
> heavy and full?
> Hold them, quiet, between my two hands,
> as I would if I could again
> your hard breasts?

Dorcey's poems describe jealousy, forgiveness, friendship, love, and sex between women—women who must sometimes enclose themselves in a protective circle against those who would condemn them. Such poems give witness to new voices willing to break the silence of once-hidden lives and suggest, in a poem like Dorcey's "Daughter" (1991, 42–43), how a woman would speak to a child she never has. Imagining this daughter, the persona bequeaths her many things, including "this whole wide world / that was not yet / wide enough for me / to bear you into."

In addition to new views on female sexuality, much recent poetry expresses multidimensional and diverse views on motherhood. In Roz Cowman's poem "Jocasta" (1986, 60), a mother talks to a child, promising to nourish him, but warning of the world beyond them:

> Tomorrow I'll unwind
> the cord that binds
> us; you will start
> the long journey
> of our kind,
> into humanity,
> through sorrow.
>
> But for today,
> I rest your head
> on breast; close
> wound, no sound.
> Safe in this stone age
> of the mind,
> we are at one,
> my son.

Turning Jocasta into the caring mother who seeks to shield her infant son from the human misery he will face, the speaker here accepts the role of the ancient lover-mother, to give her child a day "Safe in this stone age / of the mind." Refocusing our attention on the mother who had to let the child go, and away from the wife blamed for Oedipus's fall, Cowman captures how ambivalent a mother feels towards a child who must inevitably leave her protection. Like the opening poems in Eavan Boland's *Night Feed,* Cowman's poem describes the unique bonds that link mother and child.

Also focused on parent-child relationships is Sara Berkeley's poem "Mother" from *Home Movie Nights* (1989a, 29), which gives us a sense of a daughter's divided loyalties as she evaluates her mother's life when she returns to spend some time at home:

> She mothers the whole village,
> She makes you think
> Of a duck-mother, with her webbed concern,
> Spreading matter-of-fact, lifebled,
> Hurting love.
>
> A consolation of children
> Clutters her mealtime, paces her world
> There can be no untruth for them, no pretence,
> On Sundays she decks them in mother-of-pearl
> She holds them when they fall
> From the apple trees, from grace,
> She dims the shock of skinned knees.

Time stops beyond the fence here as the image of a loving, comforting, sacrificing mother is drawn within the parameters of her home. But hints that motherhood may have a darker side come from phrases like "life-bled, / Hurting love," "A consolation of children / Clutters," and the speaker's journey back into another world where "Time huddles, waiting, as we say goodbye." For a new generation of Irish poets, the glories and joys of motherhood are often tempered with recognition of the sacrifices that mothering demands.

One of those sacrifices might be to raise children alone: to choose, like the speaker in Heather Brett's "No Vacancies" from *Abigail Brown* (1991, 44–45), to create a home without a man. Constructing a new image of family, this woman positions her single chair by the fire and defines the boundaries not to be crossed. Addressing an unseen man from whom she has separated, the persona acknowledges that she may be too quick to put him in his place and to assume hers, but she argues that there are benefits to what she has chosen:

> But alone I look fondly on the things
> I have here, the bits and pieces that we have
> accumulated and collectively call mine.
> The walls are missing nothing, the house
> is furnished, we call it home.
>
> All the rooms are taken, each bed spoken for.
> Any cracks have long since been papered over
> or filled in. We have no space left, no empty
> drawers or anywhere where another might make himself
> at home: There are no candles burning in the window.

As contemporary women poets explore the implications of conventional ideas of motherhood, they also continue to make connections between different expressions of female creativity. *Mother* can refer to language as well as to children, as Moya Cannon's poem "Prodigal" from her volume *Oar* (1990, 19), illustrates. Alluding to the prodigal son's return to the father, Cannon's poem describes a return to the mother, an attempt to find solace in the "dark mutter tongue":

> Old gutter mother
> I am bereft now,
> my heart has learnt nothing
> but the stab of its own hungers
> and the murky truth of a half-obsolete language
> that holds at least the resonance
> of the throbbing, wandering earth.
>
> Try to find me stones and mud now mother
> give me somewhere to start,
> green and struggling, a blade under snow,
> for this place and age demand relentlessly
> something I will never learn to give.

The remnants of a mother tongue, the "half-obsolete" Irish language that resonates with throbbing earth, are a source of nourishment, as is the mother / goddess / muse who provides shelter, "somewhere to start." The stones and mud to protect the speaker against a world in which "Someone / businesslike in his desires / has torn out the moon by its roots" identify a conflict between nature and technology as well as between the world of business and the world of the imagination (symbolized by the moon).

Cannon's "outrageous worlds" have no intense pain or innocence, but "only the little quiet sorrows / and the elegant joys of power." A return to the "gutter mother," to the values of an older culture that linger in a mother tongue and a primitive landscape, might help. But an undercurrent in the poem suggests the difficulty of the return: the language yields only "murky" truth; the age "relentlessly" demands what the speaker cannot give. Still, the prodigal daughter turns to fragments of the language. In its own way, "Prodigal" can be read as a woman returning to a mother, as a woman poet defining her own struggles with language, and as strong a political statement as those poems by male poets that blend Irish and English in a testament to the poetic power of both languages.

In another poem, "'Taom'" (1990, 13–14), Cannon describes the consolation offered by the Irish word for an overwhelming wave of emotion: "Surfacing from a fading language, / the word comes when needed. / A dark sound surges and ebbs, / its accuracy steadying the heart." In recent poetry by Irish men, Paul Muldoon's "Clonfeacle" (1985, 20) or "Anseo" (1980, 20–21), for example, the melding of Irish words into English lines has been seen as both an aesthetic and political statement, an attempt to recognize and preserve the "fading" language Cannon describes. A woman poet like Cannon takes a giant leap when in "'Taom'" she reclaims that tongue for women as well, writing in English about the value of the mother language:

> There are small unassailable words
> that diminish caesars;
> territories of the voice
> that intimate across death and generation
> how a secret was imparted—
> that first articulation,
> when a vowel was caught
> between a strong and a tender consonant;
> when someone, in anguish
> made a new and mortal sound
> that lived until now,
> a testimony
> to waves succumbed to
> and survived.

Evidence of self-assertion and success in a quest for poetic identity, in the discovery of words, is often juxtaposed with an ingrained habit of silence expressed by female speakers in recent poems. Máiríde Woods's "Covering the Traces—A Convent Education" (1986, 91) addresses one such problem, the learned virtue of silence. Startled when someone interrupts her, the speaker in this poem hides her writing in a drawer, "Preserves the self as in some museum bottle." Early habits linger, even when a woman writer is ready for freedom: "Before that buckle fell away forever / The habit of concealment laced the soul, / Left yellowing and tidy in the drawer." Maeve Kelly, in "Feminist III," from *Resolution* (1986, 49–50), also speaks about the silence and reticence of women and about the consequences of harboring internalized anger and rage. If women speak out, her speaker says, changes will come: "Kindly condescension out the door, / Martyrs and mothers redundant, / Male poets losing monopoly." But this process of opening up is not so easy, Kelly suggests, as she considers women's responses:

> Well, lips are padlocked still.
> Speech too grave for song
> Breaks another rule of tongue.
> Open lips are for kissing.
> Paint them for that.

The multiple meanings of painting, suggesting both the making up that women do and the art they can create, clearly illustrate the conflict over choices, the woman poet's difficulty in unlocking lips meant to be kissed for that "utterance" that might liberate her.

But when women poets do speak, their words often express a different angle of vision. While much attention has been focused on the male poet's response to the Troubles in Ireland, very little has been directed to poetry by women on the same subject. The Belfast poet, Janet Shepperson, in a selection in the anthology *Trio 5* (1987), writes about the battles in Northern Ireland, and her imagery reflects a woman's perspective. "Protestant Street," we are told in the poem of that title (1987, 50), looks like a folded tablecloth, "evenly / patterned with windows criss-crossed / with net or lace." Typical of many poems written by women, "Protestant Street" emphasizes the insides of houses; the empty rooms ache with silence since the Catholic family was forced to leave. In another Shepperson poem, "Fragile" (1987, 49), a woman who walks into her garden to hang sheets hears a popping sound she cannot identify:

> She's hearing grass
> drying out, unbrowning, lifting, flicking off
> its load of water, straightening into spring.
> She listens—touching greenness—breathing sunshine.
>
> But then like a heavy cloud, a helicopter
> from the army base comes with its ponderous chugging
> and draws dark circles and flattens all the delicate
> stirring of hesitant gardens.
> She turns back to
> her soundproofed world, still cradling a handful of grass.

On the perimeter of this world hovers the helicopter ("like a heavy cloud"), ready to destroy the flowers and grass she cradles in the final lines. The poem pits a female world of gardens, sheets, and cradles against a male military one, and the woman, by turning her back on the helicopter noise, retreats into the "fragile" world the title describes. Silence and sound, crucial to the imagery of this poem, distinguish one world from the other: the woman nurturing what the helicopter destroys.

Linda Anderson, another Belfast writer, in her graphic "Gang-Bang, Ulster Style" (1987), focuses more specifically on the relationships fostered by war. A woman and a man live like "corpses clung together," his prison Long Kesh, hers the Belfast streets until she is "found out" and must be punished:

> They dragged you to their playroom.
> Now you lie limp,
> Face down,
> Dumped in a ditch.
> Routine policemen come
> Accustomed, stony-faced
> 'Turn her over, see the damage'.
>
> O, poor adventurous—
> In the name of virtue,
> They cut your flaxen hair,
> Defiled your lovely breasts,
> Before degutting you.

The violent scenes portrayed here emphasize how love suffers in such an environment and how women are punished by physical mutilation.

In a similar poem, Paula Meehan's "Caesarean Section in a Belfast Street" from *Reading the Sky* (1986, 38–39), the speaker struggles to make poetry out a newspaper account of a child born to a mother killed by a car bomb. Though the innocent woman becomes a part of history, hers is "Just another death / On page four, in the daily litany of death." The speaker-poet describes the child's first two acts as political: his birth scream and his "reach towards a breast already past / Nurturing." Addressing the child, the poet offers what she can:

> You were dragged into history
>
> By a soldier's bloody hands. He cursed history
> That soldier agent of your miracle birth
> Among the sirens and screams and ghosts of the past
> That shattered the silence of her womb. Her death
> Cry in his ears, he pulled you clear. Political
> Forces demanded he hold you in his hands. I try

> To rescue from history a song that's stronger than death.
> To celebrate your birth by a political
> Act, I'll dream a beginning, a future, a violent poetry.

Already a pawn in an endless game, the child becomes the impetus for the poet's own political act, the poem that she writes. In many of the poems about the war written by women, the emphasis falls on the ways in which war and military men destroy what women create and nurture.

The newest direction we can chart in recent poetry is the acknowledgment of links between women poets, as contemporary poets pay tribute to those who preceded them. A shared identity as women often reinforces this recognition, as national and ethnic boundaries collapse. In "Emily Dickinson" from *Home Movie Nights* (1989a, 36), Sara Berkeley in Dublin imagines the poet's life in Amherst:

> From anything that touches her she may recoil
> Go no further
> But retreat upon it all and reap
> Words that are born and unfurl under careful hands
> Words that come from her trance
> In a silent monotone.
>
> Then the Alice-like fall
> Swings from dull thud to thud of her hitting earth.
> In her long descent did she howl?
> I worry about that sound
> And watch how her own nouns
> jostle her now she is down,
> Her thoughts are an empty train, doors open,
> And no-one getting in.
>
> At times she has nodded drily at the abyss
> It is not sunny at this time so there are no shadows
> But maybe down there genius lightly spirals,
> Words landing squarely, perfect fits;
> I edge warily, all blows glancing,
> Until my mind connects with a bright shock.
> Somewhere, a train pulls off.

Working from the traditional image of the withdrawn spinster, Berkeley reimagines Dickinson as maternal, reaping words and bearing poems produced in an imaginative trance. Berkeley's speaker pictures

Dickinson, Alice-like, falling out of her writing trance, and wonders whether she howled. Borrowing some of Dickinson's imagery and language, the speaker here identifies with the American poet and waits for her own dry time to pass, for her own train to pull off.[6]

In reaching out to acknowledge the work of other women, Irish women poets have stressed the links that connect them. Clairr O'Connor's "Saffron" (1989, 55) invokes the imprisoned Russian poet, Irina Ratushinkaya, as her speaker tells about a dream she has had:

> I dreamed about you last night.
> You were holding my skull
> testing it lightly as if
> to throw it.
> . . . .
> I met you for the first time last
> night. You were smiling from under
> a fringe on the pages of a poetry magazine.
>
> You can't be too strong now after
> the hunger strikes.
>
> Last night you held out to me
> the three orange stigmas
> of a saffron.
>
> It takes eighty thousand flowers
> to make one kilogram of dried saffron.

Like Berkeley's poem to Emily Dickinson, O'Connor's seeks a connection between women poets, and the image of saffron provides the link. As muse and mentor, Ratushinkaya holds the speaker's head, testing it.

6. If we compare Berkeley's poem on Emily Dickinson to one written by the Northern poet Michael Longley (1969, 14), we note a difference that might be associated with gender. Each poem of course has its own merits. Longley sees Dickinson from the outside, dressing with care and making "perfect progress" through "cluttered rooms" towards poems that he compares to love letters; he describes a woman very much under control, undauntedly committed to her daily routine, and pictures her as detached and removed, "christening" the world with her "large philosophy." Berkeley, in contrast, imagines a recoiling, howling Dickinson, in a trance "jostling" with words. Longley's speaker admires Dickinson from afar; Berkeley's speaker identifies with her, sees them as sharing the same problems, and is more concerned with the internal psychological makeup of the woman poet. The words of her speaker, "I worry about that sound," or "I edge warily, all blows glancing," tell us that she looks to the older poet for guidance, knowing that Dickinson must have faced the same problems she does.

Inspired by the words she had read in a poetry magazine, the persona draws from the Russian poet the will to go on, knowing how Ratushinkaya must have felt when she read the work of her Russian literary forebears. Taking courage from a woman poet whose suffering makes poetry seem impossible, the speaker acknowledges both her work and the indomitable spirit that inspires others.

In Leland Bardwell's poem "Kassia" from *Dostoevsky's Grave* (1991, 66), the conflict over roles that women might play is imagined as one between marriage and writing, a choice that arose for another woman writer:

> Kassia, the 9th century Byzantine poet
> wore epigrams like bangles on her arms
> when offered marriage with the emperor
> she scalded him with wit.
>
> Banished from the court
> Columns of stone will kneel
> she said, before you change a fool.
>
> A learned fool, God save us.
> The pigs are eating pearls.

Socialized to put marriage and family first, the Irish woman poet, like Kassia, often must make difficult choices in order to write. As writers and critics have pointed out, Irish society has not always encouraged women to think of themselves beyond the parameters of the home, and Irish women face a conflict over how to balance a writing career with other choices. In her poem "Game" from *Long Tongue* (1982, 47), Anne Le Marquand Hartigan alludes to this problem. The persona notes the difference between male and female with an image of a chess game:

> Though wild knights can leap
> Sideways, and bishops diagonal
> Slide, appear from nowhere
> . . . .
> A queen can move in any direction,
> Her problem is one of choice, multiple.

One of those choices, to write, often leads women to imagine the lives of other women writers, as Eavan Boland does in "The Rooms of Other Women Poets" from *Outside History* (1990b, 20–21): "Somewhere you are writing or have written in / a room you came to as I come to this."

Increasingly, Irish women are choosing to write, to publish what they write, to promote and publicize their work. This assertive acceptance of the role of the poet, which male poets have expressed for some time in Ireland, is a crucial step in what Maeve Kelly, in "Feminist I" (1986, 28), has called refusing the "lure of acquiescence." As these women speak, they write not only about themselves, but also about the lives of other women, in Ireland and beyond.

I began this study with a question related to Seamus Heaney's *Field Work*, asking whether there were volumes like his written by women, poems with a female point of view. My answer, illustrated through the work I have examined, is that there are many, and they often picture a world different from the one Heaney portrays. Responding to the issue raised by Katie Donovan about putting women writers in an isolating spotlight, I hope I have shown that one way to see what women think, feel, and write—to know what a woman's "field work" might be—is to do just that.

To illustrate, we can end with two poems. Paula Meehan's "The Pattern" from *The Man Who Was Marked by Winter* (1991, 17–20)[7] might be set beside Heaney's early poem "Digging" from *Death of a Naturalist* (1980, 3), in which he compares and contrasts his father's potato digging to his own digging with his pen. The two poems illustrate different approaches to a similar subject, with gender an important element in the contrast.

Meehan's metaphors of knitting and patterns introduce us to a female scene where a daughter kneels before a mother, the child's outstretched hands holding a skein as the mother rolls the wool into balls. Heaney's speaker remembers himself as a child walking in his father's shadow across the fields; Meehan's speaker imagines her mother reeling her home, like wool, when she drifts away. Her early "pattern" dreams foreshadow her writing career: "I dreamt a robe of a colour / so pure it became a word." Her mother's prophetic words, "'One of these days I must / teach you to follow a pattern,'" mean different things for the knitting mother and the writing daughter, just as digging involves different work for Heaney's father and son. While acknowledging the links with the mother, the poem also pictures the daughter as a different kind of pattern maker: the pattern is the poem, the knitting together of words.

7. *The Man Who Was Marked by Winter* combines poems from two earlier volumes, *Return and No Blame* (1984) and *Reading the Sky* (1985), which are both out of print.

Although both Meehan's "The Pattern" and Heaney's "Digging" suggest the closeness and the distance between parents and children, they are also poems about poetry and how a man and a woman connect their writing with their past. "Digging" also becomes both a poem about how a poet is formed and a poem about Ireland, where potato digging acquires almost mythic status. Heaney, blessed (or burdened) with the mantle of Yeats, has, with poems like "Digging," found a place in the tradition of Anglo-Irish poetry. But, as I have noted in the beginning of my study, that has been a male tradition, and ultimately a father digging and a man writing have been historically more important than a mother knitting and a woman writing. The chances that a poem like "The Pattern" would find as large an audience as "Digging" has less to do with the merits of either poem than with the numerous factors that influence the status of women and women poets in Ireland. Few women have achieved the reputation that male poets in Ireland have. To his credit, Heaney has also written good poems, such as "Sunlight," "Clearances," and the Glanmore Sonnets, which focus on the lives and values of women (particularly his mother and his wife), but these are again images of women from a male point of view, and they highlight the relationship of the woman to the male speaker.

In the poems that I have covered, in which women create women, we often have a very different voice and vision. In comparing Paula Meehan to Seamus Heaney, we gain one insight, but in placing Meehan in the company of women writers, we gain another. As we have seen, there are many common elements in the poetry of Irish women, including the many images of mothers, of children, of handwork, and of "patterning" that writing poetry involves.

In recent poetry, as I hope these chapters have demonstrated, there has emerged a more self-conscious and self-confident female poet, ready to rewrite the story of Irish women and redefine and explore female identity and the image of women in Irish history, culture, and literature. New work by poets like Susan Connolly, Catherine Byron, Catherine Phil MacCarthy, Nuala Archer, Enda Wyley, Anne Kennedy, Joan Newmann, Mary O'Malley, Julie O'Callaghan, Katie Donovan, Angela Greene, and others, suggests that the contributions of women to literature in Ireland are increasing dramatically. Ground has been broken by these women; if we explore the terrain, they will show what can grow. Before long, we may be piecing together a tradition of Irish women poets (connecting past and present), and, when we talk of Irish poetry, we will give women their rightful place.

Selected Bibliography
Index

Selected Bibliography

Abel, Elizabeth, ed. 1980. *Writing and Sexual Difference*. Chicago: Univ. of Chicago Press.

Adcock, Fleur. 1987. *The Faber Book of 20th Century Women's Poetry*. London: Faber and Faber.

Allen, Michael, and Angela Wilcox, eds. 1989. *Critical Approaches to Anglo-Irish Literature*. Totowa, N.J.: Barnes and Noble; Gerrards Cross, Bucks.: Colin Smythe.

Allen-Randolph, Jody. 1991. "Écriture Feminine and the Authorship of Self in Eavan Boland's *In Her Own Image*." *Colby Quarterly* 27, no. 1: 48–59.

———. 1993. "Private Worlds, Public Realities: Eavan Boland's Poetry, 1967–1990." *Irish University Review* 23, no. 1: 5–22.

Allison, Jonathan. 1991. "Poetry from the Irish." *Irish Literary Supplement* 10, no. 1: 14.

Amiel, Henri-Frédéric. N.d. *Amiel's Journal Intime*. Translated by Mrs. Humphry Ward. New York: A. L. Burt.

Andersen, Jorge. 1977. *The Witch on the Wall: Medieval Erotic Sculpture in the British Isles*. London: Allen and Unwin.

Anderson, Linda. 1987. "Gang-Bang, Ulster Style." In *Pillars of the House: An Anthology of Verse by Irish Women from 1690 to the Present*, edited by A. A. Kelly, 144–45. Dublin: Wolfhound.

Andrews, Elmer, ed. 1990. *Contemporary Irish Poetry, A Collection of Critical Essays*. London: Macmillan.

Archer, Nuala. 1981. *Whale on the Line*. Dublin: Gallery.

———, ed. 1986. *Midland Review* 3 [special issue devoted to Irish women writers].

———. 1992. *The Hour of Pan/Amá*. Galway: Salmon.

Archer, Nuala, and Medbh McGuckian. 1989. *Two Women Two Shores: Poems by Medbh McGuckian and Nuala Archer*. Baltimore, Md.: New Poetry Series.

Bardwell, Leland. 1970. *The Mad Cyclist*. Dublin: New Writer's Press.

———. 1984. *The Fly and the Bedbug*. Donnybrook: Beaver Row.

———. 1991. *Dostoevsky's Grave*. Dublin: Dedalus.

Barry, Sebastian. 1986. *Inherited Boundaries: Younger Poets of the Republic*. Portlaoise: Dolmen.

Barthes, Roland. 1977. "The Death of the Author." In *Image, Music, Text,* translated by Stephen Heath. New York: Hill and Wang.

Beale, Jenny. 1987. *Women in Ireland: Voices of Change*. Bloomington: Indiana Univ. Press. Original edition, Dublin: Gill and Macmillan, 1986.

Bedient, Calvin. 1990. "The Crabbed Genius of Belfast." *Parnassus: Poetry in Review* 16, no. 1: 195–210.

Beer, Ann. 1992. "Medbh McGuckian's Poetry: Maternal Thinking and a Politics of Peace." *Canadian Journal of Irish Studies* 18, no.1: 192–203.

Belsey, Catherine, and Jane Moore. 1989. *The Feminist Reader, Essays in Gender and the Politics of Literary Criticism*. London: Macmillan.

Berkeley, Sara. 1989a. *Home Movie Nights*. Dublin: Raven Arts.

———. 1989b. *Penn*. Dublin: Raven Arts.

Boland, Eavan. 1967. *New Territory*. Dublin: Allen Figgis.

———. 1975. *The War Horse*. Dublin: Arlen House.

———. 1979. "Nationalism and Obsession in Contemporary Irish Poetry: Interview with Eavan Boland." Conducted by Adrian Frazier. *Literary Review* 22: 237–57.

———. 1980. *In Her Own Image*. Dublin: Arlen House.

———. 1981. *Introducing Eavan Boland*. Princeton, N.J.: Ontario Review Press.

———. 1982. *The Journey*. Dublin: Gallery.

———. 1986. "The Woman Poet: Her Dilemma." *Midland Review* 3: 40–47. Also published in *Stand Magazine* (Winter 1986–87): 43–49.

———. 1987a. "Editorial." *The WEB* (Dublin: Women's Education Bureau) 1 (June): 1.

———. 1987b. *The Journey and Other Poems*. Manchester: Carcanet. Original edition, Dublin: Arlen House, 1986.

———. 1987c. "The Woman Poet in a National Tradition." *Studies* 76: 148–58. Also published as *A Kind of Scar: The Woman Poet in a National Tradition*. Dublin: Attic LIP Pamphlet, 1989.

———. 1988a. "Q. & A. with Eavan Boland." Conducted by Deborah Tall. *Irish Literary Supplement* 7, no. 2: 39–40.

———. 1988b. "An Un-Romantic American." *Parnassus: Poetry in Review* 14, no. 2: 73–92.

———. 1989a. "An Interview with Eavan Boland." Conducted by Marilyn Reizbaum. *Contemporary Literature* 30, no. 4: 470–79.

———. 1989b. *Selected Poems*. Manchester: Carcanet. Dublin: Arlen House.

———. 1990a. "Eavan Boland: Outside History." *American Poetry Review* (Mar./Apr.): 32–38.

———. 1990b. *Outside History*. Manchester: Carcanet.

———. 1990c. *Outside History: Selected Poems, 1980–1990*. New York: Norton.

———. 1990d. "The Woman, The Place, The Poet." *Georgia Review* 44, nos. 1–2: 97–109.

———. 1991. "In Defense of Workshops." *Poetry Ireland Review* 31: 40–48.

———. 1992a. "An Interview with Eavan Boland." Conducted by Deborah McWilliams Consalvo. *Studies* 81: 89–100.

———. 1992b. "Writing in the Margin." *Irish Times,* Apr. 18, p. 12.

———. 1994a. *In a Time of Violence*. Manchester: Carcanet; New York: Norton.

———. 1994b. *Night Feed*. Manchester: Carcanet. Original edition, Dublin: Arlen House, 1982.

Boland, Rosita. 1991. *Muscle Creek.* Dublin: Raven Arts.

Bourke, Angela. 1988. *Working and Weeping: Women's Oral Poetry in Irish and Scottish Gaelic Poetry.* Women's Studies Working Papers, no. 7. Dublin: UCD Women's Studies Forum.

———. 1991–92. "Performing—Not Writing." *Graph* 11: 28–31.

———. 1993. "More in Anger than in Sorrow: Irish Women's Lament Poetry." In *Feminist Messages,* edited by Joan Newlon Radner, 160–82. Urbana: Univ. of Illinois Press.

Bourke, Eva. 1985. *Gonella.* Galway: Salmon.

———. 1989. *Litany for the Pig.* Galway: Salmon.

Bowen, Charles. 1975. "Great Bladdered Medb: Mythology and Invention in the *Táin Bó Cuailnge.*" *Éire-Ireland* 10, no. 4: 14–34.

Brady, Anne M. 1988. *Women in Ireland: An Annotated Bibliography.* Westport, Conn.: Greenwood.

Breathnach, R. A. 1953. "The Lady and the King, A Theme of Irish Literature." *Studies* 42: 321–36.

Brett, Heather. 1991. *Abigail Brown.* Galway: Salmon.

Brodsky, Patricia Pollock. 1988. *Rainer Maria Rilke.* Boston: G. K. Hall.

Brophy, James D., and Eamon Grennan, eds. 1989. *New Irish Writing.* Boston: G. K. Hall.

Browne, Joseph. 1985. "Eiléan Ní Chuilleanáin." In *Poets of Great Britain and Ireland since 1960,* vol. 40, part 2, of *The Dictionary of Literary Biography,* edited by Vincent B. Sherry, 411–15. Detroit: Gale.

Browne, Terence. 1975. *Northern Voices: Poets from Ulster.* Dublin: Gill and Macmillan.

Browne, Terence, and Nicholas Grene, eds. 1989. *Tradition and Influence in Anglo-Irish Poetry.* Totowa, N.J.: Barnes and Noble.

Byron, Catherine. 1988. "The Room is a Kind of Travel Also." *Linen Hall Review* 5, no. 1: 16–17.

———. 1993a. *The Fat-Hen Field Hospital, Poems 1985–1992.* Bristol: Loxwood Stoneleigh.

———. 1993b. *Settlements and Samhain.* Bristol: Loxwood Stoneleigh.

Cahill, Eileen. 1994. "'Because I never garden': Medbh McGuckian's Solitary Way." *Irish University Review* 24, no. 2: 264–71.

Cairns, David, and Shaun Richards. 1991. "Tropes and Traps: Aspects of 'Woman' and Nationality in Twentieth-Century Irish Drama." In *Gender in Irish Writing,* edited by Toni O'Brien Johnson and David Cairns, 128–37. Buckingham, U.K., and Philadelphia: Open Univ. Press.

Caldecott, Moyra. 1988. *Women in Celtic Myth.* Rochester, Vt.: Destiny Books.

Cannon, Moya. 1990. *Oar.* Galway: Salmon.

Carpenter, Andrew, ed. 1977. *Place, Personality and the Irish Writer.* Gerrards Cross, Bucks.: Colin Smythe; New York: Barnes and Noble.

Casey, Juanita. 1985. *Eternity Smith and Other Poems.* Portlaoise: Dolmen.

Caws, Mary Ann. 1986. "The Conception of Engendering: The Erotics of Editing." In *The Poetics of Gender,* edited by Nancy K. Miller, 42–62. New York: Columbia Univ. Press.

Cixous, Hélène. 1976. "The Laugh of the Medusa." Translated by Keith Cohen and Paula Cohen. *Signs* 1: 875–94. Reprinted in *New French Feminisms: An Anthology,* edited by Elaine Marks and Isabelle de Courtivron (New York: Shocken, 1981).

———. 1989. "Sorties: Out and Out: Attacks/Ways Out/Forays." In *The Feminist Reader: Essays in Gender and the Politics of Literary Criticism,* edited by Catherine Belsey and Jane Moore, 101–16. London: Macmillan.

Clark, Rosalind. 1991. *The Great Queens: Irish Goddesses from the Mórrígan to Cathleen Ní Houlihan.* Gerrards Cross, Bucks.: Colin Smythe.

Collins, Denis, and Anne Heffernan, eds. 1990. *Six for Gold.* Wexford: The Works.

Conboy, Sheila C. 1990. "'What You Have Seen is Beyond Speech': Female Journeys in the Poetry of Eavan Boland and Eiléan Ní Chuilleanáin." *Canadian Journal of Irish Studies* 16: 65–72.

Condren, Mary. 1989. *The Serpent and the Goddess: Women, Religion, and Power in Celtic Ireland.* New York: Harper and Row.

Conlon, Evelyn. 1988. "Millions Like Us." *Graph* 5 (Autumn): 4–6.

Connolly, Susan. *Boann and Other Poems.* 1991. In *How High the Moon,* edited by Theo Dorgan and Constance Short. Dublin: Poetry Ireland.

———. 1993. *For the Stranger.* Dublin: Dedalus.

Conroy, Roisin. 1980. "Images of the Irish Woman: Bibliography." *Crane Bag* 4, no. 1: 73–80.

Conway, Thomas. 1972. "Women's Work in Ireland." *Éire-Ireland* 7, no. 1: 10–27.

Corcoran, Neil. 1992. *The Chosen Ground: Essays on the Contemporary Poetry of Northern Ireland.* Bridgend, Mid Glamorgan, Wales: Poetry Wales; Chester Springs, Pa.: Dufour Editions.

Cowman, Roz. 1986. "Jocasta." *Midland Review* 3 [special issue edited by Nuala Archer]: 60.

———. 1989. *The Goose Herd.* Galway: Salmon.

Craig, Patricia. 1988. "Props and Prodigies." *Times Literary Supplement,* 2–8 Sept., 957.

Cullen, Mary, ed. 1987. *Girls Don't Do Honours: Irish Women in Education in the 19th and 20th Centuries.* Dublin: Women's Education Bureau.

Cullingford, Elizabeth. 1991. "Yeats: The Anxiety of Masculinity." In *Gender in Irish Writing,* edited by Toni O'Brien Johnson and David Cairns, 46–67. Buckingham, U.K., and Philadelphia: Open Univ. Press.

———. 1993. *Gender and History in Yeats's Love Poetry.* Cambridge: Cambridge Univ. Press.

Curran, Margaret. 1986. "The Ulster Widow's Tale." *Midland Review* 3 [special issue edited by Nuala Archer]: 98.

Curtin, Chris, Pauline Jackson, and Barbara O'Connor, eds. 1987. *Gender in Irish Society.* Galway: Galway Univ. Press.

Dalton, G. F. 1974. "The Tradition of Blood Sacrifice to the Goddess Éire." *Studies* 63: 343–54.

Deane, Seamus, et al., eds. 1991. *The Field Day Anthology of Irish Writing.* 3 vols. Derry: Field Day Publications.

DeSalvo, Louise, Kathleen Walsh D'Arcy, and Katherine Hogan, eds. 1990. *Territories of the Voice: Contemporary Stories by Irish Women Writers.* London: Virago.

De Shazer, Mary. 1986. *Inspiring Women: Reimagining the Muse.* New York: Pergamon.

Docherty, Thomas. 1992. "Initiations, Tempers, Seductions: Postmodern McGuckian." In *The Chosen Ground: Essays on the Contemporary Poetry of Northern Ireland,* edited by Neil Corcoran, 191–210. Mid Glamorgan, Wales: Poetry Wales; Chester Springs, Pa.: Dufour.

Donovan, Katie. 1988. *Irish Women Writers: Marginalised by Whom?* Dublin: Raven Arts.

———. 1993. *Watermelon Man.* Newcastle upon Tyne: Bloodaxe Books.

Donovan, Katie, A. Norman Jeffares, and Brendan Kennelly, eds. 1994. *Ireland's Women: Writings Past and Present.* Dublin: Gill and Macmillan.

Dorcey, Mary. 1982. *Kindling.* London: Onlywomen Press.

———. 1991. *Moving into the Space Cleared by Our Mothers.* Galway: Salmon.

Dunbar, William. 1932. *The Poems of William Dunbar.* Edited by W. Mackay Mackenzie. London: Faber and Faber.

Eliade, Mircea. 1957. *Myths, Dreams and Mysteries.* Translated by Philip Mairet. London: Harvill.

Evason, Eileen. 1991. *Against the Grain: The Contemporary Women's Movement in Northern Ireland.* Dublin: Attic Press LIP Pamphlet.

Eyler, Audrey, and Robert F. Garratt. 1988. *The Uses of the Past: Essays on Irish Culture.* Newark: Univ. of Delaware Press.

Fallon, Peter, and Derek Mahon, eds. 1990. *The Penguin Book of Contemporary Irish Poetry.* London: Penguin.

Feeney, John. 1980. "Eithne Gets to Grips with Sin." *Dublin Evening Herald,* 28 July, 7.

Flannery, Denis. 1992. "Ignoring the Risks." [Review of Medbh McGuckian's *Marconi's Cottage.*] *Irish Literary Supplement* 11, no. 2: 20–21.

Foster, John Wilson. 1978. "*The Second Voyage* by Eiléan Ní Chuilleanáin." *Éire-Ireland* 13, no. 4: 147–51.

Foster, R. F. 1988. *Modern Ireland, 1600–1972.* London: Penguin.

Gaffney, Maureen. 1991. *Glass Slippers and Tough Bargains: Women, Men and Power.* Dublin: Attic Press LIP Pamphlet.

Gallagher, S. F., ed. 1983. *Women in Irish Legend, Life and Literature.* Totowa, N.J.: Barnes and Noble; Gerrards Cross, Bucks.: Colin Smythe.

Galvin, Margaret. 1989. *Miresuck and Slaver.* London: Tuba Press.

Gardiner, Judith Kegan. 1982. "On Female Identity and Writing by Women." In *Writing and Sexual Difference,* edited by Elizabeth Abel, 177–91 Chicago: Univ. of Chicago Press.

Garratt, Robert F. 1986. *Modern Irish Poetry: Tradition and Continuity from Yeats to Heaney.* Berkeley: Univ. of California Press.

Gilligan, Carol. 1982. *In a Different Voice: Psychological Theory and Women's Development.* Cambridge: Harvard Univ. Press.

Green, Miranda. 1986. *The Gods of the Celts.* Gloucestershire: A. Sutton; Totowa, N.J.: Barnes and Noble.

Greene, Angela. 1993. *Silence and the Blue Night.* Dublin: Salmon.

Greene, Gayle, and Coppelia Kahn, eds. 1985. *Making a Difference: Feminist Literary Criticism.* New York: Methuen.

Haberstroh, Patricia Boyle. 1992. "Literary Politics: Mainstream and Margin." *Canadian Journal of Irish Studies* 18, vol. 1: 181–91.

———. 1993. "Woman, Artist and Image in *Night Feed.*" *Irish University Review* 23, no. 1: 67–74.

Hannon, Dennis J., and Nancy Means Wright. 1990. "Irish Women Poets: Breaking the Silence." *Canadian Journal of Irish Studies* 16, no. 2: 57–65.

Harper, Margaret Mills. 1988. "The Medium as Creator: George Yeats's Role in the Automatic Script." In *Yeats: An Annual of Critical and Textual Studies,* vol. 6, edited by Richard Finneran, 49–71. Ann Arbor: Univ. of Michigan Press.

Hartigan, Anne Le Marquand. 1982. *Long Tongue.* Dublin: Beaver Row.

———. 1986. *Return Single.* Donnybrook: Beaver Row.

———. 1991. *Now is a Moveable Feast.* Galway: Salmon.

———. 1993. *Immortal Sins.* Dublin: Salmon.

Hartman, Mark. 1971. "Poetry Publications of the Runa Press." *Dublin Magazine* (Summer): 84–111.

Harwood, John. 1989. *Olivia Shakespear and W. B. Yeats.* New York: St. Martin's.

Heaney, Seamus. 1979. *Field Work.* London: Faber and Faber.

———. 1980. *Poems, 1965–1975.* New York: Farrar, Straus and Giroux.

———. 1989. *The Place of Writing.* Atlanta: Scholars Press.

Heilbrun, Carolyn G. 1988. *Writing a Woman's Life.* New York: Random House.

Henderson, Gordon. 1972. "An Interview with Juanita Casey." *Journal of Irish Literature* 1, no. 3: 42–54.

Henigan, Robert. 1985. "Contemporary Women Poets in Ireland." *Concerning Poetry* 18, nos. 1–2: 103–115.

Henry, P. L., ed. 1990. *Dánta Ban: Poems of Irish Women, Early and Modern.* Dublin: Mercier.

Herr, Cheryl. 1990. "The Erotics of Irishness." *Critical Inquiry* 17: 1–34.

Higgins, Rita Ann. 1986. *Goddess on the Mervue Bus.* Galway: Salmon.

———. 1988. *Witch in the Bushes.* Galway: Salmon.

———. 1990. *Goddess & Witch.* Galway: Salmon.

———. 1992. *Philomena's Revenge.* Galway: Salmon.

Hooley, Ruth, ed. 1985. *The Female Line: Northern Irish Women Writers.* Belfast: Northern Ireland Women's Rights Movement.

————. 1986. "Woman Alone." *Midland Review* 3 [special issue edited by Nuala Archer]: 50.

Hutcheson, Mark. 1989. "In the Middle of the Journey." *Irish Times,* 17 June.

Innes, C. L. 1993. *Woman and Nation in Irish Literature.* London: Harvester.

Irigaray, Luce. 1985. *The Sex Which Is Not One.* Translated by Catherine Porter. Ithaca: Cornell Univ. Press.

"Irish Women Writers." 1991. Special issue of *Colby Quarterly* 27, no. 1.

Jacobus, Mary. 1989. "The Difference of View." In *The Feminist Reader: Essays in Gender and the Politics of Literary Criticism,* edited by Catherine Belsey and Jane Moore, 49–62. London: Macmillan.

————, ed. 1979. *Women Writing and Writing about Women.* New York: Harper and Row.

Jardine, Alice. 1985. *Gynesis: Configurations of Woman and Modernity.* Ithaca: Cornell Univ. Press.

Jenkins, Alan. 1982. "Private and Public Language." *Encounter* 59: 56–63.

Johnson, Máirín, ed. 1988. *Alice Alivo O: Recollections and Visions of Dublin Women.* Dublin: Attic.

Johnston, Dillon. 1985. *Irish Poetry after Joyce.* South Bend, Ind.: Univ. of Notre Dame Press; Dublin: Dolmen.

Kaplan, Cora. 1986. *Sea Changes: Culture and Feminism.* London: Verso.

Kavanagh, Patrick. 1942. *The Great Hunger.* Dublin: Cuala.

————. 1967. *Collected Pruse.* London: MacGibbon and Kee.

Keane, Patrick J. 1988. *Yeats, Joyce and the Myth of the Devouring Female.* Columbia: Univ. of Missouri Press.

Kegan, Judith. 1982. "On Female Identity and Writing by Women." In *Writing and Sexual Difference,* edited by Elizabeth Abel, 177–91. Chicago: Univ. of Chicago Press.

Kelly, A. A. 1987. *Pillars of the House: An Anthology of Verse by Irish Women from 1690 to the Present.* Dublin: Wolfhound.

Kelly, Maeve. 1986. *Resolution.* Belfast: Blackstaff.

Kelly, Rita. 1989. *Fare Well/Beir Beannacht: Poems in English and Irish.* Dublin: Attic.

Kelly, Sylvia. 1993. "The Silent Cage and Female Creativity in *In Her Own Image.*" *Irish University Review* 23, no. 1: 45–56.

Kenneally, Michael, ed. 1988. *Cultural Contexts and Literary Idioms in Contemporary Irish Literature.* Gerrards Cross, Bucks.: Colin Smythe.

Kennedy, Anne. 1994. *The Dog Kubla Dreams My Life.* Dublin: Salmon.

Kennelly, Brendan, ed. 1970. *The Penguin Book of Irish Verse.* Middlesex: Penguin.

————. 1973. "Patrick Kavanagh." In *Irish Poets in English,* edited by Sean Lucy, 159–84. Dublin: Mercier.

————. 1975. "Mother's Poems on Motherhood." *Dublin Sunday Independent,* 17 Aug., 11.

Kilmurray, Avila. 1987. "Women in the Community in Northern Ireland: Struggling for Their Half of the Sky." *Studies* 76 (Summer): 177–84.

Kline, Gloria C. 1983. *The Last Courtly Lover: Yeats and the Idea of Woman.* Ann Arbor, Mich.: UMI Research Press.

Kolodny, Annette. 1980. "Dancing Through the Minefield: Some Observations on the Theory, Practice, and Politics of a Feminist Literary Criticism." *Feminist Studies* 6, no. 1: 1–25.

———. 1980. "A Map for Rereading: Or, Gender and the Interpretation of Literary Texts." *New Literary History* 11, no. 3: 451–68.

Kozok, Heinz. 1988. "Anthologies of Anglo-Irish Literature." *Irish University Review* 18: 251–62.

Kristeva, Julia. 1982. *Desire in Language: A Semiotic Approach to Literature and Art.* Translated by Léon S. Roudiez, Alice Jardine, and Thomas Gora. New York: Columbia Univ. Press.

———. 1984. *Revolution in Poetic Language.* Translated by Margaret Waller. New York: Columbia Univ. Press.

Lakoff, Robin. 1975. *Language and Women's Place.* New York: Harper and Row.

Larissey, Edward. 1990. *Reading Twentieth-Century Poetry: The Language of Gender and Objects.* Oxford: Basil Blackwell.

Lendennie, Jessie. 1988. *Daughter.* Galway: Salmon.

Loftus, R. 1964. *Nationalism in Modern Anglo-Irish Poetry.* Madison: Univ. of Wisconsin Press.

Logan, William. 1991. "Animal Instincts and Natural Powers." *New York Times Book Review,* 22 Apr., 22.

Longley, Edna. 1990. *From Cathleen to Anorexia: The Breakdown of Irelands.* Dublin: Attic Press LIP Pamphlet.

———, ed. 1991. *Culture in Ireland: Division or Diversity?* Belfast: Institute of Irish Studies.

Longley, Michael. 1969. *No Continuing City, Poems 1963–68.* Dublin: Gill and Macmillan.

Luddy, Maria, and Cliona Murphy, eds. 1989. *Women Surviving: Studies in Irish Women's History in the 19th and 20th Centuries.* Swords, Co. Dublin: Poolbeg.

Luftig, Victor. 1989. "A Migrant Mind in a Mobile Home: Salmon Publishing in the Ireland of the 1990s." *Éire-Ireland* 26, no. 1: 108–19.

———. 1993. "'Something Will Happen to You Who Read': Adrienne Rich, Eavan Boland." *Irish University Review* 23, no. 1: 57–66.

Lysaght, Patricia. 1986. *The Banshee: The Irish Supernatural Death Messenger.* Dublin: Glendale.

MacCarthy, Catherine Phil. 1991. *Sanctuary.* In *How High the Moon,* edited by Theo Dorgan and Constance Short. Dublin: Poetry Ireland.

———. 1994. *This Hour of the Tide.* Dublin: Salmon.

Mac Curtain, Margaret. 1985. "The Historical Image." In *Irish Women: Image and Achievement,* edited by Eiléan Ní Chuilleanáin, 37–50. Dublin: Arlen House.

Mac Curtain, Margaret, and Donncha Ó'Corráin, eds. 1979. *Women in Irish Society: The Historical Dimension.* Westport, Conn.: Greenwood. Original edition, Dublin: Arlen House, 1978.

Mac Curtain, Margaret, and Mary O'Dowd, eds. 1991. *Women in Early Modern Ireland*. Edinburgh: Edinburgh Univ. Press.

Madden-Simpson, Janet, ed. 1984. *Woman's Part: An Anthology of Short Fiction by and About Women, 1890–1960*. Dublin: Arlen House.

———. 1986. "Womanwriting: The Arts of Textual Politics." *Midland Review* 3: 121–28.

Maher, Mary. 1980. "A Salute to Grace." *Irish Times*, 4 July, 10.

———, ed. 1984. *Woman's Part: An Anthology of Short Fiction by and about Women*. Dublin: Arlen House.

Máighréad, Medbh. 1990. *The Making of a Pagan*. Belfast: Blackstaff.

Malone, Aubrey. 1993. "The Astrakhan Coat." *Irish Studies Review* 4: 38–39.

Marconi, Degna. 1962. *My Father Marconi*. New York: McGraw-Hill.

Marcus, Jane. 1988. *Art and Anger: Reading Like a Woman*. Columbus: Ohio State Univ. Press.

Marks, Elaine, and Isabelle de Courtivron, eds. 1981. *New French Feminisms: An Anthology*. New York: Shocken.

McBreen, Joan. 1990. *The Wind Beyond the Wall*. Brownsville, Ore.: Story Line.

McCafferty, Nell. 1984. *The Best of Nell*. Dublin: Attic.

———. 1985. *A Woman to Blame: The Kerry Babies Case*. Dublin: Attic.

———. 1987. *Goodnight Sisters* . . . . Dublin: Attic.

McCarthy, Thomas. 1990. "Package from Mars." *Poetry Ireland Review* 30: 89–95.

McCauley, Leon. 1992. "Wuthering Depths." *Honest Ulsterman* 93: 63–65.

McCurry, Jacqueline. 1991. "'Our Lady, dispossessed': Female Ulster Poets and Sexual Politics." *Colby Quarterly* 27, no. 1: 4–8.

McElroy, James. 1985. "Night Feed: An Overview of Ireland's Women Poets." *American Poetry Review* (Jan./Feb.): 32–36.

———. 1989. "The Contemporary Fe/Male Poet: A Preliminary Reading." In *New Irish Writing*, edited by James D. Brophy and Eamon Grennan, 189–202. Boston: G. K. Hall.

McGuckian, Medbh. 1980a. *Portrait of Joanna*. Belfast: Ulsterman Publications.

———. 1980b. *Single Ladies*. Budleigh Salterton: Interim.

———. 1982. *The Flower Master*. Oxford: Oxford Univ. Press.

———. 1984. *Venus and the Rain*. Oxford: Oxford Univ. Press.

———. 1988a. "The Light of the Penurious Moon." *Honest Ulsterman* 85: 60–62.

———. 1988b. *On Ballycastle Beach*. Oxford: Oxford Univ. Press; Winston-Salem, N.C.: Wake Forest Univ. Press.

———. 1990. "An Attitude of Compassion." Interview conducted by Kathleen McCracken. *Irish Literary Supplement* 9, no. 2: 20–21.

———. 1991. *Marconi's Cottage*. Meath: Gallery. Reprint, Winston-Salem, N.C.: Wake Forest Univ. Press, 1992.

———. 1992. "Don't Talk to Me About Dance." *Poetry Ireland Review* 35: 98–100.

———. 1993a. "An Interview with Medbh McGuckian." Interview conducted by Susan Shaw Sailer. *Michigan Review* 32, no. 1: 111–27.

———. 1993b. *The Flower Master and Other Poems*. Meath: Gallery.

————, and Nuala Archer. 1989. *Two Women Two Shores: Poems by Medbh Mc-Guckian and Nuala Archer.* Baltimore, Md.: New Poets Series.

McGuinness, Arthur. 1988. "Hearth and History: Poetry by Contemporary Irish Women." In *Cultural Contexts and Literary Idioms in Contemporary Irish Literature,* edited by Michael Kenneally, 197–220. Totowa, N.J.: Barnes and Noble.

Meaney, Gerardine. 1991. *Sex and Nation: Women in Irish Culture and Politics.* Dublin: Attic Press LIP Pamphlet.

Meehan, Paula. 1984. *Return and No Blame.* Donnybrook: Beaver Row.

————. 1986. *Reading the Sky.* Donnybrook: Beaver Row.

————. 1991. *The Man Who Was Marked by Winter.* Meath: Gallery.

Mhac an tSaoi, Máire. 1983. "The Female Principle in Gaelic Poetry." In *Women in Irish Legend, Life, and Literature,* edited by S. F. Gallagher, 26–38. Totowa, N.J.: Barnes and Noble; Gerrards Cross, Bucks.: Colin Smythe.

————. 1990. "Minority Culture." *Poetry Ireland Review* 30: 96–101.

Miller, Áine. 1994. *Goldfish in a Baby Bath.* Dublin: Salmon.

Miller, Nancy K., ed. 1986. *The Poetics of Gender.* New York: Columbia Univ. Press.

Miller, Ruth. 1968. *The Poetry of Emily Dickinson.* Middletown, Conn.: Wesleyan Univ. Press.

Modersohn-Becker, Paula. 1980. *The Letters and Journals of Paula Modersohn-Becker.* Translated by J. Diane Radycki. Metuchen, N.J.: Scarecrow.

Moers, Ellen. 1978. *Literary Women.* London: Women's Press.

Monaghan, Patricia, ed. 1987. *Unlacing, Ten Irish-American Poets.* Fairbanks, Alaska: Fireweed.

Montague, John, ed. 1974. *The Faber Book of Irish Verse.* London: Faber and Faber.

Montefiore, Jan. 1987. *Feminism and Poetry.* London: Pandora.

Moran, Lynda. 1985. *The Truth about Lucy.* Donnybrook: Beaver Row.

Mother Ireland. 1988. Directed by Anne Crilly. Derry: Derry Film and Video.

Muldoon, Paul, 1981. *Why Brownlee Left.* Winston-Salem, N.C.: Wake Forest Univ. Press; London: Faber and Faber, 1980.

————. *Quoof.* 1983. London: Faber and Faber; Winston-Salem, N.C.: Wake Forest Univ. Press.

————. 1985. *Mules and Early Poems.* Winston-Salem, N.C.: Wake Forest Univ. Press.

————. ed. 1986. *The Faber Book of Contemporary Irish Poetry.* London: Faber and Faber.

Mullen, Molly. 1991. "Representations of History, Irish Feminism, and the Politics of Difference." *Feminist Studies* 17, no. 1: 29–50.

Murphy, Cliona. 1989. *The Women's Suffrage Movement and Irish Society in the Early Twentieth Century.* Philadelphia: Temple Univ. Press.

————. 1992. "Women's History, Feminist History, or Gender History." *Irish Review* 12: 21–26.

Murphy, Maureen. 1989. "The Elegiac Tradition in the Poetry of Máire Mhac an tSaoi, Caitlín Maude, and Nuala Ní Dhomhnaill." In *New Irish Writing,* edited by James D. Brophy and Eamon Grennan, 141–51. New York: Twayne.

Neville, Grace. 1982. "Medieval Irish Courtly Love Poetry: An Exercise in Power Struggle?" *Études Irlandaises* 7: 19–30.

Newmann, Joan. 1995. *Coming of Age.* Belfast: Blackstaff.

Newmann, Kate. 1992. "All Sorts of Untils." *Irish Review* 12: 173–75.

Nic Dhiarmada, Briona. 1988. "Tradition and the Female Voice in Contemporary Gaelic Poetry." *Women's Studies International Forum* 11, no. 4: 387–93.

———. 1993. "Going for It and Succeeding." *Irish Literary Supplement* 12, no. 2: 3–4.

Nic Eoin, Máirín. 1992. "Gender's Agendas." *Graph* 12: 5–8.

Ní Chuilleanáin, Eiléan. 1972. *Acts and Monuments.* Dublin: Gallery.

———. 1975. *Site of Ambush.* Dublin: Gallery.

———. 1977. *Cork.* Dublin: Gallery.

———. 1980. "Woman as Writer: The Social Matrix." *Crane Bag* 4, no. 1: 101–105.

———. 1981. *The Rose-Geranium.* Dublin: Gallery.

———, ed. 1985. *Irish Women: Image and Achievement.* Dublin: Arlen House.

———. 1986. *The Second Voyage.* Dublin: Gallery. Original edition, Winston-Salem, N.C.: Wake Forest Univ. Press, 1977.

———. 1989. *The Magdalene Sermon.* Meath: Gallery.

———. 1991. *The Magdalene Sermon and Other Poems.* Winston-Salem, N.C.: Wake Forest Univ. Press.

Ní Dhomhnaill, Nuala. 1987. "Q. and A.: Nuala Ní Dhomhnaill." Interview conducted by Lucy McDiarmid and Michael Durkan. *Irish Literary Supplement* 6, no. 2: 41–43.

———. 1988. *Selected Poems/Rogha Dánta.* Translated by Michael Hartnett and Nuala Ní Dhomhnaill. Dublin: Raven Arts.

———. 1990. *Pharaoh's Daughter.* Meath: Gallery. Reprint, Winston-Salem, N.C.: Wake Forest Univ. Press, 1993.

———. 1992a. "What Foremothers?" *Poetry Ireland Review* 36: 18–31.

———. 1992b. *The Astrakhan Cloak.* Translated by Paul Muldoon. Meath: Gallery. Reprint, Winston-Salem, N.C.: Wake Forest Univ. Press. 1993.

Nolan, Janet. 1989. *Ourselves Alone: Women's Emigration from Ireland.* Lexington: Univ. Press of Kentucky.

Nulty, Christine, ed. 1982. "Images of the Irish Woman." In *Crane Bag Book of Irish Studies, 1977–81,* edited by Richard Kearney and Mark Patrick Hederman. Dublin: Blackwater.

O'Brien, Edna. 1976. *Mother Ireland.* London: Penguin.

O'Brien, Toni Johnson, and David Cairns, eds. 1991. *Gender in Irish Writing.* Buckingham, U.K., and Philadelphia: Open Univ. Press.

O'Callaghan, Julie. 1983. *Edible Anecdotes.* Portlaoise: Dolmen.

———. 1988. *Taking My Pen for a Walk.* London: Orchard Books.

————. 1989. *When You Need Them.* Galway: Salmon.

————. 1991. *What's What.* Newcastle upon Tyne: Bloodaxe.

O'Donnell, Mary. 1986. "Male Domination/Female Serengeti." *Poetry Ireland Review* 16: 16–19.

————. 1989. "Suburban Blitz." *Graph* 6: 25–26.

————. 1990. *Reading the Sunflowers in September.* Galway: Salmon.

————. 1992. "Responsibility and Narcosis." *Poetry Ireland Review* 35: 108–12.

————. 1993. *Spiderwoman's Third Avenue Rhapsody.* Dublin: Salmon.

O'Dowd, Liam. 1987. "Church, State and Women: The Aftermath of Partition." In *Gender in Irish Society,* edited by Chris Curtain, Pauline Jackson, and Barbara O'Connor, 3–36. Galway: Galway Univ. Press.

O'Driscoll, Dennis. 1989. "For Larkin Read Kavanagh." *Poetry Review* 79, no. 1: 38–40.

O'Hagan, Sheila. 1992. *The Peacock's Eye.* Galway: Salmon.

O'Hara, David, and Michael Bouchier, eds. 1988. *Rainbows and Stone: An Anthology of Modern Irish Poetry.* Wicklow: Real Ireland Design.

O'Malley, Mary. 1990. *A Consideration of Silk.* Galway: Salmon.

————. 1993. *Where the Rocks Float.* Dublin: Salmon.

O'Neill, Michael. 1984. "Barbaric Yawp, Gibbous Voice." *Honest Ulsterman* 77: 59–64.

Olsen, Tillie. 1970. *Silences.* New York: Delacorte.

Ormsby, Frank, ed. 1979. *Poets from the North of Ireland.* Belfast: Blackstaff.

Ostriker, Alicia Suskin. 1985. "The Thieves of Language: Women Poets and Revisionist Mythmaking." In *The New Feminist Criticism: Essays on Women, Literature, and Theory,* edited by Elaine Showalter, 314–38. New York: Random House.

————. 1986. *Stealing the Language: The Emergence of Women's Poetry in America.* Boston: Beacon.

Owens, Rosemary Cullen. 1984. *Smashing Times: A History of the Irish Women's Suffrage Movement 1889–1922.* Dublin: Attic.

————, et al. 1985. *Did Your Granny Have a Hammer? A History of the Irish Suffrage Movement, 1876–1922.* Dublin: Attic.

Pagels, Elaine. 1988. *Adam, Eve, and the Serpent.* New York: Random House.

Peters, Anne. 1982. *Rings of Green.* Gerrards Cross, Bucks.: Colin Smythe.

"Poetry Supplement." 1990. *Krino* 89: 40–85. (Includes 14 women poets.)

Pope, Deborah. 1984. *A Separate Vision: Isolation in Contemporary Women's Poetry.* Baton Rouge: Louisiana State Univ. Press.

Porter, Susan. 1989. "The 'Imaginative Space' of Medbh McGuckian." *Canadian Journal of Irish Studies* 15, no. 2: 93–104.

Quinn, John, ed. 1986. *A Portrait of the Artist as a Young Girl.* London: Methuen.

Reddy, Maureen. 1988. "Line of Most Resistance." *Women's Review of Books* (Oct.): 9.

Reynolds, Lorna. 1983. "Irish Women in Legend, Literature, and Life." In *Women in Irish Legend, Life and Literature,* edited by S. F. Gallagher, 11–25. Totowa, N.J.: Barnes and Noble.

Rich, Adrienne. 1973. "Diving into the Wreck." In *Diving into the Wreck,* 22–24. New York: Norton.

———. 1979. *On Lies, Secrets, and Silence: Selected Prose, 1966–1978.* New York: Norton.

Rilke, Rainer Maria. 1982. *The Selected Poetry of Rainer Maria Rilke.* Translated by Stephen Mitchell. New York: Random House.

Roche, Anthony, and Jody Allen-Randolph, eds. 1993. "Eavan Boland—Special Issue." *Irish University Review* 23, no. 1.

Rowbotham, Sheila. 1990. *The Past Is before Us, Feminism in Action since the 1960s.* London: Penguin.

Ruddick, Sara. 1989. *Maternal Thinking: Toward a Politics of Peace.* Boston: Beacon.

Rumens, Carol, ed. 1985. *Making for the Open: The Chatto Book of Post-Feminist Poetry.* London: Chatto and Windus.

Sawyer, Roger. 1993. *"We Are but Women": Women in Ireland's History.* London: Routledge.

Shannon, Catherine. 1992. "Recovering the Voices of the Women of the North." *Irish Review* 12: 27–33.

Shannon, Elizabeth. 1989. *I Am of Ireland: Women of the North Speak Out.* Boston: Little, Brown.

Shepperson, Janet. 1987. *Trio 5.* Belfast: Blackstaff.

Sherry, Ruth. 1991. "How is Irish Writing Reviewed?" *Cyphers* 31: 5–11.

Showalter, Elaine. 1985. "Towards a Feminist Poetics." In *The New Feminist Criticism: Essays on Women, Literature, and Theory,* edited by Elaine Showalter, 125–43. New York: Random House.

Slade, Jo. 1989. *In Fields I Hear Them Singing.* Galway: Salmon.

Smith, R. T. 1993. "Altered Light: Outside History." *Irish University Review* 23, no. 1: 86–99.

Smyth, Ailbhe. 1983. *Women's Rights in Ireland: A Practical Guide.* Swords: Ward River.

———, ed. 1988. "Feminism in Ireland." Special issue of *Women's Studies International Forum* 11, no. 4.

———. 1989a. "The Floozie in the Jacuzzi: Intersextextual Inserts." *Irish Review* 6: 7–24.

———, ed. 1989b. *Wildish Things: An Anthology of New Irish Women's Writing.* Dublin: Attic.

———, ed. 1993. *Irish Women's Studies Reader.* Dublin: Attic.

Somerville-Arjat, Gillean, and Rebecca E. Wilson, eds. 1990. *Sleeping with Monsters: Conversations with Scottish and Irish Women Poets.* Dublin: Wolfhound.

Spacks, Patricia Meyer. 1975. *The Female Imagination.* New York: Knopf.

Spender, Dale. 1980. *Man-Made Language.* London: Routledge and Kegan Paul.

———. 1989. *The Writing or the Sex? or why you don't have to read women's writing to know it's no good.* New York: Pergamon.

St. Peter, Christine, and Ron Marken. 1992. "Women and Irish Politics." *Canadian Journal of Irish Studies* 18, no. 1 [special issue].

Strong, Eithne. 1943–45. *Poetry Quartos.* Monkstown: Runa.

———. 1961. *Songs of Living*. Monkstown: Runa.

———. 1974. *Sarah, in Passing*. Dublin: Dolmen.

———. 1979. *Degrees of Kindred*. Dublin: Tansy.

———. 1981. *Patterns*. Swords: Poolbeg.

———. 1985. *My Darling Neighbour*. Donnybrook: Beaver Row.

———. 1990. *Let Live*. Galway: Salmon.

———. 1993a. *FLESH . . . the Greatest Sin*. Dublin: Attic. Original edition, Monkstown: Runa, 1980.

———. 1993b. *Spatial Nosing: New and Selected Poems*. Dublin: Salmon.

Táin Bó Cuailnge. 1983. Translated by Thomas Kinsella. Philadelphia: Univ. of Pennsylvania Press.

Taubman, Mary. 1985. *Gwen John: The Artist and Her Work*. Ithaca: Cornell Univ. Press.

Todd, Janet. ed. 1980. *Gender and Literary Voice*. New York: Holmes and Meier.

———. 1988. *Feminist Literary History*. Cambridge: Polity.

Vance, Norman. 1990. *Irish Literature: A Social History*. Oxford: Blackwell.

Viney, Ethna. 1989. *Ancient Wars: Sexuality and Oppression*. Dublin: Attic Press LIP Pamphlet.

Ward, Margaret. 1983. *Unmanageable Revolutionaries: Women and Irish Nationalism*. Kerry: Brandon.

———. 1990. *Maud Gonne: Ireland's Joan of Arc*. Boston: Pandora.

———. 1991. *The Missing Sex: Putting Women into Irish History*. Dublin: Attic Press LIP Pamphlet.

Warner, Marina. 1976. *Alone of All Her Sex: The Myth and Cult of the Virgin Mary*. New York: Knopf.

Weekes, Ann Owens. 1990. *Irish Women Writers: An Uncharted Tradition*. Lexington: Univ. Press of Kentucky.

———. 1993. *Unveiling Treasures: The Attic Guide to the Published Works of Irish Women Literary Writers*. Dublin: Attic.

Welch, Robert. 1992. "Translation as Tribute." *Poetry Ireland Review* 34: 125–29.

White, James. 1971. *Drawings and Paintings of Jack B. Yeats*. London: Secker and Warburg.

Wills, Clair. 1987. "Nearer by Keeping Still." *Times Literary Supplement*, 25–31 Sept., 1435.

———. 1988. "Country Feelings." *Times Literary Supplement*, 19–25 Aug., 915.

Williams, Patrick. 1989. "Spare that Tree." *Honest Ulsterman* 86: 49–52.

Wittig, Monique. 1986. "The Mark of Gender." In *The Poetics of Gender*, edited by Nancy K. Miller, 63–73. New York: Columbia Univ. Press.

"Woman Alive!" 1987. Special issue of *Studies* 76.

Women's Work: An Anthology of Women's Poetry. 1990. Wexford: The Works.

Women's Work Is Never Done: Women's Poetry—Anthology II. 1991. Wexford: The Works.

Wood, Helen Lanigan. 1985. "Women in Myths and Early Depictions." In *Irish Women: Image and Achievement*, edited by Eiléan Ní Chuilleanáin, 13–24. Dublin: Arlen House.

Woods, Máiríde. 1986. "Covering the Traces—A Convent Education." *Midland Review* 3 [special issue edited by Nuala Archer]: 91.

Wyley, Enda. 1993. *Eating Baby Jesus*. Dublin: Dedalus.]

Yeats, W. B. 1964. *Letters on Poetry from W. B. Yeats to Dorothy Wellesley*. Edited by Kathleen Raine. London: Oxford Univ. Press.

———. 1978. *A Critical Edition of Yeats' "A Vision" (1925)*. Edited by George Mills Harper and Walter K. Hood. London: Macmillan.

———. *Collected Poems*. 1990. Edited by Augustine Martin. London: Arrow.

Index